THE
CUSTOM
OF
THE SEA

NEIL HANSON

John Wiley & Sons, Inc.
New York • Chichester • Weinheim • Brisbane • Singapore • Toronto

Copyright ©1999 by Neil Hanson. All rights reserved
Published by John Wiley & Sons, Inc.

First published in the United Kingdom
in 1999 by Doubleday, a division of
Transworld Publishers

This publication is designed to provide accurate and authoritative information in regard to the subject matter covered. It is sold with the understanding that the publisher is not engaged in rendering professional services. If professional advice or other expert assistance is required, the services of a competent professional person should be sought.

Library of Congress Cataloging-in-Publication Data:

Hanson, Neil.
The custom of the sea / Neil Hanson.
p.   cm.
Includes bibliographical references (p.).
ISBN 0-471-38389-9 (alk. paper)
1. Mignonette (Boat)   2. Survival after airplane accidents, shipwrecks, etc.   3. Cannibalism.
4. Dudley, Tom, 1853–1900.   5. Stephens, Edwin, 1847–1914.   6. Trials (Murder)—England—
London.   I. Title.

G525.H26   1999
910.4'52—dc21
99-058798

Printed in the United States of America

10 9 8 7 6 5 4 3 2 1

For Lynn, Jack and Drew

PROLOGUE

The small boat was drifting in a vast expanse of empty ocean. The sun burned down from a sky the colour of brass and even the waves seemed flattened, oppressed by the heat. The oars lay idle and the faint breeze barely ruffled the makeshift sail – four tattered shirts lashed together.

Three gaunt, wild-eyed men sprawled in the bottom of the dinghy. Their skeletal bodies were emaciated and covered in sores, their feet and legs swollen, their lips and tongues blackened. There was no movement but the slow rocking of the boat on the swell.

The dinghy was just thirteen feet long, four feet wide and twenty inches deep. Its thin planking was blistered by the sun and there was a jagged, splintered gash in the port gunwale. There was another hole on the waterline, roughly plugged with mildewed black cloth. Each time the hull flexed in the swell more water trickled from the hole to feed the pool covering the bottom boards.

A makeshift sea-anchor – some pieces of broken timber from the wreck – trailed from the boat, holding the dinghy head to wind. A torn canvas sheet, too small to offer protection from the sun, was lashed across the bow. A chronometer and sextant were stowed beneath it, but the dish-shaped metal case of the chronometer, its surface marked with dark stains, floated in the layer of scummy water in the bottom of the dinghy.

There was nothing else in the boat but two empty tins and a wooden baler. On an ocean teeming with life, the three men were slowly dying of thirst and starvation.

For over a week they had been driven stern-first by the gales, unable to turn and run before the wind for fear of being swamped. One man worked a steering oar at the stern, fighting to hold the dinghy head-to-sea, but waves broke constantly over the bows, spilling a tide of foaming water into the boat and drenching to the skin the man trying to rest, huddled in the bottom.

The other man knelt in the waist of the dinghy, dragging the baler towards him and emptying it over the side in one continuous movement. Barely keeping pace with the flow of water into the boat, he repeated the endless weary cycle a hundred, a thousand, ten thousand times. His watch over at last, he handed the baler to the next man and took his turn curled in the bottom of the boat, trying vainly to rest as sea-water cascaded over and round him, in cruel mockery of his thirst.

Their horizons shrunk by the towering seas, their world was bounded by sounds: the wind howling through the makeshift rigging, the creak of wood, the crash of waves, the swirl of water and the scrape and splash of the baler. Finally the gale began to blow itself out, the seas slackened and they slumped into an exhausted sleep.

The sun moved steadily higher in the sky and at last one of them stirred. His once-stocky figure was thin and wasted, his ribs showed through his yellowing skin and his arms and face had been burned an angry, blistered red by the sun, almost matching the colour of his hair and beard. Moving with painful slowness, he sat up, bowed his head and his cracked lips moved in a silent prayer.

After so long in the cramped confines of the dinghy, sitting, crouching or huddling on the bottom boards, none of them was able to stand upright. He peered out over the leaden sea, scanning the horizon.

'Nothing.' His voice was weak and hoarse, masking his Essex accent, but his grey-green eyes still showed a steely glint.

The others barely moved in response.

He sat down again on the bench and ran his finger along the gunwale, feeling each of the twenty-three notches carved in it. He took a clasp-knife from his pocket. There was a dark, sticky residue around the base of its two-inch blade.

He tested the edge with his finger, then began stropping the blade against the heel of his palm. The sound was almost hidden by the creaking of the timbers and the lapping of the swell against the boat, but the other two men were instantly alert, their eyes fixed on him as they sat up.

He leaned over the gunwale and cut another notch with four strokes of his knife, then folded it and put it away. He turned to reach under the canvas sheet and handed a small strip of dried meat to each of them. 'There's little enough left,' he said, his voice low and hoarse. 'And we've been four days without rain. If we are not all to perish . . .'

One of the men turned his head away as if ducking his captain's words, but the other's dark, brooding eyes held a warning. 'Let's not talk of that again. A ship will come.'

'But if one does not . . . ?'

'I tell you, a ship will come.' He moved back to the stern and gnawed at his scrap of meat.

The captain studied him for a moment, then began chewing his own piece. It was as brown, tough and dry as old leather and, without saliva, almost impossible to swallow.

After a few moments he set it aside. Moving with painful slowness, he undid his trousers. Each touch of the coarse, salt-encrusted cloth against his skin was agony. He reached into the bottom of the boat for one of the empty tins, and after sitting motionless for several minutes, a few drops of thick yellow urine dribbled into the tin. He closed his eyes and drank it in one gulp, his face slack and expressionless, then resumed his slow chewing.

PART 1

CHAPTER 1

A cold north wind was blowing off the sea, over the wasteland of creeks, marshes and mudflats. Between the banks of reeds and coarse sea-grass, thin streams, shining silver in the light from the cloud-streaked sky, wriggled sinuous as eels across the brown, glistening mud.

Raised wooden walkways on timber piles threaded through the marshes, linking the berths and small jetties lining the creeks. The carcasses of a few mouldering hulks lay on the mudbanks, slowly drowning under a relentless, choking tide of silt. Cormorants perched on them, airing their wings, as herons stalked across the mud, probing with dagger beaks for frogs, eels and fish.

Tom Dudley watched the fishing smacks making their way down-stream on the swirling water of the rising tide, past Shinglehead Point and out into the main channel of the Blackwater. The cries of birds filled the air and the wind carried the sour, earthy smell of the saltings to him; he could almost taste the salt tang at the back of his throat. He had learned his craft in these waters, but this was the last time he would ever sail them.

His stance as he stood at the helm of the yacht *Mignonette* showed his character: feet spread, broad shoulders back, meeting chest-on anything that the sea – or life – could throw at him. His keen eyes were as grey-green as the seas on which he had always earned his living, and his red hair and beard stood out in vivid contrast to the monochrome vista of mud, marsh and water.

The floodtide advanced across the saltings and broke against the sea wall. Part of it had been breached by the winter storms and the pounding waves had scoured away a broad section of the marsh beyond it, as if some sea-monster had risen from the deeps and bitten down into the land.

The defences were being repaired, as they had been countless times before, but all Tollesbury men knew that the sea was an implacable opponent. Whether it stole their land, their ships, their lives, by the sudden, savage assault of a single, ferocious storm, or the relentless attrition of a thousand tides and a million breaking waves, the hunger of the sea could never be assuaged.

Away to the north, at the furthest reach of the marshes, the wooden sails of a windmill creaked and rattled as they turned, pumping fresh water for the livestock from deep below ground. The grazing cattle plodded towards higher pasture, some pausing to rub themselves against the thick baulks of timber, black as bog oaks, driven into the ground. Their trampling hoofs had turned the earth around the scratching posts into a black morass.

The sheep grazing the saltings were also yielding ground to the rising tide, retreating towards the fenceline of up-ended railway sleepers linked by woven rushes, that gave some shelter from the bite of the wind.

Hares lying in the sea-grass waited until the last possible moment, when the tide had almost cut them off, before turning and running in zigzag lines, ears pressed flat against their heads, their feet throwing up webs of spray as they sped inland.

Two men were standing on a plank resting on the marsh, clearing one of the deep drainage ditches running inland from the sea wall. One sliced at the bank with a long-handled sedge-knife, the other followed behind him, lifting the cut squares from the ditch with a crome and dumping them on the bank.

Grey smoke was belching from the lime kiln at Old Hall, and Tom could see the barges tied up at the jetty, unloading the downland chalk for burning. He had once worked there, carrying the wicker baskets of 'blue billy' – quicklime – from the kiln to the waiting carts and waggons. The lime that seeped through the wicker and the coarse weave of his shirt had burned his back red raw.

Tom was thirty-one, the youngest of three sons of George Dudley, a local customs collector turned professional yachtsman. His mother had died when he was only six, and since his elder brothers were already at sea, like their father, he and his younger sister had been taken in by relatives.

He grew up a solitary, introspective child. His lack of inches, pale, freckled face and mop of red hair made him conspicuous among the village children, but he was brave and strong enough to face down or fight those who tried to bully him. From an early age he showed a dogged determination: when set a task he would always achieve it.

Like most Tollesbury families, life for the Dudleys was a hard year-long grind for adults and children alike. Few could afford the twopence a week school fees, and Tom was sent out to work instead whenever there was money to be earned.

Whole families decamped inland for the fruit-picking, pea and bean harvests, leaving the village deserted. The school boards eventually bowed to the inevitable and created an annual pea-picking holiday. The work was back-breaking but Tom earned a few pence a day, and when the harvest was gathered in, the farmers would allow him to collect the spent stalks, to be dried and used as winter kindling.

If at all, the children were back at school only for a few weeks before there was another mass exodus for the grain harvest. After that, there was winkling, eeling, turnip-pulling and a score of other seasonal tasks.

The school attendance officer grew weary of making fruitless calls on the cottage in Head Street, and beyond the Bible instruction at his Sunday school, Tom received almost no education at all, but when he went to sea, he took books with him, and over years of slow, painstaking effort, he taught himself to read and write.

The only real holidays in the year were two one-day fairs: Gooseberry Fair, at the end of the fruit- and pea-picking season, and the feast held in late September to celebrate the return of the many village men who had spent the summer working as crewmen on racing yachts. It was the one time in the year when money flowed freely across the bar of the Plough and Sail and the King's Head.

Tollesbury men were much in demand from the skippers of racing yachts. The bleak, marshy Essex coast and the prevailing cold, offshore winds were reckoned to produce tougher, more skilful seamen than the sheltered ports of the Channel coast. Yachting had boomed since the end of the Napoleonic wars. For the first time, offshore waters were safe for pleasurecraft and the rising prosperity of the middle and upper classes, fuelled by the Industrial Revolution, led to a rapid expansion in the rich men's pastimes of cruising and yacht-racing.

Many owners were as ruthlessly competitive in their sailing as in their business dealings. Having bought or commissioned the best available boats, they were also willing to pay good wages for the best hands, including a share of the prize money. Crews were attired at the owner's expense, with shoes, oilskins, trousers and jerseys embroidered with the name of their yacht.

The racing season began at Harwich in Essex at the start of May and the yachts then sailed clockwise around the coast, calling at the regattas at Southend, Dover and Bangor, before spending a fortnight racing on the river Clyde. They then returned to the south coast for Cowes Week and the Ryde Regatta, and the season ended in September, with a regatta and quayside fair at Dartmouth. Most of the yachts were then laid up for the winter. Their crews found employment on merchant ships and fishing smacks, or worked in boatbuilders' and repairers' yards until the following spring.

Tollesbury was just beginning to establish itself as a yachting centre in its own right, with its own small regatta in the last week of September, to mark the homecoming of the village's men. The return-ing crewmen sometimes earned an illicit bonus by bringing back rum, brandy or tobacco from across the Channel. Excisemen occasionally searched the yachts, but they made no more than a token effort to curb the smuggling; they had, after all, to live among the communities they tried to police.

Like his brothers before him, Tom went to sea, still a child, three months before his tenth birthday. He rowed out with the crew in the grey light of pre-dawn, the fading stars still reflecting in the water and the mournful cries of seabirds filling the air. His boat joined eighty or ninety other smacks crowding the fishing grounds, netting eels in their season, or fishing offshore for skate, sole, plaice, cod, whiting, mackerel, herring and sprats. The sprats were salted down in barrels for shipping to Russia, but most of the other fish was sold locally, hawked from door to door in wicker baskets.

In winter Tom caught eels in the deep mudholes in the saltings, pulled turnips from the frozen fields or joined the ships fishing for 'five-fingers' – the starfish that preyed on the oyster beds. They were sold to the farmers for manure. Other oyster predators like whelks and slipper limpets were killed and thrown overboard.

The first smacks in at the end of the day would line the shore of Woodrolfe creek and later arrivals had to unload across their decks. The starfish were piled in baskets and driven away in tumbrils to the farms around Tollesbury.

Tom would arrive home at night heavy with the stench of rotting starfish. It was filthy work, disliked by all the men, but there were few alternatives. When storms kept the fishing smacks at home there was no money at all and in some bleak winters the Dudleys were forced to join the forty other village families claiming poor relief from the parish.

Tom also worked on the oyster dredges. The crew sweated over the windlasses, hauling in dredges full of culch – the pieces of dead shell to which the oysters attached themselves. They were then sorted by size into brood, half-ware and ware. The ware – the adult, full-grown oysters – were packed into barrels for sale; the brood and half-ware were returned to the seabed or moved to private dredging grounds.

'The most valuable native oyster breeding ground in the world, or at least, the Kingdom,' was now only a memory, however, wrecked by overfishing and the sale of oyster brood to other fisheries. A few years before, over five million tons had been shipped to Whitstable alone in a single three-month period. Every Tollesbury man knew it could not be sustained, but none would step back while others continued to plunder the Blackwater. The dredgers continued to operate, but each year the catch diminished.

Tom's fingers tightened on the helm, but before giving the order to cast off, he turned to cast a last glance behind him. Beyond the marshes, a group of low cottages huddled around the squat church tower like children sheltering behind their mother's skirts. He picked out first the school and then the reed-thatch of the nearby cottage in Head Street.

As he had walked down through the village that morning, he had stopped outside the house. The door stood ajar and he peered into the kitchen, seeing the familiar iron range, scrubbed wooden table and worn rag rug on the bare brick floor. There was to be no farewell to his father: he was away on a year-long voyage to the Americas and no longer kept the house.

Tom's eye lingered on the village a little longer, then he turned his back, setting his gaze out to sea. His wife, Philippa, stood alongside him in the stern, cradling their youngest child against her shoulder. She was several years older than Tom and a couple of inches taller than his stocky, powerful figure. She did not speak, not wishing to wake her sleeping baby, but she studied his face for a moment, then reached out and laid a hand on his arm. As he turned towards her, she gave him a gentle, understanding smile.

His expression softened as he looked at her, then he raised his eyes to the horizon and paused, seeming to scent the wind. He frowned. It was backing north-westerly and freshening all the while. 'I'm afraid it will not be a pleasure cruise, my dear. There's another blow coming on.'

William Frost, the younger of the two brothers who formed his crew, stood ready at the warp tethering the *Mignonette* to her mooring. He had reached his fourteenth birthday only the previous week, but had been at sea since he was twelve. His brother, Jim, was four years older and already an experienced able seaman. They were also natives of Tollesbury and Tom had known them all their lives.

'Let go,' he said.

'Wait!'

Tom stifled a curse as he saw a figure running along the walkway towards them. It had taken all his powers of persuasion to convince the Frost brothers to make the voyage. He did not want their father to talk them out of it now, but he could not prevent Joe Frost from making one last try.

'You're not to be dissuaded, then?'

Tom shook his head. 'I've given my word to the owner. I'll not go back on it.'

Joe paused, choosing his words with care. 'Tom, there are few braver sailors on this coast, nor fairer men, but you're sailing across the world in a twenty-year-old yacht. She was built for inshore waters, not great oceans.'

'You know the yard that built it. Their boats are stout-timbered and solid, and the *Mignonette*' – he had given up trying to adapt his broad

Essex accent to the French pronunciation and called it 'Miggonette' – 'was built as a cruiser and fishing boat. Only later was she converted to a racing yacht. If she's properly handled, she'll do well enough on any ocean.'

'She's an old boat and she's been lying on the Brightlingsea mud all winter.'

Tom nodded. 'And she's been fitted out since then by a man we both know and trust.'

'My boys are on board, Tom.'

He glanced at Philippa. 'As are my wife and child. Do you think I'd risk them?'

'But they are sailing only to Southampton, not New South Wales.'

'And if your boys are not happy with the *Mignonette* after sailing her that far, they can also leave ship. You have my word on that.'

Joe hesitated, looking from his sons to Tom. 'Will you not reconsider, before this ends in disaster?'

Embarrassed and uncomfortable, the boys barely met their father's gaze.

Tom shook his head. 'I will not. It will be the start of a new life for myself and my family, and I have given my word.'

Joe stood with his hand half extended, then let it fall to his side. He embraced his sons and walked away, unwilling to watch as the yacht slipped from her mooring and began to drift down Tollesbury Fleet.

Tom kept a careful eye on the boys as they went to their work, raising sail. They had said not a word, but their father's anxiety was now mirrored in their faces.

Still backing into the north-west, the wind drove them down South Channel, past Great Cob Island. Mounds of oyster culch were spread on the shore, left to dry and bleach in the summer sun. Tom raised a hand in farewell to the men mending the sea wall from a barge. They paused to watch the *Mignonette* slip downstream then resumed their work, driving split elm piles into the riverbed and dumping boulders around them.

As the yacht cleared Shinglehead Point, she lay over to the wind, driven into a swell that was short and steep even in the sheltered waters of the estuary.

Tom's gaze was never far from the sails and he felt every tremor of the boat through the helm as he steered south-east towards the distant Kent coast. It was the first voyage in the *Mignonette* for all of them and each boat was an individual. Her ways had to be learned, her strengths utilized, her weaknesses protected.

She was a thirty-tonner, a little over fifty foot long and twelve foot in beam, with a seven-foot draught. She carried sixteen tons of lead ballast and another three tons carried externally on the keel. That made her a stiff boat, slow to roll with the swell but quick to right again as the keel weight hauled her back to the vertical.

For all her weight, she was a fast yacht and had won her share of prize money over the years. She carried a fair spread of canvas on the main mast – with her top mast up, she was rigged to sixty foot above the deck – and had three jibs rigged from the main mast to the bowsprit, and a small mizzen mast, set well aft, almost on the taff rail.

As they cleared the Maplin Sands and began to cross the Thames Estuary, the sea was speckled with sails. Barges laden with stinking nightsoil – human excrement – hugged the Essex shore, bound for the ports where it would be sold as farm manure.

Packet boats, clippers and barques were beating up the channel, racing to make port before the backing wind forced them to heave-to, while smaller craft – coasters, fishing smacks and pleasureboats – scurried for the shelter of shore and harbour. Only the steamers held a straight course, the wind laying the black columns of smoke from their stacks parallel to the water behind them as they ploughed through the waves towards the capital.

The *Mignonette* pitched and rolled in the swell. The baby awoke, crying, and a stream of milky puke poured on to Philippa's shoulder. 'Best take the child below,' Tom said. 'We'll have no shelter from the wind until we round the North Foreland.'

He set the Frosts to reef then double-reef the mainsail, but even with the jib down, the yacht still sped before the wind, its mast bent and its bowsprit plunging through the swell as water cascaded over the bows and foamed out through the scuppers.

The sky was growing still darker and above the howl of the wind, the groan of the timbers and the relentless thud of waves against the bow,

Tom heard a distant rumble of thunder. He saw a grey, opaque curtain of rain to the west, binding the black clouds to the sea. It raced towards them on the wind, lit from within by stabs of lightning.

'Tom?' Philippa's pale face appeared at the head of the companion-way. 'There's water leaking in.'

'How much?'

'An inch or so, but it's still rising.'

She tried to keep her voice calm but he heard the edge of fear in it, and held his own expression impassive. 'Don't be alarmed, it's normal in a storm.' He raised his voice. 'William, Jim, get forward and man the pumps.'

They ran to the head. The leather washers inside the barrels of the pumps wheezed like consumptive lungs as they began working the hand-pumps and the stinking bilge water poured over the side. The Frosts struggled to hold their ground as the wash from the largest waves coursed over the bows, reaching almost to their thighs. Their oilskins gleamed in the spray, showing dull reflections of the lightning strikes piercing the black sky.

The heart of the storm rolled over the ship. It was as dark as dusk. Torrents of rain cascaded from the gleaming sails, flooding the deck, and lightning forks counterpointed each peal of thunder, which came so hard and fast that it sounded like one long, booming concussion.

Even amid the clamour of the storm, Tom heard little Julian's insistent cries. He cursed himself for bringing Philippa and the baby with him instead of leaving them safe at home in Sutton, but the chance of a cruise on the yacht without the inhibiting presence of its owner had been a rare opportunity. He was also anxious to spend every possible minute with Philippa before their parting. In seven years of marriage, she had grown accustomed to his absences at sea, but even during the racing season, when regatta followed regatta around the coast, Tom was never more than a day's sail from port. He would often catch the mail train, arriving home in the early hours to snatch a day with his family before the next regatta began.

This time was different, a voyage of over ten thousand miles to deliver the yacht to its new owner in Sydney. Like Joe Frost, some of Tom's friends had tried to persuade him not to make the voyage, predicting danger and possible disaster, but other captains had made similar voyages in even smaller ships, and in over twenty years at sea, Tom felt he had learned enough to find a safe passage to Australia.

The potential dangers of the voyage worried him less than the separation from his family. Once the *Mignonette* sailed from Southampton, Philippa would have no word of him other than a letter passed to an inbound ship, if they chanced to meet one, until they made port. He would have no way of knowing if his wife and children were well or ill until he reached New South Wales, and it would be approaching a year, perhaps even longer, before he laid eyes on them again. Whatever happened to them in the meantime, he would be powerless to provide help until they too, arrived in Sydney.

He pushed that thought away as soon as it formed, gripping the helm so hard that the veins stood out on his arms. The storm rolled past and the thunder faded to a dull, distant rumble, losing itself in the empty reaches of the North Sea. The rain eased as the sky lightened, but the wind and the swell kept up their twin assaults on the ship.

The Frost brothers still stood in the bow working the pumps and foul bilgewater spewed from the side in a steady stream. Tom called to Philippa. 'What is the level now?'

'The same.'

He frowned. It was a problem that would have to be addressed, but for the moment he had his hands full simply holding the ship to its course and fighting the violent kick of the rudder as the yacht met each wave. His gaze raked the mast-top, the rigging and the straining sails, then returned to the grey march of the waves ahead of the bow. He thought about reducing canvas still further, but the gale seemed to have reached its peak and the sheltering east coast of Kent was now not far away.

He saw Margate off the starboard beam, and a few minutes later the coastline to the south began to open up. He called the Frosts back from the pumps. 'Ready to go about.'

They released the canvas of the mainsail and held it taut ready for the swing of the boom.

'Haul sail.' They released the bracing ropes, the boom swung over and the sails filled again with a crack.

'Well all.'

They returned to the head and bent once more to the pumps.

The edge of the wind was blunted and the swell lessened as they sailed into the sheltered waters of the Downs, between the Goodwin Sands and the Kent coast. Scores of other ships had also taken refuge there from the storm.

Tom kept the sails close-hauled and called Jim back to take the helm. The acrid smell of vomit filled his nostrils as he went down the companionway. He carried a stinking bucket on deck and tipped it over the side, then went back below.

Philippa was sitting in Tom's cabin nursing the child on her lap. Both were wan and drawn. 'I'm sorry,' she said. 'I feel a little better now.'

He took her hand in his and stroked the baby's cheek, then moved away through the below-decks, scrutinizing the planking. There was a small leak around the base of the bowsprit, but the ship's carpenter had not been born who could stop water coming in there in a heavy swell. More worrying was the steady trickle of water through the garboard strakes – the planking near the keel towards the stern of the boat.

He watched it for some minutes. It was no more than a slow trickle for most of that time, but when Jim allowed the bow to come round a little and a big wave caught them more towards the beam, the planking seemed to twist as the hull flexed and water poured through the seams. As the ship was righted, the leak again dwindled to a slow seepage.

Philippa was watching him. 'Is it serious?'

He shrugged. 'It will be, if it's not repaired.'

'But the boat was fitted out at Brightlingsea.'

He nodded. 'I know, I know, but ships are like sailors. Some faults only show themselves when you're at sea.'

He paused, studying the leak again. 'We've seen the worst of the weather for now. We'll make for Southampton as planned and I'll have her hauled out and repaired there. It'll eat into the profit on the voyage a little, but there'll still be a handsome return – enough to buy us a new house for a new life in Australia.' He stooped and kissed her brow. She gave him a weak answering smile before he went back on deck.

CHAPTER 2

Tom had spent his first six years at sea on fishing smacks and coasters, working his way up from cabin boy to ordinary seaman, then able seaman. When he was fifteen he joined his father as a crewman on a Clyde racing yacht, the *Condor*, under Captain Mackie.

There was the inevitable talk among the crew that he only had the berth because of his father, but one day they were caught in a full gale coming through St George's Channel and had to run before the wind. The yacht was heeled over so far that the boom was half submerged and ploughing its own parallel white furrow through the water. When the others refused orders to go out along the boom to reef the sail, Tom crawled to the end of it and did the job himself. After that there was no more talk of favourites.

During the winter he worked as cook-steward on a trading schooner, the *Lady Rodney*, out of Salcombe. It was a curious position, outside the normal chain of command of the ship. He was responsible only to Captain Cowling and had sole charge of the food stores; no one else was permitted even to enter the pantry. Like many other ships of the time, it carried live animals as part of the foodstores and Tom had to learn the craft of butchery.

The first animal Tom slaughtered was a pig. There was no one to teach him, only the instructions outlined in a dog-eared copy of *The Steward's Handbook*:

It is very essential that livestock before being killed must not be given any food for twelve hours. Plenty of water must, however, be supplied to them to prevent the blood from being loaded with an excess of food matter and thus rendered difficult from being eliminated from the smaller blood vessels in the flesh. In this condition it would very rapidly commence to decompose. The water must be given in abundance in order to keep the temperature of the blood normal and thus render it more fluid for clearing out the blood vessels . . .

Tom had given the pig copious quantities of water and ignored its ever-louder clamour for food, but when the time came to despatch it, he found ways to postpone the event by checking his stores, sharpening and resharpening his knives.

At last he could delay no longer. He tied a rope around the pig's neck and bound it down to a ringbolt in the deck. It took an effort of will to move to the next stage, for the pig kept up a terrible, almost human squealing, as if realizing his intentions.

He took a deep breath and braced himself, his legs spread to counter the steady roll of the ship. Averting his eyes, he grasped the handle of the heavy iron poleaxe and brought its pointed blade down with all his strength on top of the pig's head. The squeals ended abruptly as it slumped to the deck but, as the handbook instructed, he worked the end of the poleaxe around inside the hole, destroying the brain.

He opened up the gullet with his knife and severed the arteries on either side of the neck, catching the blood in a bucket as it poured from the dying beast. Clouds of steam filled the cold air, carrying the hot, sweet, sickly smell of blood.

Tom gagged and had to retreat for a few lungfuls of the fresher air at the foot of the companionway before he could return to complete the task. He turned the pig on to its back and cut off its head and trotters. Forcing himself to concentrate only on the next cut to be made, he sawed through the breastbone, then slit the pig from stomach to tail. A slippery tide of entrails spilled on to the stained wooden deck. Gritting his teeth, he pushed his hands inside the carcass and pulled out the remainder of them, separated out the kidneys and liver and removed the gall bladder. Next came the heart and lungs. Then he washed out the carcass with buckets of sea-water, and began to joint it, turning it from a still-recognizable body into meat.

He was never to find slaughtering and butchering animals easy, but it was his job, and he taught himself to do it as skilfully as he passed a reef earing or furled a sail.

While the captain feasted on fresh pork that night, Tom and the rest of the crew ate 'salt-horse' – rank, unidentifiable meat pickled in brine. Like many other cheapskate captains and ship-owners, Cowling had bought it from contractors who sold on barrels of salt beef bought from the naval victualling yards and condemned as unfit for Royal Navy use.

The unpleasantness of some of his work was only one of Tom's problems on board the *Lady Rodney*. She was the worst ship he had ever sailed on, undermanned, underprovisioned and with a drunken tyrant for a captain, who used his fists and floggings with a knotted rope to re-inforce his orders. Tom vowed that if ever he was master of his own ship, he would not treat his men the way Captain Cowling had treated them.

Tom and another hand, Frank Williams, jumped ship in St Michael's in the Azores and found passage home on a schooner bound for Hull. After that he served under better captains and on better schooners, but he never forgot the misery of the voyage on the *Lady Rodney*, or the vow he made to himself.

He sailed with merchant ships – the *Jane Ann*, the *Annie Grant* and the *Bohemian Girl* – to Spain, Portugal, Genoa and Newfoundland, but his heart was in yacht-racing. At the start of every season he returned to England and found a berth on a yacht, first with his father and then on his own account. For fourteen years it was his life and he built a reputation as a solid, dependable, brave character. One captain under whom he served described him as 'a sober, steady, respectable, God-fearing man and a smarter or pluckier one never sailed a boat'.

In 1873 he was able seaman on Prince Albert of Monaco's yacht, *Pleiad*, sailing out of Torquay. The following year he was promoted to boatswain on a forty-ton cutter, the *Mosquito*, out of Greenock, and by the next season he had become mate on the *Fiona*, a cutter owned by Mr Boutcher. His crew did well for him, winning over £500 in prize money that season, but he was a generous man, and more than once divided the prize between the crew.

In 1876 Tom was given his first command as a sailing master, the *Camelia*, after Captain Mackie of the *Condor* spoke to the owner on his behalf. She was a small boat out of Greenock, rated at just five tons against the *Fiona*'s eighty, but he had a good season with her that year and a better one the next, when he was first across the line fifteen times, earning over £200 in prizes, though the owner lost half of that in a private match with the owner of a rival yacht.

Tom was master of Tom Kirk's ten-tonner, the *Volga*, over the next two years, winning eight races. He moved to the *Reindeer*, a 100-tonner owned by Iain MacNab for two years after that, and then captained the *Nexie* for Mr Addie until the owner's death in 1883.

By this time Tom was well known amongst the yachting fraternity from Southampton to the Clyde, and was considered 'one of the smartest men who ever sailed a small yacht'.

He had met Philippa Julian, the mistress of Plymstock Board School, while he was sailing at the Plymouth Regatta in 1877. She was taller than Tom's five foot three and was seven years older than him. She was the daughter of a tin miner, William Julian, but he had died when she was young and she had been raised by her uncle, Richard, a school-teacher. She named him as her father on the marriage certificate.

Tom and Philippa married at St Saviour's the day after Boxing Day 1877, and lived at the school house in Oreston until she became mistress of Newtown Board School in Sutton, Surrey, in 1880. They had three children, Philippa, born just before they moved to Surrey, Winifred, born in 1881, and Julian in 1883.

Although there was no shortage of demand for Tom's services as a sailing master during the season, winter work was harder to find and often entailed long absences from home on overseas voyages. His lack of formal qualifications was no obstacle to employment on racing yachts, where experience, seamanship and, above all, the ability to get across the line ahead of your rivals were the only qualifications necessary.

When Tom first went to sea, merchant ships had taken a similarly relaxed view of qualifications. Custom and practice, not the law, ruled almost every aspect of life on board ship. The way to acquire a skill was to learn it at sea, and promotion was by merit, default or sheer necessity. You became an able seaman, a boatswain or a mate because you had shown yourself a steady, reliable hand, and you learned the trade as you went along.

Ship-owners and captains still remained free to maintain a near-feudal rule over their wooden estates, but from the middle of the nineteenth century, government regulation had begun to intrude on other aspects of shipboard life. The law now required senior officers responsible for the navigation of a British ship to hold certificates of efficiency. Having secured a second mate's certificate, an officer had to serve at least a year at sea before his first mate's examination, and then a further two years before taking his master's certificate.

With Philippa's encouragement, Tom passed his mate's certificate. His qualification of 'only mate' allowed him to skipper small yachts but he needed more service on large ships and additional qualifications if he was to secure further promotion.

He was already turning away from the sea, however, anxious to find secure work on land that would both enable him to spend more time with his growing family and allow Philippa to give up her own employment. In partnership with another man, he set up a greengrocery business in Sutton. He hoped to retire from the sea altogether, as soon as it was established, but while he was away at sea, his partner took every penny from the business and disappeared. Tom could find no trace of him or his money; it was said that he had emigrated to the colonies.

Philippa's aunt, Mrs Pettigrew, was in business in a small way as a tent-maker in Sydney, and when she heard of their misfortunes, she wrote offering to take in Tom as a partner, with a view to expanding the business to include sailmaking and yacht chandlery.

The idea tempted him, but a natural caution and his earlier bad experience in a partnership made him reluctant to risk everything on a new venture in a land that they had not even seen. He replied, asking for more time to settle his affairs, then went back to sea, captaining the *Myrtle*, a steam yacht of 200 tons, out of Wigtown in Galloway.

The following January, Tom was rehired to skipper the *Myrtle* on a winter Mediterranean cruise for Sir Charles Strickland and ten of his guests. They sailed on 7 January 1884 and had an easy enough voyage out, but the return was stormy and after battling gales and mountainous head seas, they had to put into Corunna for additional coals. When they made port at Dartmouth on 23 April, Tom found a cable waiting for him from Andrew Thompson of the Thames Yacht Agency in London.

Seamen could be recruited on any wharf and harbour in England, but good skippers and mates were rarer breeds and competing yacht owners used agents like Andrew Thompson to secure the best crews. Thompson had known Tom for some years and thought highly of him. When a gentleman from the colonies arrived at his offices in Adelphi Terrace, the Strand, one early spring morning, looking for a man to take a yacht out to New South Wales, Thompson immediately recommended Tom as 'a bold and fearless man, much sought after by the owners of yachts'.

Jack Want, a flamboyant Australian lawyer and politician, was also a keen yachtsman. His father had been a founder member of the Royal Sydney Yacht Squadron in 1862; Jack was also a member, and a former commodore of the Royal Prince Albert Yacht Club. He owned a ten-ton yacht, the *Guinevere*, but had arrived in England looking for a fast – but cheap – boat to take back to Sydney. He had chartered the forty-two ton *Terpsichore* for the 1883 season and raised hackles among the more hide-bound yachting clubs by picking up first prizes at Ostend, Ryde and Torbay.

Want's membership of the most exclusive clubs in Australia carried no weight in English yachting circles and his bluff manner was not to the taste of English club commodores. Like that other expensive rich man's fancy, horse-racing, yachting not only provided an opportunity for prodigious expenditure and ostentation, but also the practice of rigid social exclusion. The more élite yachting clubs, like the Royal Yacht Squadron at Cowes, were every bit as exclusive as the Royal Enclosure at Ascot, with great wealth a necessary but by no means sufficient pre-requisite for membership.

One of the rules of yacht-racing was that every competing boat must either carry its owner or a member of the sailing club. Breaching the rule by entering races in someone else's yacht was bad enough, but winning them was most certainly not the conduct of a gentleman. An acrimonious correspondence filled the letters columns of the sporting press and Want found himself blackballed from the leading clubs.

His enthusiasm for English yachting clubs may have been diminished but his admiration for English yachts and crews remained undimmed. He resumed his search for a yacht that could be shipped back to Sydney, anxious both for a competitive edge in races there and for the status that an English-built boat would confer on him.

The *Mignonette* seemed to fit the bill. A solid, though somewhat elderly boat, first registered in September 1867, she had been raced with some success over the previous few years. She was owned by Mr S. Hall, a member of the Welsh and New Thames clubs, who was having a new yacht built for him.

After a brief period of ungentlemanly haggling, Want purchased the *Mignonette* for £400 cash. She was too large to be shipped to Sydney as deck cargo, and he began the search for a captain to sail her there.

On Andrew Thompson's recommendation, he caught a train to Dartmouth to meet Tom Dudley. They took to each other immediately. For all Want's flamboyance he was, like Tom, a blunt-spoken and honest man, and in Tom's steady gaze, square stance and soft Essex brogue, he detected the qualities of courage, reliability and honesty that he was seeking.

He offered a handsome fee: £100 in advance, with a further £100 on delivery of the yacht. Even though Tom had to provision the boat and pay the crew from his own pocket, he would be left with around £140 after meeting all expenses – enough to buy a house in Sydney and pay the passage of his wife and family to join him. Want also told him that he could remain as master of the *Mignonette* after he reached Sydney and keep on the crew as well, if they so wished.

The offer could scarcely have been better timed, for it gave Tom the chance to see Sydney for himself and assess Mrs Pettigrew's business proposition without any financial risk, but still he hesitated before accepting. The *Mignonette* was a small, old boat for such a voyage, and for all his years at sea, Tom had little experience of deep-sea sailing and had never crossed the Line.

He asked Want for time to consider the offer and discussed it deep into the night with Philippa. He also read every account of voyages in similar craft he could find and talked with many other sailing masters. Some tried to dissuade him but most felt as Tom did, that if properly handled, a small boat would be at no more risk than a ship ten times her size. He met Jack Want again later that week and shook hands on the deal.

Tom brought the *Myrtle* into Southampton on Sunday 27 April 1884. He returned home to Sutton the next morning, and the following weekend he and Philippa travelled to Tollesbury with the baby, leaving the other children in the care of Philippa's sister. On his way across London he took out life insurance of £200 and deposited the policy in the hands of Andrew Thompson.

The shipwright who had fitted out the *Mignonette* had already brought her the few miles down the coast from Brightlingsea, and they sailed from Tollesbury on Monday 5 May.

Tom remained on deck throughout the rest of that day and the night that followed, fearing the strengthening gale as they came out of the shelter of the Kent coast. Water continued to leak through the ship's planking so fast that one or both of the Frost brothers was continuously at work on the bilge pumps throughout the voyage.

As they passed off Brighton, two bathing machines floated past them, ripped from the beach by the power of the storm and driven like drift-wood before the wind, but the gale and the seas were already abating, and they reached the Solent safely just after dawn on Wednesday 7 May.

They sailed up Southampton Water past the mass of barques and packet boats waiting their turn to unload at the wharves. Rising above them were the iron towers of the steam cranes and the huge, round drums of the old wooden treadmills, driven by the feet of scores of men, which were still used at some of the older docks to raise cargo from the ships' holds.

The *Mignonette* sailed on into the Itchen, and they moored at Northam on the west bank of the river, at half past eight. Still pale from the effects of sea-sickness, Philippa and the child left for home at once, leaving Tom to follow once he had organized the repairs to the ship.

As soon as they had tied up, the Frost brothers were ready to jump ship, frightened by the defects in the yacht that the rough passage from Essex had revealed. Jim acted as spokesman while William hung back behind him, his eyes averted and his cheeks crimson with embarrassment.

31

'We wish to leave the ship, Captain Dudley,' Jim said.

Tom paused for a moment, weighing his words. 'It's been a difficult voyage from Tollesbury, I'll grant you, but I'll have her hauled out here and the planking repaired. She'll be as sound as any ship then.'

'Just the same, we want away.' Jim twisted his cap in his hands. 'You gave your word to our father.'

'Indeed I did, and none can say that Tom Dudley doesn't keep his word, but I would be disappointed to lose you. I'll be taking on an extra pair of hands, a mate, before we sail. The leaks will be plugged and the work less hard. Will you not sail with me? Australia could be the making of you.'

'We know our mind on this, Captain Dudley. It is not to be altered.'

Tom hesitated a moment longer, then gave a resigned shake of his head. 'So be it, then. I'll pay your wages and your fare back to Tollesbury, unless you're looking to join another ship here?'

'We plan to.'

'Then I'll speak for you with any captain you find.' He held out his hand. 'Good luck. Come and find us in Sydney, if your voyages should ever take you that far.'

Tom had the *Mignonette* hauled out at Fay's Yard in Northam. He knew it by reputation as the best, and best-value, yard in the area. He paced up and down alongside the yacht as it lay on its side, its keel exposed, while the shipwright peered at the timbers and prodded them with the blade of his knife. 'The garboard strakes are rotten. They'll have to be replaced.'

Tom nodded, already knowing that much. 'Use what you can of the existing timbers when you're replacing them,' he said. 'I don't want to lose the profit on the voyage before I've even set sail.'

The man grunted, still probing the timbers with his knife. 'The keel-wood's soft too.'

'If I replace that, I'll be sailing her to the colonies for nothing. Can you make it sound without replacing the keel?'

The shipwright glanced at him. 'I can, but it'll not last many more winters.'

Tom smiled. 'It'll not need to. They tell me there's no such thing as winter where this yacht's bound.'

'Just the same, tell the owner the keelwood needs watching. If it rots much more the ship'll open up like a dock whore's legs. Anything else?'

'Yes, shorten the bowsprit by a couple of yards, and take the mizzen mast out of her as well. I want her cutter-rigged. She's over-canvased, good sailing in light winds, but top heavy in a big blow.'

A mizzen sail slightly improved a yacht's handling on the wind and the yawl rig also increased the overall spread of canvas, or enabled a captain to carry a smaller, more easily handled mainsail, but with a crew of four the weight of even a saturated mainsail would present no difficulties and the *Mignonette* already carried more sail than would be safe in the conditions they would face in the Atlantic and Southern oceans.

'The mizzen mast and the bowsprit are easy enough done, at any rate,' the shipwright said.

'And you'll allow me the value of the mast against the new planking?'

He laughed. 'I will, such as it is. Twenty-year-old sticks have no great value, except as firewood. Is that everything?'

'No, put a coat of copper paint on her hull. It'll keep the barnacles from fouling her. I need every scrap of speed she can give me.' He paused. 'And you could spread word that I'm looking for a crew – mate, able seaman and a boy. We're bound for New South Wales. I'll pay well for the right men and the provisions will be ample and good.'

'No salt-horse, then?'

He shuddered at the thought. 'None of that. Fresh pork while it lasts and canned beef after that.'

CHAPTER 3

Tom returned home while the repairs to the *Mignonette* were carried out but he was back in Southampton on Wednesday 14 May to begin the search for a new crew. It was a still morning and a pall of smoke hung over the city, drifting over the rooftops to merge with the river mist.

The streets were jammed with traffic. Carts, carriages and hansom cabs rattled past, horseshoes striking sparks from the cobbles, and the warm smell of dung mingled with the acrid stink of soot and smoke in the air.

Lower on the hillside, the streets leading down to the quays were full of a jostling tide of people, most of them pinched and poor-looking. The gutters of the meaner streets ran with filth, and the dark alleys and refuse-strewn courts stank of stale urine. There were piles of human excrement, crawling with flies.

Like every port, the warren of cobbled streets, lanes and alleys surrounding the wharves and warehouses was crowded with taverns and grog shops. Some had purpose-built pits in which dog-, cock- and rat-fights were staged. There were scores of brothels and the music- and dance-halls were also thinly disguised knocking-shops. Many of the prostitutes were little more than children.

The scabrous business of the port was conducted side by side with more respectable trades – shipping agents, ship's chandlers, roperies and sail lofts, provision merchants, marine stores, pawn shops and curiosity shops full of shells, coral, native artefacts and seamen's carvings, scrimshaws and ships in bottles.

As in every port, there was a tattoo parlour, where drunken young seamen were brought for one of their painful rites of initiation. As well as nautical motifs, like mermaids or anchors, many had a large crucifix tattooed on their chest, in the hope of ensuring a Christian burial if they were wrecked or drowned and washed up on a heathen shore.

The tattoo parlour also pierced ears, and even before drink and whores, a single gold earring would be a young seaman's first purchase after being paid off from his maiden voyage. Unlike coin, the gold he wore in his ear could not readily be spent or stolen, but it was the currency that might save him from starvation or secure him a passage home if cast up or abandoned on some distant coast.

The boarding-houses, slums and tenements that accommodated the seamen between ships were also home to stevedores, labourers, lumpers and hauliers, watermen, warehousemen, ballast men and colliers, balladeers and broadside-sellers, the mudlarks who scoured the harbour and riverbeds for valuables at low tide, and the beggars, thieves and whores who preyed on all of them.

A number of seamen's charities, including Sailors Homes, the British & Foreign Sailors Society, the Royal National Institute for the Preservation of Life from Shipwreck and the Destitute Sailors Asylum, had been set up in the first half of the century. The more prudent seamen found lodging with them, or in the decent boarding-houses run by former sailors and offering a clean, comfortable bed and a decent meal.

Other lodgings were rat-infested slums and rookeries, their floors crowded with filthy straw mattresses open to people of both sexes and all ages. Young children would sleep alongside drunken men and whores, destitutes on parish relief, the sick, the crippled, the old and the dying. The worst lodgings were run by the 'land sharks' – crimps and boarding-house masters – who made their living by delivering drunk, drugged or unconscious seamen to captains of outward-bound ships. The captains paid the crimps a commission and never queried the methods by which they obtained these unwilling recruits.

Fishermen, merchant seamen or anyone else foolish or unfortunate enough to be loitering near the dockside had always been ripe for the press-gangs dragooning men into service with the Royal Navy. If there were insufficent men to be found there, the press gangs would move inland. If they still could not find enough victims, it was not unusual for notorious prisons like Newgate and the Fleet to be emptied of able-bodied prisoners.

The practice of press-ganging men for the Navy had been in existence for centuries, but that of crimps snaring crews for merchant ships was a largely nineteenth-century evil. Crimps, or more usually the runners operating on their behalf, would meet inbound ships, often boarding them with grappling irons and offering liquor and the best whores in town as inducements to seamen to jump ship with them at once. The men were often only too willing to make shore at the first opportunity andmost captains turned a blind eye, either bribed to win their acquiescence or merely relieved to be free of the burden of paying the crewduring the largely idle time in port before the next voyage.

The runners' victims were brought ashore and delivered to the crimps, who would ply them with drink and drugs, surround them with whores, part them from their wages and often ship them out again the same night. A few waterside boarding-houses had trap-doors through which the unconscious victims could be lowered into a waiting boat without even leaving the building. They were rowed away across the harbour and handed over to any ship's captain willing to pay the crimp's fee.

The unfortunate sailors were confined below decks and not released until their new ship was already at sea. They then had no choice but to work for whatever pay the captain chose to offer, with the added indignity that the commission of the men who had kidnapped them was deducted from their wages. If they refused to work, the flesh would be flogged from their backs.

Seamen just returned from a year or more away might open their eyes to discover themselves outward-bound once more on another hell-ship with no money in their pocket and their first two or three months' wages lost to the crimp's commission.

Some operators were not above passing off a dead body, pulled from the harbour, collected from the street after a fatal brawl, or bought from the custodian of the Dead House – the morgue where unclaimed bodies were stored. Soused in gin or rum, it would be delivered to a ship – just one more unconscious crew member – and the deception would not be discovered until the ship had sailed and the crimp's commission had been safely secured.

Many of the tailors fitting out seamen for ocean voyages also operated practices that were as venal as those of the crimps. They would take sailors' advance notes – the letters of credit given by a ship's captain to enable his crewmen to equip themselves for the voyage – but while measuring the seamen for their clothes, the tailors would once more ply the seaman with whores and drugged drinks. The comatose victim would be carried to his ship by the tailor's runners and wake to find that his advance note had disappeared. The tailor often shared the proceeds with the ship's captain. All the seaman had to show for it was a sore head and – if he was lucky – a sea-chest full of often worthless second-hand clothes, which might even have been stripped from dead bodies.

So many seamen were victims of the crimps, boarding-house masters and tailors that the ceremony of 'selling the dead horse' was a feature of most voyages around the Horn or the Cape. A symbolic wooden horse whittled by one of the crew was pitched into the sea to celebrate the end of the time that the seamen had worked for nothing to pay off the commissions and advance notes.

Long after the press-gang had been outlawed, crimps continued the forced recruitment of seamen; well into the twentieth century men were still being delivered to ships unconscious, or comatose through drink or drugs.

Tom steered well clear of the crimps and boarding-house masters of Southampton, preferring to find a crew that was both willing and able by spreading the word around the boatyards, yachting agents and dockside taverns. He had little difficulty in finding the men he wanted. Although not comparable with earnings on a good racing yacht, the rates of pay he was offering were above the norm for ships on the Australia run, and food, which was often charged against the men's wages, was included. It was also of much better quality than that likely to be supplied on most merchant ships.

The ship's articles specified that each man was to receive a weekly ration of six pounds of beef, three and three-quarter pounds of pork, one pint of peas and seven pounds of 'hard tack' – ship's biscuit. In addition there was one and a half pounds of flour per week, used for the fresh bread baked on Sundays, one-eighth of an ounce of tea, two ounces of sugar, and a daily water ration of three quarts. There would be no alcohol on board. Although not a teetotaller, Tom was a moderate drinker who preferred a sober crew, unfortified by grog.

He also offered the customary arrangement of finding return voyages for his crew aboard British vessels at standard wages, or paying the cost of their passages home, though there was the promise of work for all of them in Sydney if they wanted to stay.

Edmund 'Ned' Brooks was the first to sign, engaged as able seaman and ship's cook at five pounds ten shillings a month, with the offer of continuing work at the same rates on the *Mignonette* in Sydney. He heard about the berth through the shipwright at Fay's Yard, where he worked as a rigger between jobs at sea.

A native of Brightlingsea, just up the coast from Tollesbury, he had been at sea since the age of twelve and had known Tom since the early 1870s, when they had crewed rival racing yachts. He was three days short of his thirty-eighth birthday when he signed the ship's articles, but whether through error or befuddlement with drink, he gave his age as thirty-nine.

He had been in steady work for a number of years, spending the summers as a yacht hand and the winters on the steamers of the Union Lines, most recently the *Athenian*, and it surprised Tom that Brooks did not have better accommodation than his dingy lodgings at the County Tavern in Northam, run by Mary Egerton.

Brooks was taller and more powerfully built than Tom. He had a swarthy countenance, and his dark eyes and brooding expression, framed by his jet-black hair, gave him a permanently sullen air. He smiled rarely. When he did, he showed a mouthful of tobacco-stained teeth like weathered tombstones. His speech was peppered with curses, for which Tom had no liking, but he was a highly regarded yacht hand, and had raced for four seasons under Captain O'Neill, one of the most successful skippers of racing cutters.

A lavish new yacht was nearing completion at Fay's Yard, which O'Neill was to skipper that season. Brooks had the offer of a berth on her and the prospect of a share in her prize money, but he preferred to cast in his lot with Tom and the *Mignonette*, telling him that he wanted to make a new life for himself in the colonies.

He was a heavy drinker, as many seamen were, ashore or afloat, but there were also rumours in Northam and Brightlingsea that he had abandoned a wife and children. Tom had heard the stories and charged Brooks with them, but he vehemently denied it on his oath, and Tom felt he had no option but to trust him. Whatever the question marks over his domestic arrangements, Brooks was a first-class yacht hand and Tom knew he was lucky to have secured him for the voyage.

He chose James Haines as mate, offering him seven pounds a month. Originally from Turnchapel in Devon, where Tom had met him while living in the neighbouring village of Oreston seven years before, Haines was now based in Southampton. He had held a Master Mariner's certificate for six years and his last ship had been the *Lord Elsington* out of Newcastle.

The last crew member to sign up was also the youngest. Richard Parker came from Itchen Ferry, in the parish of St Mary Extra. It was just over the water from Fay's Yard, on the far bank of the river from Southampton. He was engaged as ordinary seaman at one pound fifteen shillings a month. Like the others, he had the option of continuing as a crewman on the *Mignonette* after they reached Sydney.

Tom liked him at once and would not have disagreed with the description of the boy later volunteered by one of his peers: 'Honest, civil and obliging, whilst his physique gave promise of his becoming a smart man.'

Richard was slightly less than honest in one respect, however. He was so keen to take the berth on the *Mignonette* that he lied about his age, claiming to be eighteen, when in fact he had only just turned seventeen.

He was the youngest of four sons of Daniel Parker, a fisherman and yachtsman, master of the yawl *Medora*. Richard's brothers were all sailors too. The eldest, Daniel, was a hand on the yacht *Marguerite*, Stephen worked on the Itchen ferries and William was another yacht hand. Richard also had a younger sister, Edith.

His father, known as 'Old Chick', had been a well-known local character and a noted batsman with the village cricket team, 'a regular old Itchen ferryman, fishing in the winter and yachting in the summer, and he was the champion in wielding the willow on the village green'.

He had died in 1881, aged sixty-one, when Richard was fourteen. The death left him an orphan, for his mother had died when he was only seven. It gave him an immediate bond with Tom, who had suffered a similar family tragedy, and their backgrounds were alike in other ways. Like Tollesbury, Itchen Ferry was then an isolated community, in which virtually every man earned his living from the sea. Richard had been to the St Mary Extra school in the shadow of the churchyard on Pear Tree Green, where his parents were buried, but his teacher could make nothing of him and he left school unable to read or write. He lived rough for a while before being taken in by Captain Jack Matthews, under whom he was serving on the racing cutter *Daphne*. None of Jack Matthews's own children were old enough to go yachting or fishing with him, and he became a surrogate father to Richard. The owner of the *Daphne* had also taken a liking to him, and had already offered him a berth for the 1884 racing season.

Although he had been brought up to boats from his cradle, Richard's experience was confined to inshore fishing and yachting in the Solent, and he had never been to sea. When some of his friends told him that a boy was wanted for an ocean voyage in a yacht lying at Northam, he crossed on the next ferry to apply for the berth.

When he came home that night, he told the Matthewses he was going out to New South Wales in the *Mignonette*. They were horrified and tried to talk him out of it, but he was determined to go. 'If I can get away for twelve months, I'll do myself some good. I want to go abroad and make a man of myself.'

Jack shook his head. 'Dick, you ought not to think of going to Australia in so small a vessel.'

'I shan't hurt,' Richard said. 'The ship's all right.'

The arguments went on for the next four days, and Jack enlisted some of his friends, and his brother John, the master of the *May*, to try to persuade the boy to change his mind. He insisted, though, that he had to try to better himself. 'Captain Dudley is a good man and intends to teach me everything he can. You'll have a good wage from me, I'll come home a proper seaman, and I'll be able to read and write as well – Captain Dudley promised me that.'

He was backed by many of his peers around Itchen Ferry who told him, on the basis of hearsay and seamen's tales from around the docks, that he would be sure to make his fortune if he could only get out to Australia.

In his desperation to win the Matthewses' approval for the voyage, Richard told them he had been promised a wage of a pound a week, more than twice as much as he was actually being paid. They continued to be implacably opposed to his going, but the one person who might have been able to persuade him to change his mind, his eldest brother, Daniel, was away at sea. In his absence Richard was immovable.

Jack Matthews's anxiety was understandable. He did not know Tom or the *Mignonette*, but he knew enough of ships and the sea to be concerned about the fitness of the craft for such a voyage, and he was deeply worried about what Richard might face in this or a subsequent berth once he was far from home on the high seas.

In the early days of British sea-power, life afloat was described as, 'Continual destruction in ye foretop, ye Pox above board, ye Pleague between Decks, Hell in ye Forecastle and ye Devil at ye Helm.'

Nothing much had changed in the intervening centuries. It was not until 1854 that the Merchant Shipping Act imposed a requirement on a shipping master to take action if a death had occurred through violence on a ship. Before that it had been left to the discretion of the captain of the vessel.

Life on board the vast majority of ships, whether they were of the Royal Navy or a merchant shipping company, continued to be nasty, brutish, and often short; as late as 1880, one seaman in sixty met a violent end at sea. The next most dangerous occupation, mining, had a death rate of only one in 315.

A ship was a dictatorship, and captains and senior officers could – and sometimes did – get away with murder. Masters and mates routinely used knotted ropes and belaying pins to enforce their orders, floggings were frequent and there were other, even more barbarous and illegal punishments, such as keelhauling. A long rope was passed right under the ship and a seaman was then thrown into the sea and dragged from one side to the other under the keel. It often resulted in serious injury or death.

One US mate was put on trial after amusing himself by firing shots at the seamen up in the rigging. One had been hit and fallen to his death. The mate was tried for murder but acquitted.

Government regulation had begun to curb the worst excesses of the industrial robber barons on land and during the latter half of the nineteenth century it was extended – albeit with painful slowness, against the concerted opposition of ship-owners – to the shipping industry. The regulations were directed at the safe carriage of cargoes and passengers, however, not the protection of seamen from tyrannical captains and rapacious owners.

Beginning with the Merchant Shipping Act of 1854, the newly established Board of Trade began to chip away at the edifice of custom and practice that had grown up over the centuries. Among its duties was the registration of all British ships and of grain and timber cargoes. Grain's propensity to shift dangerously in transit, the buoyancy of timber and the habit of carrying deck cargo on timber ships, made the vessels that carried those cargoes often dangerously unstable.

The board carried out inquiries into wrecks and casualties and supervised the testing of anchors and chain cables. It also investigated allegations of misconduct by officers and deaths at sea, and oversaw – notionally, at least – the engagement, discharge and payment of seamen, the protection of them from crimps, the repatriation of seamen discharged abroad and the relief of distressed seamen.

It held continuous records of discharge, investigating and punishing desertion or crewmen's failure to join ships, and was given responsibility for supervising the examination and certification of ships' officers.

Crews had to be signed on formally and discharged at a Marine Office under the eye of a Board of Trade official, but many ship-owners and masters simply flouted the law. The number of sailors and ships involved set limits to the control that the board could exercise, even around the wharves and dockside taverns, crimps and boarding-houses, let alone on the high seas.

The board was also given responsibility for ensuring the sea-worthiness of ships, with particular attention to the overloading and undermanning of emigrant ships, after a string of disasters around the middle of the century. A huge growth in emigration had led to a shortage of passenger ships. Between 1846 and 1854, 2.5 million people had left the United Kingdom for Australia and America. Although partly fuelled by famine in Ireland, the emigration was also inspired, and to some extent financed, by previous generations of emigrants who were now eager that their families should join them in the New World.

Large numbers of ships were converted to carry passengers, many of them utterly unsuited to the task. In seven years, sixty-one passenger-carrying ships were wrecked at a cost of 1,600 lives. The rate of losses forced government to legislate, and passenger, particularly emigrant, ships were subject to new controls.

While the carriage of passengers became better regulated, the scant legislation relating to crewmen laid down only the most minimal standards. The minimum area for a sailor's quarters, for example, was only an eighth of the cubic space and a fifth of the floor space required by the War Office for barracks accommodation for soldiers.

If life for men in the Royal Navy was often grim – and the growth in traffic to the Black Sea resulting from the Crimean war had further increased the demands upon them – the ships in which they sailed were at least usually in a state of manageable repair. Merchant seamen had no such guarantee and the decrepit 'coffin-ships' of some corrupt ship-owners were notorious.

The owners were protected by a powerful parliamentary lobby. When the Board of Trade attempted to explore the causes of the appalling level of losses of merchant shipping at sea, prominent ship-owners set up such a clamour against 'legislative interference ... and restrictive practices which favour our foreign rivals,' that, far from introducing further legislation, Lord Palmerston's government was persuaded to repeal the existing laws governing deck-loading and the provision of watertight bulkheads.

Preventable losses multiplied as the Government withheld its scrutiny and insurance removed most of the financial risk to ship-owners. Britain's increasing control of the high seas led to falling insurance rates as the threat from pirates and corsairs was reduced. Greater competition in the insurance market also saw the traditional policy of paying out only 75 to 90 per cent of the insured value replaced by payment in full.

It had previously been in the interest of all owners to ensure that their ships were overhauled after each ocean voyage, and for safety reasons it was also the invariable practice to have a minimum of three inches of hull clear of the water for every foot of cargo space, measured from the keel to the main deck.

However, once full insurance was available, there was every incentive for the more avaricious ship-owners to overload their vessels, increasing the potential profit from each voyage by as much as 50 per cent. If the ship went down, the insurance at least covered the loss and often yielded a handsome profit, for some owners were insuring elderly vessels and their cargoes for considerably more than their true value.

It could be even more profitable for an owner to have his ship sink than deliver its cargo intact. One London owner insured a vessel that cost him £300 for £1,000. Another ship bought for £7,500 but insured for £10,000 sank with the loss of twenty lives. The owners collected a £2,500 profit, and the seamen's wives and families were left destitute. There was no compensation for the crew . . . if they survived.

Even with ships and cargo worth tens of thousands of pounds, the liability of any individual underwriter was unlikely to exceed a couple of hundred pounds. None had the time or the available information to inquire into the provenance or condition of every ship he was asked to cover. It was cheaper and easier to pay the claim than attempt to mount an investigation into a loss on the high seas or on some distant coastline.

It was impossible to prove that coffin-ships were being deliberately wrecked or sent to sea in a condition that made foundering inevitable, but there was no doubt that many hundreds of seamen were sailing to their deaths each year in ships that were profoundly unseaworthy. If they complained or refused to sail, they were imprisoned, for the law was emphatically on the side of the owners.

A full-rigged coaling ship, the *Epaminodas*, grounded twice while loading at the Tyne docks and shipped water at the rate of two and a half inches an hour. The ten-man crew refused to sail for Genoa in her and were promptly gaoled for three months by the South Shields magistrates.

Another ship loaded in London was condemned by a Lloyds surveyor as 'utterly unfit to go to sea' and her crew deserted *en masse* at Deal. They were gaoled and a fresh crew recruited. All were lost when the ship went down in the Atlantic.

As the *Lifeboat* – the journal of the Royal Naval Lifeboat Institution – complained: 'Any unprincipled ship-owner or his agent has the power to send and even to force a well-insured, unseaworthy ship to sea against the judgement and will of her master and crew, to their almost certain destruction.'

One man set out to challenge this national scandal. Samuel Plimsoll had been elected as MP for Derby on a pledge to force legislation that would protect merchant seamen, but his attempts to introduce a

Merchant Shipping Survey Bill in 1871 were talked out by ship-owning MPs.

Disgusted, Plimsoll determined to arouse public opinion in his support. The means he chose, a book entitled *Our Seamen*, was published in December 1872. In it he denounced the unseaworthiness of a significant proportion of the merchant fleet, the callous and often barbaric treatment meted out to the crews and the greed and criminal negligence of corrupt ship-owners.

In refutation of claims that he was sensationalizing isolated or trivial incidents to further his own political career, Plimsoll quoted an august and unimpeachable source, the *Lifeboat*:

> In 1869, 177 wrecks happened when the wind was either perfectly calm or at most there was not more than a gentle breeze blowing. 660 vessels were lost in moderate, fresh and strong breezes. Of the 606 total wrecks on our shores, not counting collisions, 74 arose from defects in the ships or their equipment, such as imperfect charts and compasses, etc . . . It is overwhelming to contemplate the loss of life from these avoidable wrecks.

Our Seamen appealed for the compulsory surveying of all merchant ships and ended with a clarion call to its readers: 'It is on you, who read these lines, that this great, this life-giving duty now devolves – you personally, not Parliament only, nor Government merely, but you.'

Britain was now at the height of her economic powers and dependent on shipborne trade for her continuing prosperity, but the British people were roused to complain that the human price being exacted from British seamen was too high.

Ship-owners tried to place the blame elsewhere. One owner, who had lost eighteen ships in ten years, blamed every one on 'the incompetence of the masters and crews'. All united in denouncing Plimsoll as 'hare-brained', a 'notoriety hunter', a man who sought 'to prohibit death by Act of Parliament', and, even worse, 'a landlubber'.

A contrary view was expressed in a letter sent by a ship's mate to his fiancée just before boarding his vessel. Having complained of the overloading of his ship, he added, 'It's a great pity that the Board of Trade doesn't appoint some universal loadmark and surveyors to see that ships are not sent to sea to become coffins for their crews.'

Reluctant to lose face with his shipmates and face gaol for desertion, he sailed with the ship. It was his last communication. He drowned when it sank during that voyage.

Plimsoll gave voice to his own fury and the anger of the public in a display of open defiance to the House of Commons:

> I desire to unmask the villains who sit in the House, fit rep-
> resentatives of the more numerous, but no greater villains, the
> ship-owners of murderous tendencies outside this House. They
> have frustrated and talked to death every effort to procure a
> remedy for this state of things.
>
> The Secretary of Lloyds does not know of a single ship that
> has been broken up by the owners because she was worn out for
> thirty years. They are bought up by needy and reckless specula-
> tors, by whom they are sent to sea with precious human lives on
> board. Hundreds and hundreds of brave men are continually
> being sent to their deaths and their wives are made widows and
> their children made orphans, so that a few speculative
> scoundrels, in whose breast there is neither the love of God, nor
> the fear of God, may make unhallowed gains.

The Unseaworthy Ships Bill, including the requirement that every ship should carry a conspicuous 'Plimsoll Line' on its hull, received its second reading on 30 July and became law, but it was to be another four-teen years before responsibility for the positioning of the Plimsoll Line was taken out of the hands of ship-owners and given to the Board of Trade. Meanwhile losses continued at a terrible rate – between 1879 and 1899, 1,153 ships went missing and 11,000 lives were lost.

CHAPTER 4

Having found his crew, Tom took the three men to the Customs House the next morning to sign the ship's articles before the shipping master. Richard had not even told the Matthewses he was going to do so. Of the three, he was the only one who made a mark instead of signing his name.

Tom noticed the boy's embarrassment. 'There is no shame in it, lad. I was unlettered myself as a boy, but I taught myself to read and write and with a little help from me, you shall do the same. We have time enough. I warrant that, by the time we reach New South Wales, you'll be signing your name with a flourish.'

He promised to give Richard some schooling on the voyage and arranged to take some books on board for the purpose. He also took prayer-books to sea to celebrate an Anglican service on board every Sunday.

When Richard went home that afternoon and told the Matthewses he had signed articles for the voyage, Mrs Matthews burst into tears. There was now no possibility of him withdrawing without risking imprisonment. 'Well, Dick,' she said, 'if you are determined to go, I hope everything will be all right and, please God, you will come home again.'

They bought him a sea-chest and all the clothes and oilskins he would need for the voyage, but they could not hide the disquiet they felt.

Tom spent the remainder of Thursday, 15 May purchasing stores, ready to sail on the morning tide the next day, but by then Haines had been alarmed by gossip from Fay's Yard about the state of the ship's timbers, and told Tom he would not sail with him. Having signed articles, he was liable to arrest and imprisonment for desertion but instead Tom tried to reason with him, even offering him an extra pound a month to make the voyage. Nothing would persuade him to change his mind.

Once more Tom postponed his departure and returned to the docks and yacht agencies to find another crewman. He recruited Edwin Stephens as mate at the eight pounds a month he had been offering Haines, securing his agreement by promising him the captaincy of the *Mignonette* once they reached Sydney.

As Stephens was previously unknown to him, Tom made thorough enquiries about his character and background. Stephens had a pleasant, open countenance, beneath a thinning thatch of sandy-coloured hair. He was tall and broad-shouldered, but spoke with a diffidence that belied his powerful frame. He was thirty-seven and married with five children. He was also well regarded in the community, a devout Christian, and a member of the Above Bar Congregational Church, the YMCA and the Cape of Good Hope Masonic Lodge. He was devoted to his children, and indulged them whenever he was home from the sea, to the despair of his wife. She often complained, 'You'll spoil those children with your softness.'

'Is it not a harsh enough world that they'll face when they grow up?' he said. 'Must they only be dealt hard words and blows as children too?'

'The world is a hard place whether we like it or no. The sooner they learn that, the better for them.'

Stephens's father, a master mariner like his son, had drowned at Cowes in April 1868, but his mother and sister were still living in Southampton, near his home at 73 Northumberland Road, Nicholls Town.

The Stephens family were relatively well off, for his father had been in well-paid, regular work, and as the only boy in a family with seven daughters, Edwin led a sheltered and somewhat spoilt childhood. Unlike Tom, he did not go to sea until he was three months short of his fourteenth birthday.

His father had worked for the Isle of Wight Steam Packet Company all his life, but his son joined the Peninsular and Orient Line. He began as a cabin boy but rose rapidly through the ranks, becoming an ordinary seaman within eighteen months and able seaman two years later. He obtained his second mate's ticket in 1869 and joined the Union Line the same year, taking his first mate's certificate twelve months later.

He was a very experienced deep-sea sailor, who had already been to the Cape several times. As he told Tom, 'All my life I have been sailing to the southward.' He could have looked forward to eventual promotion to captain with the Union Line, but for an incident in 1877 that blighted his career. It also caused Tom to pause before employing him. With such a small crew, he was dependent on the complete competence of each man to fulfil his duties.

In poor visibility, the 2,000-ton steamer, the *European*, had hit a reef and sunk while returning from the Cape with the mails, thirty passengers and seventy-six hands on board. Captain Ker was the company's agent in South Africa and had little recent sea-going experience. Stephens was chief officer and navigating at the time. The last landfall had been Cape Finisterre, but low cloud and a sea-fret had stopped them from taking a sun-sight for two days. Navigating by dead reckoning, he set a north-easterly course across the Bay of Biscay, aiming to pass well clear of Ushant.

Early on the afternoon of 5 December they stopped to take soundings. Although the chart showed the depth at their estimated position to be 73 fathoms, no bottom was found with 100 fathoms of line. Since any depth of 100 fathoms or more is taken as being on the open sea, a safe distance from land, they steamed on to the north-east.

Three hours later they again tried and failed to take a sounding, but still pressed on, though the charts showed that Stephens's estimate of the ship's position had to be almost fifty miles wide of the mark. A further three hours later they found a bottom of shell and sand at 40 fathoms.

Ushant was still shrouded in fog, but Stephens and Ker decided they were ten miles north of it, even though the chart showed mud and silt, not shell and sand in that location, and a different depth.

Stephens had just gone off duty at the end of the second dog-watch, when the look-out cried out, 'Light on the port bow.'

They put the helm hard to starboard and stopped engines. Then the look-out called, 'Breakers ahead.'

The captain ordered full ahead in an effort to clear the rocks, but his ship was carried on to the Basse Meur rock. The light they had seen was the Ushant light. The passengers, hands and mails were all saved but the ship was lost.

A formal inquiry found the captain guilty of gross, culpable negligence. As a subordinate notionally carrying out the captain's orders at all times, Stephens escaped direct criticism, but he knew that his guilt was at least as great as his captain's and admitted as much at the hearing. He was never employed by the Union Line again.

He subsequently served on the ships of G. T. Harper and Company in the Black Sea trade and also worked for his father's old employers, the Isle of Wight Steam Packet Company, but his pay was barely half that of a chief officer on the Union Line. The work was also irregular – he was unemployed when Tom offered him the berth on the *Mignonette* – and with a wife and five children to support, he was already thinking of emigrating to Australia to make a fresh start.

Whatever Tom's reservations about a man who had made such a disastrous navigational error, he found Stephens's blue-water experience very attractive. Although Tom had served as a sailing master for years, his own ocean-going experience was very limited and he had never practised the complicated process of establishing longitude at sea.

He was also impressed with Stephens's honesty. He made no attempt to minimize his errors and freely admitted his own culpability in the sinking of the *European*.

'You are willing to take me on despite that?' Stephens said. 'And entrust me with the navigation?'

'I am. I've made enquiries about you in Southampton and heard nothing but good about you. The *European* was a terrible mistake, but as far as I can ascertain, it is the only one of your career.' He smiled. 'I have made mistakes myself and I would not wish to be judged for ever because of an error I had made years before.'

Before beginning to load the supplies for the voyage, Tom set his new crew a hard, dirty but necessary task. Every door and hatch below decks was opened and the ship's stores, tools, spare sails and spars were either removed or spread out to allow air to circulate around them.

He built a slow fire of charcoal on an iron hearth laid on the ballast of the keel, covered it with damp bark, then poured a mound of sulphur on to the smoking fire. Every open seam on the boat had already been caulked, but now the hatches and the slide over the companionway were also closed, battened down and sealed. Tom and his men went over the ship, caulking any chink from which smoke still issued.

They spent the night ashore and the next morning the hatches were opened again, allowing the cool spring air to circulate through the below-decks and blow away the last lingering stench of sulphur. As he walked the length of the yacht below decks, Tom saw tiny yellow sulphur crystals in the cracks of the timbers, glowing in the faint light like primroses in the dark soil of a forest floor.

Along with the cold, spent ashes of the fumigating fire, they found and removed five dead rats. Tom also felt confident that any lice, fleas and other vermin were now equally dead.

He set the crew to work loading the ship with supplies for the voyage and supervised the stowing of the stores himself. In storm conditions, a yacht lying to under a small headsail is often thrown on to her beam ends. It may happen as often as three or four times an hour, but no harm comes to the ship providing the cargo and stores do not shift. If they have not been properly stowed, however, they will be thrown to the side as the yacht rolls and the additional instability may make her founder. The majority of ships that foundered and sank did so because the cargo or the ballast had shifted under the stress of weather. Those carrying loose cargo were particularly at risk, and a part-cargo of any sort was always more dangerous than a full hold.

The *Mignonette*'s lead ballast was fixed to the keel and could not move but the hold would only be half full of stores. As a result, provisions were stowed with particular care. Once the huge water butts and the other heavy stores were in place, the four men laid stout planks across the top of them and fixed them in place with stanchions extending from the planks to the beams supporting the deck. The stanchions were then wedged and braced until they were locked so solidly into position that even a hurricane would not have shifted them.

By Friday morning the job was complete, but wanting to allay some of the anxieties aroused in Philippa by their rough and leaky passage from Tollesbury, Tom decided to postpone sailing until the Monday, to enable him to return one last time to Sutton. A watchman from Fay's Yard was recruited to guard the ship and its stores, while the men dispersed for a final weekend at home.

Tom arrived back at eleven thirty on the Monday morning, 19 May, after a sleepless night and an uneasy parting from his family. He was a solid, practical man, not much given to shows of emotion, but as he had closed the garden gate that morning and looked back at his wife and children, his eyes had filled with tears. If anything went wrong . . . He dug his nails into his palms, driving the thought away. He forced himself to smile and gave a confident wave as he turned away from the gate, though the sight of his children's tearful faces tore at his heart.

By the time he reached Southampton his mood had shifted to his customary stolid acceptance of whatever fate had in store for him. He had prepared himself, his boat and his crew as well as he knew how, and he was in God's hands now.

The senior members of his crew were sharing little of his enthusiasm for the voyage and all of his misgivings. Continuing rumours circulating around Fay's Yard about the state of the ship's timbers had now unsettled Ned Brooks, who was trying to withdraw, though he later claimed: 'I did not consider there was any risk in undertaking the voyage. Having always been brought up to the sea and small yachts and boats, I did not think there was any more danger in going to Sydney in the *Mignonette* than there would be in crossing the Channel. My friends, however, or everyone who spoke to me on the subject, tried to persuade me not to go.'

Tom went straight to the County Tavern in Northam, where he found Brooks surrounded by a number of cronies and already reeking of drink. Brooks greeted Tom belligerently. His dark eyes stared at Tom over the rim of his battered pewter mug, as he took another swig of his ale. Then he stood up, his powerful figure looming above Tom. He put his face close to Tom's, his voice mocking him. 'It's me you've come for is it, Captain Dudley? I'll not go with you. I'll not sail in that ship.'

Tom recoiled from the stink of sour ale on Brooks's breath, but stood his ground, unafraid, keeping his anger in check, and his voice firm and level. 'I have a ship waiting and a tide to catch. It is no wish of mine to have you thrown in jail, but you have signed articles for this voyage. And if I must do it, I will.'

'Be damned with you and do your worst.'

One of Brooks's cronies laughed and slapped him on the back, but another took hold of Brooks's sleeve and spoke to him. Brooks cursed and shook off his arm, but the look he directed at Tom, still standing impassive in front of him, showed less certainty.

Tom lowered himself onto a bench at the other side of the table. 'Come on, Ned, you've given your word man to man, and shaken my hand on it. Finish your drink and then let's be away.' It took two more hours of argument to persuade him to board the *Mignonette*.

Stephens also had to be fetched from his house twice, but in his case it was his wife who was the major obstacle to be overcome. He had taken the berth on the yacht much against her wishes, and on the day of sailing she tried all she knew to persuade him not to make the voyage.

Stephens did not share his wife's doubts, although he seemed frightened to argue with her, and hung back behind Tom, as if he, not Stephens, was married to her. Tom reasoned with her, and in the end prevailed. Stephens left his wife and mother sobbing on each other's shoulders, but when he tried to say farewell to his children, tears also began streaming down his own face. 'Goodbye, my little ones,' he said. 'Be brave and strong for your —' Then his voice failed him. Twice he tried to recompose himself, but finally, unable to finish the sentence, he turned and stumbled away and followed Tom down to the mooring.

He later said: 'I never had the least anticipation that the *Mignonette* was not seaworthy. Not being a yachtsman, I made enquiries before I shipped whether it would be safe and they all said that if she was properly handled, we should ride better than in a big vessel.'

The sole enthusiast among the crew was Richard Parker, who was so excited about the journey that he left home at five that morning, although he showed some regret as he said his farewells. 'As he said goodbye, he kissed us both and hung upon our necks for several minutes,' Mrs Matthews said. 'I shall never forget it. He seemed then sorry that he was going to leave us and this was the first time he showed any regret for the resolve he had taken. That was the last I saw of him for I did not see the *Mignonette* leave the river.'

Before he joined the ship, Richard walked over Pear Tree Green to the churchyard. He took his bearings from an ornate, four-sided obelisk, a memorial to a prominent local family, engraved with the names of generations of dead. His eye lingered for a moment on one of the inscriptions '... and their children, Rebecca aged one day, Caleb aged three days, Reuben aged six months and Alice aged one year and ten days'.

His sympathy for the losses suffered by that family was tinged with resentment: even those brief lives had left some mark upon the world. No stone or tablet recorded the burial place of his parents. He walked towards the east window of the church, overlooking the little school that he had briefly attended, and stopped by a sloping patch of grass studded with spring flowers. He bowed his head over the grave and said a farewell to his father and to the mother he barely remembered, then turned and walked away under the arch of yews shading the church gate.

The ancient pear tree on the green was in flower and the scent of the blossom was carried to him on the wind from the sea. He walked down Sea Road towards the quayside, passing the uneven, sloping green where, on Saturday afternoons, his father had earned extra coppers for himself and guineas for the local gentlemen who wagered on his skill with a cricket bat.

At the bottom of the hill, he crossed the railway track and reached the huddle of houses and taverns along the shorefront between the slip and the ferry landing. Only a foot or so of seaweed-encrusted timber showed above the water on the slipway. The low sun glinted on the water and the ferries on their endless shuttling across the Itchen cast long shadows on to the far bank.

He caught the next ferry over to Northam, alighting near the copse of masts of the yachts pulled out of the water for repairs and careening at Fay's Yard. Near the bottom of the slip, the *Mignonette*'s own tall mast bobbed in the current as the tide began to turn. Downstream, the muddy course of the Itchen merged into the broad expanse of Southampton Water.

Richard relieved the watchman on the yacht and stowed his sea-chest and gear under the cramped berth allocated to him, the smallest, hard-up against the chain-locker in the head. In rough seas, the deafening rattle of the cable against the sides of the locker would make it all but impossible to sleep, but as the youngest, most junior member of the crew, he had no choice but to accept the dog's berth on board.

Brooks and Stephens arrived much later, each escorted to the yacht by Tom and still casting frequent glances back towards the shore. After his experience that morning, Tom chose to have the dinghy hauled aboard at once. It required careful handling, for it was a frail craft, 'clinker built' from layers of overlapping, downward-facing planks of quarter-inch mahogany, fixed by clenched copper nails.

Once the dinghy had been stowed over the fore skylight, there was no turning back for the crew. The only way off the ship was to swim for the shore, and of the four, only Tom had ever learned to swim. Many seamen deliberately chose not to do so, fearing that, if shipwrecked, they would deprive themselves of a swift, merciful end, only to endure the horror of shark attacks or the slow torture of starvation instead.

Tom called them together around the helm. 'We're a small ship and we have a long voyage before us, but do your duty like men and we'll do well enough. If we all pull together you'll find me a fair and friendly captain.' He smiled. 'Friendlier than I've had need to be today at times. Now we've said our farewells, there's a fair wind to speed us and a new land waiting for us. To work, there's much to be done before we're ready to make sail.'

They sailed from Fay's Yard on the afternoon tide, casting off at high water at five thirty. Brooks and Richard – the strongest pair – worked the windlass to raise the anchor. It was heavy work. It weighed a hundredweight and hung from 300 feet of chain. The windlass rang like a bell as it turned, sending the rusty iron links of the cable clattering into the chain-locker one by one. The anchor at last broke surface and swung dripping from the bow. Brooks and the boy ran to cat it, their trousers flapping loose around their legs. They lashed it tight against the hull as Tom gave the steam-tug, the *Mezphi*, the signal to tow the *Mignonette* clear of the Itchen.

Gulls wheeled and cried overhead as they moved downstream. Richard looked back beyond the huddled houses at the water's edge, over the rising ground and the green fields studded with clumps of trees. Before they slipped from sight, he caught a last glimpse of Pear Tree Green and the dark huddled mass of the yews surrounding the church.

Tom had the helm as the *Mignonette* dropped her tow in South-ampton Water, near the moored battleship, HMS *Hector*. He gripped the rail of the bulwarks as he glanced back towards the shore, feeling the reassuring warmth and solidity of the weathered wood under his hand. 'All ready? Hoist sail.'

He heard the whine of rope through the blocks as his men hauled at the halyards. No two ships ever sounded the same; by the time they had been at sea a few days he would know the sounds of the *Mignonette* so well that he could pick it out from other ships with his eyes closed.

The heavy mainsail was hoisted and sheeted home. The jibs and top-sail followed and as the sails filled, the *Mignonette* leaned over before the wind, rolling with the groundswell as they met the open water. With all plain sail set in the south-east breeze, their point of departure had soon disappeared from sight and the coastline lay like a bank of low cloud on the sea.

Tom gave an approving nod as he watched his crew. Stephens and Brooks were both cool and slick in their work, but they also took time to guide the eager if inexperienced Richard.

They would work the standard hours – four hours on watch, four hours off, seven days a week – a minimum of eighty-four hours a week, and much more in bad weather. The watches ran from midnight to midnight and a bell was rung every half-hour: one bell at the end of the first one, up to eight bells, which signalled the end of the watch.

Tom and Richard took the first watch, but the other two also remained on deck, reluctant to go below while the familiar coast-line remained in sight. The mixture of emotions was the same for all of them, regret at leaving loved ones behind, and excitement, coupled with a little fear at the journey ahead.

At the end of the first watch, Tom handed over the helm to Stephens and went below to inspect his kingdom. The familiar musty smell of below-decks greeted him: old, damp wood, men's stale sweat, tar from the ship's caulking, and no matter how often the pumps were manned, there was always the faint but acrid odour of bilge water.

His cramped cabin, aft behind the companionway, contained only his berth, a straight-backed wooden chair and a map-table already spread with charts and the ship's log, weighted down with pieces of pig-iron.

The table stood directly under the aft skylight, the only source of light other than a single lantern hanging from the cross-beam. The sextant and chronometer were stowed beneath the table, though as mate, Stephens, not Tom, had the responsibility of calculating the ship's position and keeping the log.

The galley and food-store, Brooks's domain, stood at either side of the narrow, dark passage leading towards the crew's quarters, roughly partitioned out of the hold where Essex fishermen had once stored their catch. A kettle was warming on the iron stove. The plank walls and ceiling of the galley were stained and smoke-blackened, and so steeped with the odour of bacon grease that no amount of cleaning or fumigation could remove all trace of it.

There was no cargo in the remaining hold space, only stacks of coal and firewood for the galley, the ship's stores, butts of fresh water and a pen containing two small pigs. Tom stopped to scratch their heads, remembering his days as cook-steward.

They would feed on the scraps from the fresh provisions loaded in Southampton but when they were exhausted, first one pig then the other would be slaughtered. Tom hoped to buy more provisions at Madeira and the Cape to eke out their stocks of canned beef.

CHAPTER 5

Ships had carried live animals as part of their stores for centuries, though chickens, ducks and other fowl, and the eggs they laid, were invariably reserved for the use of the captain and his senior officers.

The longboats were often pressed into use as temporary livestock pens and a pigsty was constructed in the hold. If they were lucky, crewmen would get one mess from every pig that was killed and would also be given the less choice cuts from sheep and occasionally cows, though unlike pigs, which seemed to thrive on it, the larger animals did not take well to life at sea. On larger ships, sows would even round the Horn or the Cape with no worse discomfort than the men, though the litters of piglets with which they began the journey steadily diminished in number to meet the appetite of the crew.

Once the fresh meat was exhausted, seamen were fed on the 'salt beef' specified in naval regulations. The contractors who supplied the Navy during the Napoleonic wars grew rich on the trade but were despised by every seaman. The meat was pickled in barrels of brine and was invariably of questionable provenance, sometimes from a cow but often pork or other, less palatable meats. Its nickname 'salt-horse' reflected the men's suspicions about its true origins and it was also called 'salt-junk'. Pieces of bone, hoof and other extraneous matter were often found among the tough and unidentifiable cuts.

The process of preserving food by boiling it and sealing it in tins had been discovered by a Frenchman, Nicholas Appert, in the first years of the nineteenth century, and as early as 1813, the English firm of Donkin and Hall supplied the Channel fleet with an experimental supply of canned beef; but though the advantages of the new process were obvious, the comparative expense led to it being issued only on long-distance expeditions, particularly to the Arctic.

Canned meat was not available on the commercial market until 1830 and did not become a regular part of the Royal Navy diet until the middle of the century. Merchant ship-owners persisted with the cheaper salt beef far longer than that, its quality as variable as the seas on which they sailed. The worst was the decommissioned Royal Navy meat that Tom had been forced to eat on board the *Lady Rodney*.

When cases of scurvy were reported in the papers in 1876, Samuel Plimsoll once more addressed the House of Commons. 'The Government keeps seven years' store of provisions in the Gibraltar and Malta garrisons. This pork and beef, simmering out there in pickle for seven years, is brought home and the hoops are knocked off the barrels down at Deptford. That which is rotten and bad is sold to the soap-boilers. The rest is put into clean casks and fresh pickle by our government and then sold to ship-owners.

'One ship arrived at San Francisco last autumn after burying twelve of her men with this horrid disease on the passage, with one dead man on board and twenty-two men who were sent to hospital, two of whom died there. I demand for our sailors that they shall no longer be fed with food that they would not give their dogs.'

His demand was not answered for many more years. The last barrels of salt beef to be carried on a British vessel were shipped in 1920.

The 'bread', which was the other staple of the naval diet, was an equally misleading term. Until 1855 bread was exclusively hard-tack – ship's biscuit baked at the victualling yards, the Royal Victoria at Deptford, the Royal Clarence at Portsmouth and the Royal William at Plymouth. It was baked to the consistency of mortar and considered so imperishable that it was stored in canvas bags, to which insects and vermin found easy access.

It was an automatic gesture of every seaman to tap his hard-tack on the table before eating it to knock out any maggots and weevils. One nineteenth-century seaman, Dalrymple Hay, described hard-tack so riddled with them that the only way to make it palatable was to lay the entrails of a freshly caught fish on top of a mound of it. The maggots and weevils came out of the biscuit into the entrails, which were then thrown away. The process was repeated until no more emerged and the hard-tack was then described as 'fit to eat'.

A Bristol baker, Henry Jones, had patented a method of making self-raising flour and a bread-oven for use on board ship in 1845. He immediately offered his invention to the Navy Victualling Office. After waiting ten years for a positive reply, Jones sent details of his invention and copies of his correspondence with the Admiralty to every Member of Parliament. Within a month self-raising flour was issued to every Navy ship, and for the first time in their history, seamen had the pleasure of soft-tack – bread – alongside their ship's biscuit, though it was served only on Sundays.

The rations specified for Tom's crew included flour from which, like in the Navy, bread was baked on Sundays; but even in 1884, their other 'bread' was still hard-tack which continued to be supplied to ships until the early years of the twentieth century.

In the Napoleonic era the only variation in the dull, constipating diet of beef and bread had been a small amount of pease pudding and, if the seamen asked for it, a little vinegar. The intervention of naval surgeons led to the inclusion of vegetables from 1825 onwards but these were usually only available in the early part of a voyage. By the second half of the century more variety had been introduced. Cook-stewards could add rice, split peas, pearl barley, flour, tinned potatoes, turnips and other root vegetables, currants and raisins, and even mustard and pepper to make the food more palatable.

What seamen drank on board ship had also gone through a long and curious period of evolution. Before the Victorian era, there was no way to keep a ship's water sweet. Stored in wooden butts, it quickly became foul-smelling, fetid and undrinkable. At each port of call, all the butts – full as well as empty – had to be hauled out of the water room in the hold, emptied and refilled. The effort of handling the huge and very heavy barrels made ruptures the most common occupational injury in the Navy.

Seamen only drank water at the beginning of a voyage, while it was still palatable, and in the course of a battle, when buckets of 'fighting water' were tied to the stanchions on deck. It was often contaminated with gunpowder, or even blood and flesh from the wounded, but in the heat and intensity of battle it was still drunk.

At all other times, seamen drank beer instead of water, a thin and often sour brew from the Navy's victualling yards. Each man was allowed a gallon a day and naval regulations laid down that the beer must be finished – or so sour that it was undrinkable – before any substitute drink could be supplied. If the ship was in home waters, more beer was purchased. In foreign ports, 'beverage' – any light wine of the local region – was bought, but the regulations also stipulated that spirits could be substituted if no beer or wine was available. In the Caribbean that inevitably meant rum, mixed fifty-fifty with water and known as grog.

It became one of the staples of Navy life. Although the rules laid down that it could be drunk only once the beer had been exhausted, in practice, and eventually even in the regulations, a daily grog ration was issued. Initially two gills – half a pint – a day, it was progressively reduced over the course of the nineteenth century.

A seaman could either drink his ration when it was issued or save it, but if he gave or sold it to one of his fellows he would be flogged. Despite these attempts at strict control, the drunkenness that character-ized gin shops and taverns ashore was equally rife on board ship.

By 1825 Navy ships were being issued with iron tanks, which kept water sweet for much longer. Small tenders were used to transport water to the boats and the heavy tanks – placed on the keel and replac-ing some of the sand and shingle formerly used as ballast – were drained and refilled by pumps.

In the tropics the water was treated heavily with oatmeal to purify it, and by the 1860s naval surgeons had at last persuaded the Navy to start mixing it with lime juice. This made it more palatable and greatly reduced the incidence of scurvy. Even with these improvements, how-ever, the supply of water remained a problem for sailing ships, which were often becalmed for long periods.

A method of distilling fresh water from sea-water had been invented 250 years before, and in 1595 Richard Hawkins, known by his contemporaries as 'the compleat seaman', took a still with him on a voyage to the South Seas. Captain Cook carried one on his second voyage.

Throughout the seventeenth and eighteenth centuries, inventors continued to design ever more sophisticated stills, but despite their obvious value, they were never issued to Royal Navy ships, though some naval captains obtained them at their own expense. In 1825 Dr Alphonse Normandy developed a still that produced a gallon of water from every six of sea-water, but perhaps fearing that it would be put to other, more illicit purposes, the Navy continued to refuse to countenance its use.

The dangers of ships sailing without a still – and the continuing gulf between officers and men – was demonstrated in a voyage by HMS *Xenophon* in 1845, which became becalmed off the coast of Mexico and began drifting with the current.

After sixty days it passed close to land, but the approaches to the coral beach were too shallow for the ship's boats. The inhabitants rowed out to the ship and offered to fetch water – at a heavy price – but the captain, who had his own private water tanks on board and an equally plentiful supply of wine, refused.

The *Xenophon* drifted away from land again and the men's ration was reduced to half a pint a day, although the livestock on board – the captain's sheep and hens – were given water in abundance. The men were forced to catch the water draining from the captain's daily bath and drink it even though they were flogged for doing so. Secure in his quarters, the captain continued to perform his ablutions while his men began to drink vinegar and sea-water. Some went insane, others died of thirst. The *Xenophon* at last reached Gil Blas and found water after ninety-seven days adrift.

Rough justice of a sort was done when the captain was court-martialled. However, this was not for condemning many of his men to death from thirst while he bathed in the water that might have saved them, but for sending a smaller, less well-armed ship to fight a naval engagement while he commandeered its cargo and claimed the captain's traditional 10 per cent share of the value for himself.

The *Mignonette* had been built as an inshore boat, not for long sea voyages, and had no iron water tanks. The supplies Tom and his men had loaded were contained in old wooden butts in the hold. One of the last duties of the dawn night watch was to refill the breaker – a small barrel of drinking water set in a wooden stand at the foot of the companionway – from the butts.

Tom squeezed through the narrow gap between the huge barrels and walked forward to the crew's quarters, ducking under the hammocks slung from the beams. The stores in the steerage right against the bow were packed with coils of rope, spare spars and sails, lengths of planking, carpenter's tools, oakum and pitch for caulking the ship's timbers, linseed oil for waterproofing their oilskins, and a host of other vital equipment, all neatly stacked and stowed.

As he peered into the steerage he could hear the rhythmic thud of the waves against the bow, the liquid, musical sound of the water rushing under the stem of the ship, and the slap of bare feet on the deck above him as Richard went forward to check the jib.

By the time Tom returned on deck, night had fallen. There was only the rush of the sea and the creak of the blocks to break the silence under the milky, shimmering light of the stars and the shadows of wind-driven clouds passing over the sky.

The *Mignonette* passed the Needles – the rocks at the westernmost tip of the Isle of Wight – at midnight. At daybreak the duty watch turned to, clearing the decks, filling the water-breaker and coiling the loose ropes and trailing rigging. With a fair wind to speed them, they made good progress down the Channel. By noon they were off Portland and they cleared Start Point during the following night.

At ten thirty on the morning of 21 May, they met and boarded a schooner, the *Lady Evelyn*, working its way up the Channel. Tom handed the captain some letters for home and was given a little spare water to top up his casks. The letters, posted on the *Lady Evelyn*'s arrival in Plymouth, led Philippa to believe that Tom had put in to port there.

At midday the *Mignonette* reached the Eddystone Light, traditionally regarded as the point of departure from England for ocean-going ships. It was an emotional moment for all of them, their last contact with England and possibly their last ever contact with their native land. The log recorded, 'We took our departure and our last sight of home.'

The next morning the dawn broke grey and cold, with mist shrouding the horizon on every side. A feeling of melancholy overcame them as the gathering light revealed the endless, unbroken march of the sea.

At once Tom set them to work, burying any lingering feelings of regret under the burden of hard physical effort. While Brooks went below to make breakfast, Tom sent Richard and Stephens forward to rig the head-pump and wash down the decks. Then they began working their way slowly and methodically over the ship's rigging. They started by examining and repairing the running ropes. Where there was any trace of wear, they fitted chafing gear – pads of leather, old rope or canvas – to ease the friction on it.

Whenever the standing rigging showed any signs of slackness – a constant occurrence in even the most gentle sea and wind conditions – all the seizings and tackles had to be removed, the rigging made taut and all the gear replaced. The tension of every rope acted on that of several others, so that none could be altered in isolation, and the men had to work outwards from the key-ropes, tightening some, easing others, until the shrouds, stays and rigging were in perfect equilibrium, and the wind made them hum, to Tom's ears, like the strings of a harp.

The men were never idle. When not working on the rigging or the pumps, or increasing or reducing canvas, they laboriously unpicked tangled, knotted masses of old rope, bought for coppers from ship's chandlers, then rolled them into balls of rope-yarn which, like a farmer's twine, had a multitude of uses. Rope too worn to be treated in that way was picked into oakum – the soft constituent fibres of the rope – which was used in caulking the seams, painting and cleaning.

On a larger ship, such menial tasks would have been beneath a first mate's dignity, let alone that of the captain. The mate's prime duties were to supervise the stowing of the stores and cargo, keep the ship's log and ensure that the captain's orders were carried out. With a crew of four, however, every hand had to be turned to work and Stephens and Tom did their share with the rest.

They cleared Ushant at eight o'clock that morning, 22 May, but the mist and rain mercifully obscured from sight the scene of Stephens's disastrous navigational error in the *European*.

For once the Bay of Biscay did not live up to its fearsome reputation. The winds were light and the swell moderate as the *Mignonette* ploughed on her south-westerly course, beating up to windward in long stretches. Tom stood at the weather side of the helm on each tack. 'Helm's a lee. Raise tacks and sheets.' The canvas was let go, then held taut ready for the swing.

'Haul sail.' The crew released the bracing ropes and the boom swung round.

'Well all forward.'

'Well all aft.'

Tom kept a close watch on the *Mignonette*'s ageing timbers. Some water still leaked around the heel of the bowsprit, but the work done at Fay's Yard appeared to have stemmed the worst of the other leaks, though a trickle of water seeped through the seams as the hull flexed in the swell. He set Brooks and the boy to work with pitch and oakum, caulking and leading the timbers, but in heavy seas, both men off-watch were still kept at work pumping the bilges with the hand-pumps.

They were now well established in the ship's routine, working in pairs on four-hour watches, except in late afternoon and early evening, when the two-hour dog-watches ensured a rotation so that the crew who had two of the three night watches one day – the first, middle and dawn watches – would only do one the next.

All hands were usually on deck during the dog-watches, but even when the first night watch was called at eight in the evening, the off-duty men would often remain on deck, for when the weather was warm and set fair, all preferred clean air to the stale, fetid odour of bilge water below decks.

Now out of sight of land, Stephens used the chronometer and sextant to take a noon sun-sight on the days when the skies were clear, then retired to the cabin to make the series of long, complex calculations that would reveal their position. However, precise readings were difficult to obtain from a small yacht and when the sun was obscured he had to rely on the often inaccurate methods of dead reckoning and 'log, line and look-out'.

Navigational techniques had altered little since the turn of the century. The magnetic steering compass was housed in the binnacle directly in front of the helm, held on gimbals to keep it horizontal, whatever the angle of the ship. Its circumference was divided into thirty-two points, which did not correspond to an exact number of degrees, but gave the helmsman a clear distinguishing mark to which he could hold the ship's heading.

The distance run by the ship was measured by a log dropped into the water at the bow and retrieved from the stern. The time it took to cover that known distance was noted and by calculating the ship's speed relative to the drifting log the mate could estimate the number of miles they had covered since the last reading.

The *Mignonette* was equipped with a less primitive log, a cylinder housing four rotator blades like the screw of a steamer. A mechanical counter kept tally of the revolutions, allowing an estimate of the distance travelled, though the effects of tides and currents also had to be allowed for. They could add or subtract as much as forty miles in the course of a day's sailing.

Tacking against the wind, variable winds and violent weather made logging the ship's progress a far from accurate procedure and often the navigator was forced into dead reckoning that was perilously close to guesswork. As the fate of the *European* indicated, it could easily be many miles out.

When close to land, regular soundings were also taken with lead and line to help pinpoint the ship's position, but the ultimate guarantee of a ship's safety was always the alertness of the look-outs. A good seaman had a restless eye, always shifting his gaze between the weather side of the boat, the masthead, spars and rigging above him, the sea around and the horizon ahead. He was also alert to the most minor and, to a landsman, insignificant changes in the sea and sky.

This was not merely to give early warning of a change in wind or weather. Proximity to land could be detected by signs visible long before the keenest eye could spot the coast itself. Even a change in the pattern of clouds or an unusual tint to the sky might be enough to alert an experienced seaman.

The dark colour of the deep ocean became paler and fish were usually more numerous close to land. Kelp, driftwood and other floating flotsam might show the presence of an offshore current. The on- and off-shore breezes and the flight of birds that mimicked them – outward at dawn and returning at dusk – could also be detected miles from land.

The other senses also played a part. The outflow of large rivers could be found miles out to sea from the opacity of the silt-laden water and its less salty taste. Breakers could be heard long before they were visible and the scents of land – earth after rain, smoke, swamps, or pungent vegetation like eucalypts – might be carried far out to sea on the breeze.

There was no coast within hundreds of miles of the *Mignonette*, however, and Tom used the calm weather to instigate a thorough cleaning and overhaul of the ship ready for the heavier weather to come in the southern latitudes.

The work of tarring down the rigging was hot, filthy and gruelling. They changed into their oldest sea-clothes, worn, holed and already stiff with tar. A bucket of pitch was heated in the galley and hauled up to the masthead, where they daubed it over the ropes, using a handful of oakum as a brush. They worked downwards, tarring the stays and shrouds, the ties and runners, and the lifts and foot-ropes around the mainmast. When they had finished they were as black as the ropes they had been working on.

They used bundles of spare canvas and rags to block up the scuppers, then pumped water into them and washed themselves in their primitive bathtub, scouring their skin with coarse soap until the worst of the tar had been removed. They used more sea-water to wash their clothes and towed them behind the boat on a rope for a few minutes to rinse the soap from them. Then they knotted them roughly around the rails to dry and began work on the deck.

While Richard polished the ship's bell, the binnacle and the brass windlass head until they gleamed, the others scraped the tar spills from the planking with knives, washed the decks and scuppers and swept them with brooms. Tom then covered the decks with a thin layer of coarse, gritty sand from the hold, ready for the laborious process of holy-stoning.

A long flat slab of soft red sandstone, bored at either end with holes from which lengths of rope protruded, was brought up from below decks. Brooks and Richard took a rope each and began to drag it backwards and forwards over the deck, scouring the planks with the damp sand. Smaller, hand-size stones were used in the angles around the hatchways, bulwarks and the galley stove pipe projecting from the deck. The hatch covers and companionway were hauled up and given the same treatment, then Brooks manned the head pump and hosed the decks clean.

As it dried, the sun-bleached wood shone white in the sunlight and it was warm under Tom's bare feet as he patrolled the deck, testing the sails and checking the tension in the shrouds and stays, his restless gaze never still.

Sailing ships making for Australia avoided the shorter route through the Suez Canal because the winds were less reliable than the Atlantic trade winds. Instead, they usually followed a Great Circle route, aiming to pass close to St Paul's Rocks in the South Atlantic, not far from the coast of South America.

They then picked up the south-east trades and followed a curving track wide of Tristan da Cunha, to latitude forty or even further south. The powerful westerlies of the roaring forties drove them well to the south of the Cape of Good Hope and, unless there was an emergency, they would not enter port or even come close to land until reaching Australia.

The big sailing barques could handle the enormous seas and heavy gales of the roaring forties. Small yachts were different, but before setting out Tom had scoured the back numbers of yachting magazines for the logs of other yachts making the passage to Australia, and he had chosen a route used by many past captains.

As he was later to say, 'I felt it safer to set a course closer to land than the Great Circle which the barques follow into the southern latitudes in pursuit of the roaring forties that carry them across the southern oceans. I felt we would have less wild weather if we followed a course to the east and north of theirs.'

He planned to sail to Madeira, where he would stop to reprovision the ship, and to the Cape Verde Islands, before making for Cape Town. After a further stop for reprovisioning, he would set a course almost due west to Australia, keeping above latitude forty, in less reliable, but lighter winds. He hoped to reach Sydney in a maximum of 120 days, an average daily distance of 120 miles. It was an optimistic target for a yacht of the *Mignonette*'s size, but not impossible.

For a man with his limited deep-sea experience, in a small, frail and elderly boat, his choice of route was entirely understandable. If anything happened to the ship, however, he was putting himself in dangerous waters, well to the north and east of the usual sailing route but a long way to the west of the steamer route to the Cape.

The first Sunday out dawned fine and fair. As Stephens held the helm, Tom took Sunday service on the after deck. He read from the Bible and led them in a hymn, and they said prayers in turn for themselves and their loved ones at home.

For the remainder of the day those off-watch took their ease about the deck. Stephens and Brooks darned their clothes and rubbed linseed oil into their worn oilskin coats, or chatted and smoked their pipes. A shadow crossed Brooks's face as Stephens began talking eagerly of his wife and children and his hopes and plans for them. After a few moments Brooks muttered something, then stood up and strode to the bow, where he leaned on the rail, staring out over the waves.

Tom began teaching Richard his letters. He prided himself on never sitting down on deck, lest it set a bad example and encouraged idleness in his crew, and he remained standing as the boy squatted cross-legged at his feet. Under his tutelage, Richard laboriously spelled out a letter to the Matthewses in his uncertain, childlike hand. It read only, 'I am happy and comfortable, all on board are well. We have had a fine and pleasant passage all the way,' but his face was flushed with pride when he had finished. It was the first letter he had ever written in his life. They would post it on reaching Madeira.

As Richard continued to practise his writing, Tom talked to Stephens. 'Will you stay in Sydney?' he said. 'Mr Want seems a good man, if not to some English tastes. There would be many worse owners.' He laughed. 'I've sailed yachts for some of them.'

'I plan to stay there,' Stephens said. 'If my Ann will join me.'

'You haven't told her?'

'I mean to. I – I didn't know how to broach it with her. I'll send her a letter from Madeira.' He seemed to flinch at the thought and hurriedly changed the subject. 'But what of you, Captain? Will you not take up Mr Want's offer for yourself?'

He shook his head. 'If Mrs Pettigrew and her business are as she says, I intend to join her in it.' His face darkened. 'But I mean to be more careful in my choice of business partner than I have been in the past.' He intercepted Stephens's questioning look and told him of his ill-fated venture.

A school of dolphins showed on the surface nearby, breaking his black mood. They tracked the yacht for several miles, swimming just under the water, the sunlight dancing on their skins as they alternately surfed the pressure wave at the bow and broke surface on either side of the boat in arcing loops that left rainbow-sprays of water hanging in the air. The *Mignonette* sailed on with every inch of canvas set under the hard light of the sun, a pyramid of blinding white sail reflecting in the green water rippling past the ship.

Brooks had no eye for the beauty of the scene. He had grumbled of toothache for two days and rose to the morning watch the next day with his face so swollen that his eyes were mere slits.

'Something will have to be done,' Tom said.

Brooks shook his head, making inarticulate protests through a mouth that would barely open.

'We've a little laudanum,' Tom said, 'but that is for something more serious than a toothache. You can wait until we make port in Madeira and take your chances with a local sawbones there, but we've three days' sailing before us, even if the wind holds. Better, surely, for me do it for you. It's not the first tooth I've had to pull.'

Brooks hesitated a while, then gave a reluctant nod. His eyes widened in fear as Tom pulled his knife from his pocket.

'You're never going to cut it out of him?' Stephens said.

'No. I'm going to make certain of the right tooth.' He held Brooks's mouth open as far as it would go, and tapped each of his teeth in turn with the back of the knife blade until Brooks roared with pain. Tom sent Richard below for the rope-yarn and pulled a long strand from it. He looped it over the tooth and knotted it, then took a couple of turns around his fist and gripped it taut. 'Hold his head still,' he said.

Stephens and the boy clamped Brooks's head between them. Tom let the cord fall slack, then jerked it taut again with a sudden snap. There was a rising howl of pain from Brooks that ended in a yelp as the tooth was ripped out and dropped on to the deck.

He pulled himself free of the other two and stumped around the deck cursing and kicking at the bulwarks, and spitting blood and fluid over the rail into the sea. By the time he had completed his circuit of the deck, the swelling was already beginning to subside and he paused to shake Tom's hand and thank him.

Tom laughed. 'You'll do well enough now, but I doubt the ladies will fall for that smile of yours so readily in the future.'

CHAPTER 6

Land clouds rising in the distance ahead of the *Mignonette* told of Madeira while the island still lay invisible in the vastness of the ocean. They began to take soundings at each change of the watch and before long, Tom caught the dull, distant rumble of breakers.

They reached the island on the evening of 2 June. They sailed down its eastern coast, smelling the sunbaked earth and the resin from the pine forests, and hearing the roar of the Atlantic rollers breaking against the rocks.

They entered Madeira Roads at midnight. The hills rose steeply behind the harbour, towards the mountains at the island's heart. The port of Funchal was in near darkness, with only a few torches flickering along the quayside, but ships showing the flags of a dozen different nations rode at anchor in the Roads or were tied up at the quay.

After so long on the open sea, the heat from the sheltered land was oppressive. The others sprawled out to sleep on the deck as soon as they had dropped anchor, but Tom and Richard stayed at the rail for some time, immersing themselves in the sights, scents and sounds of a strange land, carried to them on the breeze.

Before the sun was barely above the horizon the next morning, the *Mignonette* was besieged by bumboats. There were men with scrawny chickens and squealing piglets trussed like turkeys, fishermen offering the pick of their catch, water-sellers and a host of other waterborne hawkers with ropes of onions and garlic, flasks of wine and rum, flowers, pineapples, melons, limes, oranges, peaches, figs and olives.

'Keep close watch on them and let no man on deck,' Tom said. 'They're as likely to thieve as trade with us.'

Brightly painted whores were also rowed out by their pimps, and the pleasures they could give were extolled to Tom and his crew. Brooks was leaning over the rail talking to one when Tom ordered him away. 'We're sailing on the next tide. There's work to be done and no time for whoring.'

Stephens checked the ship's longitude against his calculations, and then they all helped with the gruelling process of taking on water. The stanchions were taken down and the empty butts hauled out of the hold. The water-sellers rowed them away, scoured them with sand, then refilled them with sweet water from the springs in the hills above Funchal. All four members of the crew were required to haul them back on board, straining on the ropes against the dead weight of the casks as they dragged them over the rail before lowering them back into the hold.

Tom bought fresh fruit and vegetables from one of the boatmen and a sackful of limes to flavour the drinking water. He also bought a pig, bartering with tobacco for everything he needed.

All four men sent messages home. Richard posted his letter to the Matthewses, and Brooks also scribbled a note, shielding it from the others with his arm and concealing the name and address on the envelope

Tom sent Philippa a terse cable, 'All is well,' but he also wrote her a long letter, pressing hibiscus and bougainvillaea petals between its pages. Some were stained with tears. When he had sealed the envelope, he walked to the bow and stood there alone, his back to his crew, staring out over the ocean that separated him from home.

Stephens sent an even longer letter to Ann, explaining for the first time his plan to emigrate and asking her if she and the children would join him in Australia. He told her to send a reply to the Cape. Since the mails went by fast steamship, it would reach Cape Town before the *Mignonette*'s scheduled arrival date.

They sailed at eleven thirty that morning, having remained in port only twelve hours. Ahead lay the horse latitudes, north of the Tropic of Cancer. Stephens was able to fix their position again six days later, when they passed within sight of San Antonio, the northernmost island of the Cape Verde group. Still well stocked with water and supplies, Tom did not put into port, preferring to make all speed for the Cape.

That night he saw a group of stars as bright as any in the sky, just above the southern horizon. He had heard seamen talk of it in the night watches, but had never before laid eyes on the Southern Cross. Every mile they sailed to the southward sent it higher in the sky, climbing the vault of the heavens.

The Cross was both a link to their destination and a reminder of how far they had already travelled from their home. On cloudy nights the darkness was total, almost palpable, and Tom could feel as well as know the thousands of miles of sea that separated him from his loved ones.

He kept every possible inch of sail on the *Mignonette*, making over a hundred miles a day as the wind drove them on. Dolphins continued to play around the yacht's hull and flying fish arched from the sea in graceful parabolas. They skimmed the crests of the waves, barely seeming to touch the water before they were airborne again on their outspread wings.

Three flying fish crossing on the wind during the night flew into the sails and fell stunned to the deck. Brooks collected and cooked them and after each subsequent moonless or cloudy night, there was always a small harvest of fish to be gathered from the deck.

In twelve days they saw only one ship, an Italian barque out from Liverpool, but on Sunday 14 June Tom heard a call, 'Sail ho!' and hurried on deck.

'Where away?'

'Starboard beam.'

A barque was cleaving the water towards them. He saw the English colours at the masthead and stifled a pang of homesickness at the thought of its homeward-bound crew. The barque's deckhands were scrambling aloft to reduce sail and Tom set Brooks and Richard to work to do the same.

He hailed the barque as the two vessels nosed towards each other, rocking gently in the moderate swell. 'Captain Dudley of the *Mignonette*. What ship are you?'

'Captain Fraser of the *Bride of Larne*, forty-one days out from Liverpool. Where are you from?'

'Southampton, bound for New South Wales.'

'Are you in need of anything?'

'Thank you, we have letters for home, but all our wants are already supplied.'

As soon as the sails were furled, the ship's dinghy was lowered and Tom and Stephens rowed across to the barque with the crew's letters. Tom shared a drink with Captain Fraser, exchanging news of sea conditions and ships they had sighted, while Stephens and the mate of the *Bride of Larne* argued over their conflicting estimates of their present longitude. There was over a hundred miles' difference between the two, but with the benefit of a recent fix on their position in the Cape Verde Islands, Tom was sure that Stephens was not in error.

They parted company with Captain Fraser at four that afternoon. As they rowed the dinghy back to the *Mignonette*, Tom saw a pilot fish in the water. 'Look sharp,' he said. 'I never saw a pilot fish that wasn't close-followed by a shark.'

As they scrambled up on to the deck, they saw a grey swirl in the water and the dinghy banged against the hull as the wake of the shark shook it. The fin broke surface, laying a thin trace of foam across the swell as the great fish passed in front of the bow and moved back along the other side of the ship. Tom saw Brooks and Stephens exchange a glance. A shark circling a boat was regarded by all seamen as a sure omen of a death on board.

On the following Tuesday, 17 June, twenty-nine days after leaving home, the *Mignonette* crossed the equator at a longitude of twenty-six degrees, forty minutes west, by Stephens's reckoning. He and Brooks had both crossed the Line many times before but for Tom and Richard Parker it was their first time.

With no alcohol on board, there was none of the usual drunken ritual to celebrate the crossing, but even the normally unbending Tom submitted to the indignity of a commemorative ducking from his crew.

Brooks and Richard took the next watch. It was a warm night with only a light breeze and there was little to do but keep a hand on the helm as they talked, passing the night hours with tales of the sea.

'So, Dick,' Brooks said, 'you've crossed the Line. You're a proper seaman now. What's your mind? Will you be staying with us in New South Wales, or is the sea in your veins?'

The boy flushed. 'There's more of the world I'd like to see first.'

Brooks glanced at him and smiled. 'Don't be too eager to sign your life away. There are many worse captains than Tom Dudley. I've been on ships that I would have cut off a hand to leave – a tyrant for captain, brutes for officers and a rabble of footpads and cutpurses for crew, sold to the ship by the crimps.'

He broke off to relight his pipe, confident he had the boy's whole attention. The blue smoke drifted upwards, barely troubled by the faint breeze. 'The crimps always had a piece of paper with what they said was the man's mark, but the officers were never too choosy. They had a crew and that was all that concerned them.

'I've known of men who went to a tavern for a wet when they were paid off from one ship, and woke the next morning to find themselves at sea on another with empty pockets, and working the first month for nothing to pay the cut of the crimp who'd robbed them and put them there.

'In some ships the food was so mean and putrid it would have starved a rat, and the cost was still docked from your wage. I sailed on one where the captain was so close-pursed that we ran out of rations ten days from land. We were so hungry we ate our tobacco and a leather wallet.' He intercepted Richard's doubtful look. 'It is as true as I'm standing here. The water ran out five days later. We caught and killed six rats, drank their blood and ate their flesh.'

Richard shuddered, but Brooks was now warming to his theme. 'Desperate men will resort to even harder measures. A ship I heard tell of, the *Frances Mary*, was hit by a monstrous wave that smashed the spars, swept every object, including the ship's boats, from the deck and stove in the stern. One man was drowned by the wave, another was found dead, dangling from the rigging. The survivors including the captain's wife and another woman, Ann Saunders, huddled together on the forecastle in a tent they made from a scrap of canvas. Two vessels passed them, but they offered no help and sailed on.

'From want of water, some drank their own urine and sea-water. They crawled on their hands and knees around the deck and died raving mad. The first perished after a week – his body was thrown over the side. The next died ten days later, after they had been adrift for seventeen days. He was quartered and hung up for food. The next day another man died and his liver and heart were eaten. Over the next twelve days, another seven men perished. All were bled and eaten.

'When the cook died, his betrothed, Ann Saunders, snatched the cup from the mate, cut her late intended husband's throat and drank his blood, insisting she had the greatest right to it. She claimed that it was "God's will" that the blood should not pass her for another.

'She had more strength in her calamity than most of the men. She performed the duty of cutting up and cleaning the bodies. She would sharpen the knives, bleed the man in the neck, drink his blood and cut him up.

'The captain's wife also ate the brains of an apprentice who had survived three previous shipwrecks. She declared them "the most delicious thing she had ever tasted". Only six were still alive when they were picked up by a frigate.'

Stephens had been below, but he had come on deck while Brooks was talking. He lounged against the rail, smoking his clay pipe and studying Richard's half-frightened, half-sceptical expression. 'It's a true enough tale, lad, and there are many others who have suffered the same fate.

'I once sailed on a collier, the *Euxine*. She was built as a paddle-steamer, but when I joined her, the engines had been removed and she worked under sail. She left South Shields ten years ago this month past, captained by Peter Murdock. She was bound for Aden with a cargo of coals for the steamships that refuelled there. I should have been on that voyage, but I heard of a better berth on a bigger ship and did not sign articles with the *Euxine*.

'On the first of August, the cargo shifted in heavy seas. The next three days were spent levelling it in the holds – terrible work – but four days later smoke was seen coming from the hatches. The coal had caught fire of itself, as happens often enough on such ships. They battened down the hatches and changed course for St Helena but they could not control the fires and on the eighth of August all thirty men abandoned ship.

'They stayed close by, hoping the fires would die out, but by morning the ship was ablaze from stem to stern and they set out in a convoy of three boats for St Helena. The last boat, under the command of the second mate, James Archer, with seven men aboard, lost contact with the others that night.

'At first there seemed little cause for alarm. Their boat was a thirty-footer, with two masts and a fore-boom, carrying mainsail, stay-sail and jib. They had tools, a sextant, chronometer and chart, and they were well provisioned – a ham, a cheese, two cases of biscuits, tins of meat, four pounds of plug tobacco. They had only two small casks of water, however, and it was rationed to a pint a day per man.

'Twelve days' sailing brought them close to the latitude of St Helena, but the second mate was a poor navigator and he could not find land. After two days he gave up the search and resolved to sail northwest-by-north, using the trade winds to make for Brazil. It was a distance of more than two thousand miles.

'They cut rations to half a biscuit and one cup of water a day, but the weather worsened and on the twenty-seventh of August, just an hour before midnight, the boat capsized. The boatswain was drowned – I was told he had thrown himself overboard while at the helm, leaving his fellows to their fate.

'The others righted the boat but soon afterwards it capsized again, and then again. A boy who had shipped as able seaman also drowned but the other five clung to the boat all night, then righted it in the morning. Their plight was now dreadful: they had lost everything – masts, sails, sextant and all their food and water.' He broke off to scan the sea ahead of them, as Richard waited, wide-eyed. 'On the last day of August they agreed to draw lots. The first one to draw the short lot three times would be killed. Amongst the men was Francis Gioffous, a small Italian boy of about thirteen years, who spoke hardly any English.'

He paused and tapped the side of his nose. 'He wasn't a popular member of the crew. He was the unlucky person on each of the first two drawings, then refused to cast a third lot. One of the crew then drew for him and once more the shortest stick was in that man's hand – or so it was said. They left the boy to pray while they looked for a sail one last time, then a crewman killed him.'

He gave a grim smile. 'Leastways, that was the second mate's version. I heard it from one of the other crew that the boy jumped overboard after the second lot was drawn. They seized him before he could drown himself, dragged him back on board and murdered him. His throat was cut with such force that he was decapitated. They drank the blood, ate

78

the heart and liver and put the body and limbs into the lockers of the boat. Five hours later they saw a sail and were rescued by a Dutch barque, the *Java Packet*, bound for Batavia.'

Despite the warmth of the night Richard shivered. 'What happened to the men?'

'They reached Batavia early in November and Singapore a week later. They were held for a few days, then sent back to England. There was even talk of trying them for murder, but they were released as soon as they reached London.'

He ruffled the boy's hair. 'You'll have heard many a tall tale on the night watches, Dick, but these are true. It is the custom of the sea, and has been practised more times down the centuries than there are stars in this sky above us.'

CHAPTER 7

The *Mignonette* was into the doldrums now, the region between the south-east and north-east trade winds, where the ocean surface was fretted into clashing cross-seas and troubled by eddying currents, and brief, fitful squalls from every point of the compass were interspersed with long periods of flat calm.

Before morning even the faint breeze had died away. The four men slept on the open deck, out of the stinking heat below decks. The sails hung limp and heavy around the mast and the lassitude extended to the crew. Stephens leaned against the helm with a vacant look on his face, Richard picked a few desultory strands of oakum and Brooks made slow work of patching a sail. Only Tom still moved with restless energy, pacing the deck, tugging at the rigging, testing the shrouds and stays and scanning the horizon around them.

In mid-afternoon, an hour before the first dog-watch, a lazy breeze got up and a cloud appeared to westward, spreading and darkening as it sped towards the ship.

'All hands, turn to,' Tom called.

They pitched the oakum and mending kit down the companionway and closed the slide over it. They had only moments to shut the hatches, douse the sails and lash all solid before the squall was on them, roughening the surface of the sea and filling the remaining canvas with a wind so warm it brought no relief from the heat.

All the men stripped off their clothes, their torsos white against their sunburned, sea-blacked arms and faces. The fat drops of tropical rain felt warm on their skin and rinsed the salt from their bodies.

Almost before the squall was past, Tom called, 'Loose the sails,' striving to squeeze every ounce of momentum from it to drag the yacht on its slow way southwards, out of the doldrums and into the region of the trade winds; but almost at once the wind died away. The rain-soaked planking began to steam as the heat drew the moisture from it and within a few minutes it was as if the squall had never been.

Towards sundown the next day, the sky began to darken with cloud and the hot, humid air seemed heavy with anticipation. Tom had the jib hauled in and the mainsail reefed ready for the storm, but though the sky continued to blacken, there was not a breath of wind and the sails still hung limp around the mast.

He paced the deck, the slap of his bare feet on the planking echoing in the oppressive silence. An eerie light seemed to glow over the ship. Richard raised his gaze to the masthead and let out a cry. A shimmering halo of light surrounded it.

'Don't worry, it'll do us no harm,' Tom said. 'It's a corposant – St Elmo's fire.'

It continued to glow for a few minutes, hovering around the top of the mast, sometimes rising or descending a few feet, but then it was extinguished as quickly as a snuffed candle. A moment later there was a savage clap of thunder, and sheet lightning – a wall of white fire – crackled around the horizon.

There was still no breath of wind and the sea was flat calm, but thunder continued to rattle like a naval broadside. Curtains of rain tumbled out of the sky and water poured from the scuppers as if the ship was beating into a heavy sea. The rain stopped as abruptly as it had begun and the storm moved on, but flickers of distant lightning continued to pierce the darkness for several hours.

The next day, a breeze at last got up and they sailed on into the South Atlantic in a freshening south-easterly, the first harbinger of the trade winds. Long thin cirrus cloud streaked the sky, aligned from north-west to south-east, pointing the way to the Cape.

Tom had the top mast taken down, reducing the height and weight of the *Mignonette*'s rigging and canvas in anticipation of the rougher winter conditions ahead. Tom, Stephens and Richard all worked barefoot. Only Brooks regularly wore his seaboots. Each night, when he was off-watch, he rubbed them with linseed oil to waterproof them.

They sailed on to the south for another week, tacking in long reaches against the wind as the light, high clouds of the trade winds streamed overhead. On 25 June, there was a change in the wind and weather. Tom was below when there was a cry from Stephens: 'All hands ahoy.'

As Tom ran towards the companionway, not even pausing to put on his oilskins, he heard the crack of the sails as a squall shook them. A fresh north-westerly was upon them. He cast a look to the weather side of the ship and saw a dense bank of cloud and mist, extending from the sky to the ocean, driving over the waves towards them. The surface of the water was darkened by the wind and stippled by rain. A short, ugly swell was beginning to rise, pitching the boat from side to side.

The yacht lay over to the strengthening wind and there was a frantic scramble to reef and furl the sails. Brooks and Richard were already at work on the mainsail. The boy tried to pass the reef earing, but the squall shook the sail with such force that twice it was snatched from his grasp, setting the canvas rattling and banging against the mast. Tom grabbed the boom alongside him. 'Be sharp, lad, or it'll have the mast out of her.'

Rain stung their skin like whips as the cloud swallowed them up and they were exposed to the full force of the wind. The ship heeled further over under the spread of canvas still exposed, and every movement of the ship was magnified threefold. Richard's face was green and he turned his head, groaned and vomited. The wind threw it back in his face.

'Get below,' Tom said. 'You're no use to us and a danger to yourself here.'

As the boy struggled back along the deck, Tom passed the reef earing himself. He glanced to his left. 'Haul in, Brooks.'

Rain lashed around the two men, their bodies bent over the boom, as they hauled at the sodden canvas. Tom's soaking clothes were plastered against his body, but he barely noticed the cold, using all the strength in his stocky frame to hold and lash the sail.

They scrambled forward to take a reef in the foresail, but the wind was still strengthening and they were soon back to double-reef the mainsail, and stuff the jibs as well. The bowsprit had been cut back by six feet before the voyage, but as Tom crawled to the end of it to stuff the number-one jib, with the seas crashing around him and the wind bidding to tear him loose from his precarious perch, he wished he had shortened it a further yard at least.

Even close-hauled, the boat lay hard over, her mast bent like a whip. The bowsprit carved through the waves, the spray flying over the forecastle as the sea broke over it, foaming away down the scuppers. They battened down the forward hatch and lashed the helm, then Tom went below again. Richard was slumped at the bottom of the companionway. 'I'm sorry, Captain, I—'

Tom held up his hand. 'My first time on an ocean voyage I was sick as a cur-dog for a week. I'd never met weather like it before – racing yachts run for home when a big blow comes on. You'll be right enough by and by.'

The boy's attempted reply ended in another groan. Tom went back to his cabin and stripped off his wet clothes, but he dressed in dry gear before lying down on his berth, certain he would be called again before his watch began.

The ship pitched ever more steeply as the sea got up before the gale. The lantern over Tom's head swung in a wide arc, casting a ray of light like the intermittent beam of a lighthouse on to the rough wood of the bulkead against which he lay.

All through that night the wind strengthened and Tom woke to hear rain still hammering on the deck above his head. The pitching of the ship had disturbed the sediment and filthy water in the bilges and a stench as foul as the gas from the bottom mud of a pond corrupted the air.

The waves smashed in endless repetition against the hull, each blow echoing through the ship like the thud of an axe on wood. Every timber in the ship seemed to be creaking and groaning, underscored by the relentless bass battering of the sea against the bow.

Tom clambered out of his berth, pulled on his oilskins and went on deck. Stephens was huddled over the helm, with Brooks forward on look-out. The sails were drum-taut and the shrouds and stays tight as fiddle strings as the wind howled over the rigging, sending the loose ends of ropes snaking through the air.

White spume flew as the bow plunged into the waves and rose again with a groan from the timbers. Each time sea-water coursed over the deck and flooded out through the scuppers, but the calloused soles and splayed toes of Tom's feet gave him a sure grip on the slippery planking.

The force of the gale was still increasing, and a heavy beam sea was running. Tom took the helm from Stephens. 'Ship the number-three jib,' he said. 'I'll run her off a couple of points to keep the sea more on our quarter.'

The north-westerly gale kept up for five days. They sailed on under a single-reefed mainsail, making fast time towards the Cape, but the pitching of the ship made it impossible to cook or even boil water to wet the tea. They chewed hard-tack, tinned turnips and lumps of cold, greasy meat, and drank cold water. The tang of the limes Tom had bought in Madeira now barely hid the water's staleness.

On Monday, 30 June, 'the wind shifted abruptly to the south-south-west, blowing very hard. I had the mainsail and foresail in and bent the storm trysail, but we could scarcely sail her at times, there being so much sea.'

The trysail was a sheet of canvas secured direct to the mast and bulwarks without a boom or yard; in the storm conditions in which it was used the danger from flying timbers exceeded any advantage the boom or yard might have conferred.

Late in the evening of the next day, the wind suddenly dropped. As always after a gale, everyone was irritable and exhausted, every joint aching from the pounding and jerking as the yacht was pitched about by the swell. Their hands were scarred by sea cuts from hauling on the wet, coarse ropes.

'I hope we see no more storms like that for a while,' Richard said, sipping the first mug of tea he had had in days. Tom scanned the lowering sky. 'The gale is only half over, lad. We've entered the eye of the storm.' He was about to say more, but then fell silent. Why tell the boy that the seas already raised by the days of gales would be whipped into even bigger waves by the further storm to come? He would find out soon enough. Meanwhile, he was better left in ignorance.

All the next day, 2 July, they lay becalmed, but in the evening a light breeze began. As it freshened, it seemed to blow in fitful gusts from every point of the compass, but then settled into the west-south-west, strengthening rapidly.

Just before the rushing clouds blotted out the night sky, Tom looked up at the heavens. Even the stars and constellations, a sailor's only fixed points far out on the ocean, had shifted almost beyond recognition. The Pole star, the first star any navigator on the northern oceans learns to recognize, had long disappeared below the horizon. The Great Bear had also sunk from sight.

The constellations of the southern skies shone in their place. The Southern Cross was now high overhead and Tom also saw the great galaxies of the southern skies, the Magellan Clouds, for the first time. Two were as bright and dusty as the Milky Way, the other as dark as if a fog bank had rolled over it.

Then the black, lowering clouds of the gathering storm blanked out the heavens and the sails began to crack as the wind ripped and tugged at them. The seas rose to fifteen, then twenty feet as the gale grew ever stronger, and flecks of grey spume like gull feathers flew through the air.

They hung on under a whole mainsail, squaresail and second jib, but by four the next afternoon it was blowing very hard out of the south-south-west, with massive seas. They reefed the mainsail and squaresail, and at eleven that night the mainsail ripped free.

The wind was blowing like knives. Above the shriek of the gale there was a snap like a pistol shot as a rope parted. A corner of the sail flapped loose for a second and then Tom heard a rending tear in the canvas. Deafened by the noise of the storm and blinded by the rain driving into their faces, they groped their way forward and began to furl the torn sail.

The canvas was heavy with water and drum-taut under the force of the wind. Tom took the centre, where the work was hardest, with Brooks on his left and Richard to his right. Inch by inch they dragged in the billowing, snapping canvas. Three times it broke free, with a wild crack, as an even more savage gust shook the mast. The sail bellied out over their heads, then lashed back at them with a force that almost shook them from the deck.

It took almost forty minutes' punishing work before the sail was in and the storm trysail set. It was brand new, made of the toughest canvas, set close to the deck, but even the little purchase the wind could take on it was enough to all but tear the eyes from it as the ship was driven on.

The ripped mainsail was bundled below and Tom strode aft to take the helm from the exhausted Stephens. Steering the close-hauled ship through such a heavy sea took every ounce of strength and all the skill he had learned in his years at sea.

Every wave battered against the hull and slewed the yacht around, threatening to push it broadsides to the mountainous seas and broach it. The least error could see a wave break over the deck to tear away the superstructure, rip out the mast like matchwood, and sweep them all to their deaths.

Four hours later, when Stephens again took over the watch, Tom remained at his side, scared to trust another man's seamanship in such conditions; but eventually fatigue drove him below to rest. He took off his clothes, wrung the water from them and draped them on the bulkhead as he collapsed into his berth. They were still dripping when he dragged them on again a bare hour later and went back on deck to answer the inevitable call of 'Hands ahoy,' as another rope broke free.

For two days the *Mignonette* was battered by the storm, labouring in the heavy seas. The gusts were so violent that the yacht was often driven bodily to leeward. Every yard of ground they had made towards the Cape in the previous week was lost again as they fled before the assault of the wind.

The rope lashing the helm snapped under the strain and Tom and Stephens held it by force of will as much as muscle until Brooks could secure it again.

When he went below to snatch a few moments' rest, the pitching of the ship spilled Tom from his berth so often that he was forced to sling a hammock. The sensation was almost as alarming: the hammock held vertical while the ship swung through a ninety-degree arc around it.

There was also another, more worrying, sign of the force of the storm. The planking repaired at Fay's Yard – the garboard strakes next to the keel – was seeping water again. As he lay in his hammock, he could see it glistening in the light of the swinging lantern.

By 5 July the weather was even worse. The sky was thick with rain and a ferocious gale was still blowing from the south-south-west. The wind was shrieking through the rigging and the sails cracked as the gusts tore at them. He heard a tortured creaking from the mast as it flexed and bent.

As the *Mignonette* ploughed on through the swell, the water in the lee scuppers was often waist-deep. The whole surface of the ocean was flecked with foam and great ropes of spume flew through the air. A heavier cross-sea was running than Tom had ever seen, a maelstrom of churning, clashing water. Huge waves seemed to appear from every direction and all the helmsman could do was keep the bow in line with the worst of the wind and seas and pray that a rogue wave would not overwhelm them.

The waves grew ever higher and steeper, reaching to forty feet, their glistening faces almost vertical, capped with curling crests of grey foam. It was an ominous sign, striking a chill in Tom's guts. Far from any shore, waves broke only for one reason: because the unstable mountains of water were collapsing under their own massive weight. Anything in the path of one of those leviathans as it broke would be crushed.

As he tried to advance along the deck to mend a broken shroud, whipping to and fro across the deck, the wind battered him so hard that he was forced to crawl, clutching at the bulwarks to stop himself being swept overboard.

He crept forward in the brief lull as the *Mignonette* hit the trough of the swell and the following wave blocked the wind for a moment, then flattened himself to the deck as the yacht was driven upwards to the crest and the gale howled and tore at him again. His hair lashed at his face and as he raised his head, tears streamed from the corners of his eyes and he could feel the force of the gale pushing his eyeballs back into their sockets.

As he reached up to catch the flailing end of the shroud, a gust hit him like a punch. He sprawled helpless, toppling end over end, and a breaking wave swept him bodily along the deck. He hit the edge of the hatch with a force that drove the air from his lungs, then spun away and was left spreadeagled against the bulwarks, within inches of the sea boiling around the ship.

As the wave receded, he dragged himself back from the brink and lay flat on the deck, gasping for breath until he saw the next wave coursing over the planking. He scrambled to his knees, clutching the bulwarks for support, and dragged himself back to safety.

A yacht he was captaining had once been pooped by a following wave on a run across the Irish Sea but even then, in a ship so full of water it was inches from foundering, Tom had never felt the fear that gripped him now. In the heart of the storm, with the shrieking wind gusting to eighty knots and the waves forty and fifty feet high, for the first time in his life he became truly aware that he might die at sea.

All four men were now grey-faced with exhaustion. Even when they were not at work on deck or at the pumps, the wild pitching of the ship made it impossible to rest, and none had slept for more than a few minutes since the storm began.

Tom had the afternoon watch with Richard and as he readied himself to call the next watch at four o'clock, he made up his mind to 'heave to until the weather abated and the sea ran down a little'.

Stephens and Brooks came on deck after lying below in their oilskins, trying in vain to sleep. Tom told Stephens to take the helm while the squaresail was taken in. 'We'll have to reduce canvas or the gale will have the sticks out of her. She can ride out the storm under a backed jib and storm trysail.'

After hauling down the squaresail, they began securing everything before Stephens brought the yacht head to wind. Peering into the storm, he would try to pick a gap between the biggest waves in which to come around, but in the ten or twenty seconds as the ship swung slowly to face the wind, losing headway all the while, the sea would force her over until the keel was all but exposed.

Any big wave hitting her then, as she lay broadside to the sea, could broach and bury her. Even if she escaped that fate, the vicious stresses as the keel weight dragged the ship back to the vertical might snap her mast or spring her timbers.

Tom had no choice, however. The swell was becoming ever shorter and more ugly, and the gaps between the precipitous wave crests were now no more than a handful of seconds. If they continued to run before the wind, the *Mignonette* would not long survive such huge waves breaking over her stern. The only hope was to turn her head to the wind and ride out the storm.

When the wind was too strong for almost any sail to be carried without the risk of capsize, or when the following seas were so short and ugly that a yacht could not run before the wind without risk of the waves breaking over the stern and burying her, a sailing master could bring his craft around to lie-to before the gale.

Square-riggers had storm-staysails, which were used only for the purpose of bringing and holding the ship head to wind, but a yacht like the *Mignonette* would lie to under a backed jib and trysail.

Flying downwind a few moments before, the manoeuvre would bring the yacht to a standstill in short order. Without any further intervention from the helmsman, the bows would hold themselves within a few points of the wind, allowing the shock of the waves to be borne by the windward bow, with little water being shipped.

The helm would be lashed, but this was done as much to stop it thrashing from side to side as for any effect on the attitude of the ship, which would hold station and ride every wave while the crew snatched what rest they could, for the ship effectively sailed itself as long as the sails held.

If the force of the gale ripped the canvas free, however, the yacht was in immediate danger of foundering as the wind pushed her broadside before the sea. The only remedy then was to cut the lashings on the helm and bring her round to run before the wind until another sail could be jury-rigged.

The work of securing everything on deck took half an hour to complete. Brooks was reinforcing the lashings on the dinghy while Tom used the butt end of a hatchet to nail canvas over the aft skylight before giving the order to bring the *Mignonette* about.

At the helm, Stephens glanced around him and froze. A freak wave was sweeping down on them, a wall of water obscuring the horizon. It seemed to reach to the height of the masthead, sixty feet above the deck. A curling crest of foam spread along its entire length and spilled in streaks down its vertical face like the breaks in a waterfall.

The trough at the foot of the wave was so deep that it looked like a black hole in the sea. He gave a strangled cry and called, 'Look out!' at the same time jamming the helm hard over to meet the wave square on, but the sea broke clean over her.

The stern of the *Mignonette* plummeted downwards as it was plunged into the trough before the wave, throwing the bow up into the air. Then the grey wall collapsed and crashed down on the yacht, burying it under tons of water. As the wave struck, the *Mignonette*'s every timber shook to its core.

Stephens tried to cling to the helm, but was hurled back against the rail. He felt the bulwarks give way and fell with them, dangling over the boiling sea, his legs kicking like a hanged man's, until the water from the monstrous wave at last flooded away.

Tom and Richard were on the lee side of the boom. At Stephens's cry, Tom ducked to look under the boom and saw a mountainous sea coming down on top of them. He caught hold of the boom. It was a wonder it did not break under the force of the wave.

Tom clung to the boom as his feet were swept from under him and hung there, like a ship's pennant streaming in the wind. There was no up or down, no light or darkness, only the crushing weight of water and the relentless power trying to tear him free from the grip he had locked around the boom. He had no idea if it was still attached to the mast or had been ripped away and swept over the bulwarks; all he could do was cling to it as his lungs screamed for oxygen and the blood hammered in his ears.

Still at work lashing down the dinghy, Brooks had also seen the wave coming, a tremendous sea reaching half-way up to the masthead. He took two turns of the rope around his arms and hung on.

As the wave swept the deck and engulfed him, the rope bit through his skin, burning deep weals into the flesh of his arms. The sail was rent and torn away in an instant.

Stephens dragged himself back on to the broken deck, but to his horror, he saw that the weather topsides and the bulwarks abaft the beam were stoved in. He cried out, 'My God, her topsides are stove in, she is sinking.'

Tom went to windward, only to find the mate's words were true: her butt ends on the starboard side had been laid clean open, where the force of the wave had torn the garboard strakes from the keel.

The dinghy was tied down over the fore skylight and Tom shouted to Brooks above the howling of the wind, 'Help me lower the dinghy.'

Brooks tried to cut the lashings off, but as he struggled with them, Tom gave him an axe and he cut them off with two blows. He made one part of the ship's painter fast to the boat before they shoved her off.

They manhandled the dinghy over the side, but in the process they contrived to hole its flimsy, quarter-inch planking. It began to fill with water as the waves crashed over it.

Stephens still held the helm. Tom shouted to Richard to go below decks with him and bring up the breaker of water from the foot of the companionway. As he held it over the rail, Tom grabbed his arm. 'Don't drop it into the dinghy, you'll stove in the bottom. Throw it into the sea and we'll pick it up.'

Already half-empty, it floated high in the water and at once began to be carried away on the wind. Brooks and Richard clambered down into the dinghy.

Brooks called to Tom and he let out some rope on the painter, allowing the waves to carry the dinghy round to the stern of the yacht. He took a turn of the rope round a cleat on the taff rail, then threw the other end of it to Brooks.

Ignoring the waves breaking over the boat, Tom hurried to the companionway. He peered down into the gloom below decks, glimpsed the swirl of foam and heard the ugly gurgle of water as it flooded through the boat.

He hesitated for a moment, then lowered himself down the companionway, battling through the chest-deep water to his cabin. The watertight cases of the sextant and chronometer were floating on the icy water swirling around him. He struggled to the bottom of the companionway and threw them up on deck, but Stephens had now abandoned the helm to join the other two in the dinghy, and the next wave breaking over the stricken ship washed the instruments overboard.

Tom was now alone on the sinking yacht. He knew it could keel over at any second, but he forced himself to stay below. He entered the galley and grabbed six tins of what he thought was canned meat floating among the debris, then heard a shout from Stephens: 'Captain, she's sinking!'

He hurried on deck as he felt the yacht lurch. Still clutching the tins, he tried to clamber down from the stern, but then jumped for the dinghy, as he felt the yacht shudder and begin to founder beneath him. He fell heavily, sprawling in the near-waterlogged boat. Only one tin found its way in the boat with him.

The remainder of the armful of tins had dropped into the sea. They scrabbled for them as they were tossed on the waves, but only managed to snare another one.

Tom pulled himself up at once and seized one of the oars as Stephens took the other, and Brooks jerked free the rope binding them to the ship. The gunwales were barely clear of the surface as waves continued to break over the dinghy and water flowed in through the hole in its side. Brooks grabbed the wooden baler and began baling for their lives. Richard used the hat of his oilskins to scoop out more water as Tom and Stephens bent to the oars, hauling the boat astern of the *Mignonette*.

They were the bare length of the dinghy from it when the outline of the bow rose vertically into the darkening sky as the yacht began to sink by the stern. It loomed above them for one terrifying moment, then the ship slid downwards and the waves closed over it. It was less than five minutes since the mountainous wave had struck her. A single giant bubble of air broke surface, the death rattle of the *Mignonette*.

CAPTAIN DUDLEY, OF THE YACHT "MIGNONETTE."

(From a Photograph by the London Stereoscopic Company, Cheapside.)

1

ABOVE: Tom Dudley's sketch of the *Mignonette*.

BELOW: The *Mignonette* in racing trim, 1882.

THE ILLUSTRATED LONDON NEWS

REGISTERED AT THE GENERAL POST-OFFICE FOR TRANSMISSION ABROAD.

No. 2370.—VOL. LXXXV.   SATURDAY, SEPTEMBER 20, 1884.   WITH EXTRA SUPPLEMENT   SIXPENCE. By Post, 6½d.

THE LOSS OF THE YACHT MIGNONETTE.—FROM SKETCHES BY MR. EDWIN STEPHENS, THE MATE.

The way in which they stowed themselves in the dinghy.

Sailing before the wind: How the dinghy was managed during the last nine days.

How the dinghy was managed in the heavy weather: with the stern sheets up aft, and the "sea anchor," made of the water-breaker bed and the head-sheets grating.

3

FOUNDERING OF THE MIGNONETTE

ARTICLES FOUND IN BOAT

Chronometer with Captain's letter to his wife on lid

Chronometer

Bradshaw's railway guide

THE SAD STORY OF THE SEA: FOUNDERING OF THE MIGNONETTE, AND THE CASTAWAY CREW.

From *Illustrated Police News*, 20 September 1884.

AS THE MIGNONETTE WENT DOWN.

From *Illustrated London News*, 20 September 1884.

1. The dinghy in which the survivors spent 24 days at sea.   3. Quadrant, with writing on the lid.
2. Lid of chronometer, with the Captain's letter to his wife.   4. Chronometer.

THE LOSS OF THE YACHT MIGNONETTE.

St Anthony's Lighthouse at the entrance to Carrick Roads, Falmouth, *c.* 1900.

The inner harbour, Falmouth, late nineteenth century.

The Market Strand Basin, Falmouth, *c.* 1870.

CHAPTER 8

In the immediate traumatic stress of a shipwreck, the body is flooded with adrenalin. Heart rate and blood pressure increase, the surface blood vessels constrict, minimizing heat loss and feeding more blood to the muscles, and the liver releases more sugar.

Without the necessary experience, knowledge and strength of will, however, much of this energy can be misdirected and shipwreck survivors often make catastrophic mistakes during this brief initial period of intense activity.

As the adrenalin ebbs and realization of the enormity of their predicament dawns, men respond in different ways. Some become dazed and disorganized, incapable of action or decision, and await the end with dumb passivity. Others react with strength and resolution, but over time, the physical effects of thirst and starvation aggravate the psychological impact of being adrift on the ocean and the mental and emotional stability of even the strongest man begins to falter.

Keeping to a routine, formulating plans to improve the chances of rescue, and keeping up morale by prayer, meditation, conversation or song, enhance the prospects of survival. Those who survive for days and weeks in an open boat do so on strength of will more than any physical characteristics, but ultimately even the strongest-willed person will be tempted to evade reality through dreams, fantasies or simply torpor. Dehydration, malnutrition, sleep deprivation, and the effects of sunburn and exposure will eventually lead to delirium and hallucinations.

Some will be driven to the extreme of self-destruction: suicide. Others will adopt the other extreme of self-preservation: the practice of cannibalism.

In the fading light they rowed through the slick of debris from the wreck. They found the chronometer and sextant as they were tossed on the swell and they also rescued the wooden base of the water-breaker, but the barrel itself had disappeared and the other four tins of provisions had been swept away. The only other items they managed to salvage were the wooden grating from the head sheets, which had floated off as the yacht sank, and a handful of sodden oakum.

Brooks pulled the oakum from the waves and used it to make a rough plug for the hole in the dinghy's side, slowing the rush of water into the boat. 'The seas were mountainous high and at times it was dreadful. We had formed a hole in our boat but we had managed to stop the great rush and had got her free when a great sea came in and filled her up to the thwarts, but we again managed to get her free and we all of us offered up prayers to be brought through our present danger.'

They baled with everything to hand, using the two halves of the chronometer box as well as the baler, but the level in the boat still rose higher as each wave flooded in faster than they could throw water over the side.

Tom shouted to Brooks. 'We must head her into the sea or she'll founder.'

Half drowned by the waves crashing over them, the others kept baling, while Tom worked with frantic haste. He lashed together the breaker stand, the wooden grating and all the boards that could be spared from the boat and then threw them over the bow. The rope tightened with a snap and the dead weight of the makeshift sea-anchor began to drag the dinghy head-to-sea.

Each giant wave still seemed certain to bury the frail boat under tons of water, but each time the bow rose to meet the wave towering above them and followed it down into the trough. There was barely a moment's respite before the next wave was upon them.

Despite their fatigue, they were driven by the adrenalin of fear and maintained the frantic pace with the baler until the water level inside the boat at last began to fall. Nothing more could be done until daybreak and the men were too tired and dispirited to speak.

Tom stared into the darkness. He began to think of their situation: no water and only two one-pound tins as their stock of provisions, it was just becoming dark, the seas were mountainously high at times. He thought about his family back at home, and he was filled with dread.

Each man baled for an hour, then took a turn on watch, while the others, still soaked to the skin, snatched what rest they could.

The dinghy was still pitching on a steep swell when around eleven that night, as near as Tom could judge from the moon, he was jolted from a fitful doze by a thud against the underside of the boat. It was followed by a grinding noise and the dinghy lurched to one side. For a moment he thought they had run aground but there was no sound of breaking waves, no phosphorescent surf-line to be seen on the black sea.

Tom peered over the side and sensed as much as saw a swirl in the water ahead of them. A great shark, almost as long as the dinghy itself, sped back towards them, knocking its tail against the frail boat.

Tom saw a glint of moonlight on its grey, leathery hide as it broke surface. There was another crash as the shark thrashed its tail against the side of the boat. Waking from their daze, the other men gripped the gunwales and turned their frightened faces towards him.

The shark moved a short distance away, but then appeared to swim to and fro, as if keeping station ten or fifteen yards from the starboard side of the dinghy. Tom felt a surge of fear as it turned and surfaced again. He grabbed one of the oars and slapped the flat of the blade down on the sea. Even in the midst of the gale, the crack was like a musket shot and the splash of white foam caused the shark to veer away. There was a swirl of water and it disappeared.

Tom felt his heart pounding as he scanned the waves, but the seconds passed without any sign of its return. Then Brooks gave a cry. It had broken surface on the other side of the boat. Tom saw the glistening hide knifing through the water towards them, and scrambled across the dinghy, sending the gunwale dipping level with the water.

He stood half upright, swaying with the rhythm of the boat, and held the oar high above his head. As the shark closed on the dinghy, Tom brought the oar down on its head with all the strength he could muster. He was forced to his knees as the boat rocked wildly. There was a splash of white water and the shark dived beneath the boat and disappeared.

It returned several more times over the next hour, but each time Tom drove it away by battering it with the oar. At last they settled into an uneasy rest, praying for the dawn.

By first light, the worst of the storm had passed, though the towering seas were still heavier than Tom had ever known. He told Stephens, the tallest member of the crew, to haul himself upright to look for a sail and scan the sea for a sight of the missing water-breaker. It was a thin hope: the sea and wind could have driven it miles from them during the night, and after searching the ocean all around them he shook his head in despair.

Tom looked along the length of the dinghy. It was barely thirteen feet long, four feet wide and just twenty inches deep. Richard's pale, frightened face stared back at him, searching his expression for some glimmer of hope. There was little that Tom could offer. Stephens looked outwardly calm but Tom could see a muscle in his cheek tugging in an insistent nervous tic. Only Brooks's lined face remained stolid and expressionless, staring back at his captain, awaiting his orders.

'We can decide nothing until we know our position,' Tom said. 'Stephens, set to with the sextant. Brooks and Parker, bale while I plug this hole a little better.'

He took out his clasp knife and cut a few inches from the bottom of the legs of his trousers. As he pulled the sodden oakum out of the hole, water once more began to gush into the boat. It slowed to a trickle as he began to pack the hole with the black cloth. It took him almost an hour to secure it to his satisfaction, then he sat back on his haunches and motioned Stephens to join him in the bow, away from the others.

'Where are we?' He kept his voice low, not wishing to further alarm the boy, who had no real sense of how far from land they were and how desperate was their plight.

Ordinary seamen like Parker and Brooks had no knowledge whatsoever of navigation, particularly the complex process of establishing longitude. Few seamen had the education or interest in it and fewer still had the necessary funds, for ships' officers had to purchase their own navigation equipment. The expense of sextants and chronometers meant that sometimes even officers responsible for the navigation of their ships didn't carry them, and one expert witness to the 1836 Select Committee investigating the causes of shipwrecks admitted 'very many' instances of ships being three or four hundred miles from their estimated position.

It was also the deliberate policy of ship-owners and officers to keep their crews in ignorance. The one means by which a ship's captain ensured that his men could not rise up in mutiny against an often tyrannical rule was that only he and his senior officers had the necessary skill to navigate the ship safely back to port. The mysteries of navigation were therefore strictly controlled; it was an offence punishable by flogging for an ordinary seaman to attempt to keep his own log or take his own sightings.

Once they were out of sight of land, neither Brooks nor Richard had the slightest idea of where they were or which way to steer. Without Tom and Stephens to navigate, they would find land only by accident, not design.

'By dead reckoning we were twenty-seven degrees, ten minutes south and nine degrees, fifty minutes west when the ship sank,' Stephens said.

'Where is our nearest land?'

The mate shrugged. 'We could not be much worse placed. We are almost midway between St Helena seven hundred miles to the north and Tristan da Cunha perhaps seven hundred and fifty miles to the south-west, and even further from the coast of Africa.'

'The Cape?'

'South-east perhaps fifteen hundred miles, but we are still in the south-east trades at these latitudes. Whatever sail we manage to rig, we will not make ground to windward.'

'South America, then?'

'But that is more than two thousand miles.'

Tom thought for a moment, then turned to face the others. 'We are already well to the west of the steamship route to the Cape. We'll sail before the wind and make what speed we can towards the route of the barques and clippers. God willing, a ship will find us soon.'

'Or we may strike land,' Richard said, with a nervous, hopeful look.

Tom merely nodded.

Brooks remained silent. Although he knew nothing of latitude and longitude, he had been at sea long enough to realize the vastness of the ocean on which they were adrift.

Tom thought carefully before he spoke again. Ordinary seamen may have been ignorant of navigation, but they knew enough of maritime law to be aware that, when a ship sank, the captain's authority went down with it. From now on he could lead only by example. If they chose to disobey or unite against him, there was nothing he could do.

He cleared his throat. 'Our situation is poor. We have no water and little food, and we must conserve what we have.' He glanced at Brooks. 'What is in those tins?'

'Turnips.'

It was not the answer he had hoped for, but he held his expression unchanged. 'We shall not open them yet.' He paused, but no one argued with him. 'We will divide the day into four watches and take turns baling and steering.'

Brooks shook his head. 'The boy can bale but he does not have the skill to steer the boat. He is too young.'

Tom nodded. 'He will take his turn only when sea conditions allow. I'll take the first watch, Brooks the second, Stephens the third. We must also keep the boat trimmed. The boy and I will take berths in the stern, the other two forward. We will have to keep her head-to-wind, but if we rig a sail, we can make some progress sternways.'

Brooks interrupted him again. 'We have no sail.'

'Then we must fashion one out of our shirts.'

Brooks glanced at Stephens, and after a moment's hesitation, he shook his head. Richard gazed uncertainly from one to other.

'You would defy me?' Tom said.

'Are we to risk our death of cold or sunstroke to move a little faster before the wind, when we have not the least idea where we are heading?' Stephens said.

Tom checked, surprised at opposition from that quarter. 'We have our oilskins.'

'And we will suffer heatstroke if we wear them,' Stephens said.

'But we must make for South America.'

'We will all be dead long before we reach it.'

Tom saw Richard's frightened, hopeless look as he digested Stephens's words.

'But it is the only way,' Tom said. A ship may cross our path.'

Stephens nodded. 'It may, but we are far from the shipping lanes and it is no more and no less likely to do so here than at any other place on this ocean.'

Tom ignored him for the moment and looked towards the others. 'Will you not do as I ask?'

Neither of them replied.

Tom turned away to hide the anger on his face. He began pulling at the bottom boards of the dinghy. 'Then we must at least raise these.'

Brooks hesitated, then helped him to free the boards. They wedged them upright in the stern.

As Tom looked round he saw Richard kneeling against the side of the dinghy, urinating into the sea. 'Stop!'

Startled, the boy paused in mid-flow.

'We cannot survive without water,' Tom said. 'You know as well as I that drinking sea-water will send us mad. We have no fresh water, all that we have is our own.'

It took a moment for Richard to grasp his meaning. 'No. I will not do that. Are we dogs or men?'

'We are men who may die of thirst if a ship does not find us soon. Richard, if you are to survive, you must drink it.'

Richard hesitated, then reached for the wooden baler.

Tom shook his head. 'It is contaminated with sea-water. Use this.' He passed him the metal case from the chronometer. Richard urinated into the case, but stared at it for a long time before he put it to his lips. He swallowed a mouthful but then gagged and vomited over the side.

Tom reached out and rested a hand on his shoulder. 'You must make yourself drink it, or you will not survive.'

'I cannot, sir,' he said, but after a few deep breaths, he again raised the case to his lips. He drained it in one gulp, shuddered and wiped the back of his hand furiously across his mouth.

Tom held the gaze of each of them in turn. 'We must do what we have to do to survive. And survive we will.' He paused. 'Now, it is Sunday morning. Let us say a prayer together that the Lord will see fit to save us and restore us to our families.'

They bowed their heads and joined him in prayer, the murmur of their voices lost in the immense void of sea and sky.

Tom took the first watch. Despite the confident face he had tried to present to his crew, he had little genuine hope of survival. While the others closed their eyes in semblance of sleep, he unfolded the certificate wedged inside the back of the chronometer case, their sole piece of paper. He fumbled in his pocket for a stub of pencil and began scribbling a farewell note to his wife on the back of it.

> July 6th 1884. To my dear wife – Phil Dudley, Myrtle Road, Sutton, in Surrey. *Mignonette* foundered yesterday. Weather knocked side in. We had five minutes to get in boat without food or water. You and our children were in my thoughts to the end. God bless and keep you. Your loving husband, Tom.

He folded the letter tightly and placed it in his inside pocket, then leaned on the oar as he stared, unseeing, at the endless ocean swell.

Stephens had been watching him. He asked Tom for his knife and scratched an even more terse note of farewell to his wife in the varnished surface of the sextant case, then added the boat's estimated position. The scratching of the knife blade against the wood was the only sound other than the scrape of the baler and the slap of waves against the hull.

They drifted all that day without sight of a sail. In the evening, Tom made a fresh attempt to get them to give up their shirts. 'The wind is with us. We must make headway to westward into the track of the sailing ships.'

Once more Brooks shook his head. 'We will be burned by the sun, half frozen at night, and a sail is as likely to capsize us as to send us westward. I say no.'

Tom looked at the others. 'And are you with him or me in this?'

They both averted their eyes.

The next day dawned without sight of a sail. The sight and sound of the waves lapping at the boat was a constant reminder of their thirst. Tom's throat felt tight and sore and his lips were swollen and cracked. Early in the morning he told Brooks to open the first tin of turnips. He took out his knife and drove it into the top of the tin, using the wooden baler as a hammer. He worked the knife around the top and peeled back the lid. 'Five pieces. Divide one piece between two and give us each a little of the fluid. We shall ration the rest to last us until tomorrow night.'

The taste of the turnip was intensely sweet, and it seemed so cool as it slipped down Tom's parched throat. He felt saliva start to his mouth, but the bare mouthful of fluid gave only fleeting relief.

Stephens managed to take a rough altitude of the sun at noon and guessing the declination, fixed their latitude at roughly twenty-four degrees, fifty minutes south, almost on the line of the Tropic of Capricorn. The winds remained strong, driving them north-west, closer and closer to the equator.

The burning heat gave them no respite. Richard leaned over the side to splash his face, the boat lurched and suddenly he was in the sea. Tom could not say whether he had jumped or fallen. The thought of sharks chilled his blood, but he did not hesitate; neither Brooks nor Stephens could swim.

He tore off his shirt and threw himself into the sea. When he broke surface there was at first no sign of the boy, but as he was carried upwards on the swell he saw an upraised arm and Richard's face, with his mouth gaping open. Then the sea closed over him again.

Tom thrashed the water with his arms, driving himself towards the boy. The sea was empty, but for the boat. Then, through the grey-green water, he saw the pale shape of an upturned face and dark hair floating on the surface like seaweed.

He dived below the waves and grabbed Richard as he began to sink again. He kicked for the dim light of the surface above them as the dead weight of the boy and their waterlogged clothing threatened to drag them both down.

Kicking again, he clawed at the water with his free hand towards the surface, seemingly an eternity away. There was a roaring in his ears and stabbing pains in his chest. The stale air in his lungs bubbled up to the surface.

He held his breath until he could do so no longer, then took a convulsive, instinctive breath. Water filled his mouth and throat. Then he felt the slap of a wave against his face.

Coughing and choking, he drew air into his lungs and heard the boy gag and retch alongside him. His arms began to flail again. Tom cursed him. 'Be still. You'll drown us both. Be still.'

Still supporting the boy with one arm, he began to battle the swell towards the boat. Already exhausted, his stroke was feeble and ragged, and at each wave-crest the dinghy seemed as distant as ever. He felt his strength ebbing and drowsiness began to overcome him. Reaching the boat no longer seemed so important. He was tired; he would pause and rest for a few minutes, then swim on.

His head slipped beneath the waves. He choked and spat water, then struck out for the boat again. He heard a splash and a swirl of water, and froze, bracing himself for the impact as a shark tore him apart. Instead he heard another splash and through the spray he saw the black outline of an oar.

He grasped for it, missed, flung himself forward and caught it. He hauled himself along, hand over hand until he reached the side of the dinghy. Richard seemed barely aware of his surroundings, but Tom dragged him round to face the dinghy. 'Take hold of the gunwale.' He shook the boy. 'Take hold of the gunwale. Both hands.'

A moment later he felt the burden lift from his arm as Richard took his own weight for the first time. Tom clung to the side of the dinghy, too weary for the moment to do more. 'Keep watch for sharks,' he said.

They hung there for several minutes. Fearing a capsize, Tom worked his way round to the far side of the dinghy and hung from the gunwale as a counter-balance, while the others tried to haul the boy back into the boat. The dinghy rocked, then settled, as he slumped on to the bottom boards. Aided by Brooks and Stephens, Tom dragged himself over the gunwale with agonizing slowness, then curled up next to the boy, too weary to speak or move again.

The next day was a black day. Hunger was a constant dull, nagging pain, but thirst threatened to overwhelm them. Splashing their faces, necks and arms and wetting their hair seemed to help, but it offered little more than momentary relief.

Tom's throat was parched and his tongue sore and swollen, and the sea-water he had inadvertently swallowed made his thirst even more extreme. He rinsed out his mouth and gargled to ease his thirst and encouraged the others to do the same, but he watched carefully as they did so, giving constant warnings of the dangers of swallowing any. The temptation to lean over the gunwale, scoop up some sea-water and drink it down was overpowering, but with the blind certainty of every seaman, he knew the terrifying consequences.

There was ample anecdotal evidence to support Tom's belief. The tales told by the survivors of shipwrecks and passed on in ships' forecastles and during the long hours of the night watches all had the same conclusion: shipwrecked sailors who drank sea-water experienced delirium, insanity and death.

> The sailor then started to drink sea-water and soon became delirious. On one occasion he told me he was going for a walk and went over the side. After a struggle I managed to drag him back into the boat ... I struggled with him throughout the night of the eleventh day. By the morning I, too, was becoming weak and delirious and could not restrain the sailor any longer. He went overboard some time on the twelfth day.

> Six of the survivors [were] taking occasional drinks of salt water. I warned them they would die a terrible death if they persisted. They obeyed me for a day or two but I soon found them again taking surreptitious drinks of sea-water. As they drank more and more they rapidly became delirious, imagining they could see rivers of water and snow ... Three of them jumped overboard shortly after drinking the salt water.

> The poor man's face was a ghastly sight. His eyes protruded straight out of their sockets, while his lips were drawn back over his teeth in a bestial smile. His lips and teeth were covered with a thick white froth. His whole body shook periodically with great convulsions. Suddenly, as three or four men were trying to hold him down, the man ... threw them off and leapt for the side of the boat.

The dangers of drinking sea-water were accepted without question until the early 1950s, when a Frenchman, Dr Alain Bombard, claimed that a castaway who drank small quantities of sea-water from the beginning of his ordeal, rather than waiting until thirst overwhelmed him, could survive. To prove his theory, he set out to cross the North Atlantic in an inflatable boat, *L'Hérétique*, carrying no supplies of fresh water with him. 'I had no rainwater for the first twenty-three days . . . During the whole of that period I proved conclusively that I could quench my thirst from fish and that the sea itself provided the liquid necessary to health . . . I drank seawater for fourteen days in all and fish juice for forty-three days. I had conquered the menace of thirst at sea.'

Dr Bombard's triumphalist conclusion was not entirely accurate. The metabolism of fish allows them to excrete the salt from the food and sea-water they absorb. The fluids Dr Bombard extracted from the fish he caught were enough to dilute the small quantities of sea-water he drank. Had he drunk it on its own, he would not have survived.

Other mariners, including Thor Heyerdahl aboard *Kon Tiki* and Sir Francis Chichester on *Gypsy Moth IV*, also drank small amounts of sea-water without ill effect, and other experiments have shown that mixing it with fresh water in a ratio not exceeding five to one is not harmful, but any higher proportion can be fatal.

The old seaman's superstition that drinking sea-water sends you mad and kills you is absolutely correct. It does so because it dehydrates the body. Sea-water is a concentrated solution of sodium chloride and other salts, and has a higher specific gravity than fresh water. Through a process of osmosis – the tendency of solvents to diffuse through a porous partition, the stomach wall, into a more concentrated solution – water from the rest of the body is drawn into the stomach in an effort to dilute the sea-water.

The body's response to this dehydration is thirst, stimulating the urge to drink, but if that drink is also sea-water, the downward spiral continues. The sufferer gulps down more and more in a vain effort to slake this raging thirst, but each mouthful only exacerbates the problem. As they become progressively more dehydrated, the cells of the body contract, and shrinkage of the brain cells causes the delusions and insanity. The opposite effect occurs if a child swallows large quantities of chlorinated water after falling into a swimming-pool. It has a lower specific gravity than fresh water and passes through the stomach wall into the body, swelling the brain cells and causing fits in the child.

Although Tom Dudley was unaware of the fact and urged his men to drink their own urine, the urea contained in it has a similar, if lesser dehydrating effect. Despite Dr Bombard's experiment, unless there is also a sufficient supply of fresh water to dilute it, drinking sea-water or urine will hasten dehydration and death.

CHAPTER 9

When they shared out the next ration of turnip, Tom held his piece in his mouth as long as he could, but most of the moisture had already evaporated from the tin and within a few minutes it felt as rough and dry as pumice. It was all he could do to chew and swallow it.

A lassitude had crept over them all. Their throats were so tight and sore that they barely spoke, staring into the green water, each alone with his thoughts. Towards dusk they ate the last of the first tin of turnips and shared the dribble of viscous, almost congealed fluid in the bottom of the tin. It was a relief when nightfall shrouded the others from Tom's sight.

Early the next morning, 9 July, Brooks saw a dark shape on the surface, just off their bow. For a moment terror gripped him, certain that the shark had returned to the attack. Then he recognized the shape of the creature and roused the others with a shout. 'A turtle! To the oars before it dives.'

The turtle was sleeping on the surface, no more than twenty yards off the port side of the boat. A few strokes of the oars brought them within range. Tom gripped the back of Stephens's shirt as he hung over the side of the boat, his fingers scrabbling for grip on the turtle's flippers as it struggled to break free.

Stephens lost his hold on the front flipper and threw himself further forward, his head dipping below the surface as he grabbed for it again. Then he straightened up, coughing and gasping, but clinging to the turtle. He dragged it over the side and dropped it on to the bottom boards, where it lay helpless on its back, its flippers waving.

Tom pulled out his knife. 'We must drink the blood,' he said. 'It will do us more good than the meat.'

He picked up the empty tin of turnips, then set it aside and reached for the chronometer case. Stephens held the turtle still as Tom slipped the case under its head and severed its neck with a single slash of his knife. Its struggles in its death throes sent blood pulsing into the metal bowl.

Craning his neck to watch Tom, Brooks had allowed the dinghy to drift beam-on to the waves. The next one broke over the gunwale, flooding the bottom of the boat and filling the chronometer case with sea-water. The men stared at it aghast.

Richard leaned forward. 'It is only a little water, surely we can drink it still?'

Tom hesitated for a second, then threw it over the side. 'It is contaminated with sea-water. It will send us mad.'

Stephens stared at the red stain merging with the green water, then rounded on Brooks. 'If you had minded your work, we, not the fishes, would have been drinking that.'

Brooks clenched his fists and half rose to face him. 'You mind your words or you'll be the one feeding the fishes.'

Tom was again stooping over the turtle, catching the last few drops of blood as they dripped from its neck. He did not raise his eyes, but his voice cut through their shouts. 'You'll both sit down. Fighting amongst ourselves will only hasten our end.' He held out the case. 'There's little enough. Each man must take only his fair share.'

He handed it first to the boy, then passed it to Stephens and Brooks, and took the last and smallest share himself. There was barely a mouthful of the congealing blood remaining. It was warm, sweet and sickly and hard to force down but he felt a little strength returning almost as soon as he had swallowed it.

Richard baled out the dinghy, then Tom set down the chronometer case in the bottom of the boat and began to butcher the turtle. He severed the tough flippers and laid them in a row on one of the cross-members, then tore the the turtle from its shell.

He removed the head and entrails and threw them over the side, but he dropped the heart and liver into the metal case and cut them in quarters. All four men fell on them ravenously, despite the fishy stench. Almost at once, Tom felt stronger.

He cut the turtle's flesh into strips and Stephens hung them around the boat to dry. There were only a few pounds of meat, but they were so overjoyed at their good fortune that, in the euphoria of the moment, they ate the rest of the second tin of turnips as well, savouring the sensation and the sweetness.

For over a week the gales continued. They were driven stern-first by a south-easterly gale – the trade winds that had failed them on the *Mignonette* – unable to turn and run before the wind for fear of being swamped. Even with the sea-anchor out, the bow of the dinghy constantly sheered off a few degrees either side of the wind. One man worked a steering oar at the stern, fighting to hold the dinghy head-on to each rising wave, but they broke constantly over the bows. At times they were a few seconds from foundering as the water level inside the boat rose to within inches of the gunwales. Everyone joined in frantic baling of the boat with anything that came to hand – the chronometer case, an empty tin or the wooden box that housed the sextant – until the water level began to drop again. Finally, on 13 July, the storm at last blew itself out, the seas slackened and they slumped into an exhausted sleep.

Each dawn Tom dragged himself up to search the horizon for a sail. Although he knew there was no land within hundreds of miles he could not stop himself from scanning the sky for the greenish tint of light reflected from the shallow water of a lagoon, or a telltale cloud formation – a patch of fixed cumulus in a clear sky or a thin line of the cloud – that indicated an island or a coastline nearby. There were no such signs on that day or on any of the succeeding days, only the endless march of the waves to the horizon.

At each passing squall or cloud they held out their oilskin capes to catch the rainwater. They put them on back to front, and held out their arms, as Stephens later said, 'waiting with burning throats and stomachs, and praying to the Almighty for water until the squall had passed. If we caught a little, how thankful we were.'

Many squalls seemed almost to mock them. On several occasions rain pocked the surface of the sea within sight of the dinghy, yet not a drop fell on them. The first of any rain that did fall had to be cast away, used only to clean the salt from their oilskins, and few squalls yielded more than a mouthful of drinkable water. Often even that would be spoiled by waves breaking over the boat before they could drink, but one storm gave them each about a pint.

As he drank it down, forcing himself to sip it and roll each mouthful around his mouth before swallowing it, Tom felt saliva in his mouth and the constriction of his throat ease for the first time in days.

It was to be the last rain for four days, however, and soon they were again suffering in the savage heat. They could talk for no more than a few seconds before their hoarse whispers turned into hacking coughs.

Tom cut off a bone button from his oilskins and placed it in his mouth, hoping it would ease his thirst like a pebble in the desert. It seemed to soften a little in his mouth and there was a faint taste on his tongue. As he sucked it over the next few hours the button grew smaller and eventually dissolved completely. He cut off another and another over the succeeding days, until they had all been used.

Every couple of hours they rinsed their mouths and gargled with sea-water. Late one burning afternoon, Tom thought he saw the boy swallowing a mouthful. 'Lad, we are all driven mad with thirst, but you must not drink that.'

The boy's sallow cheeks flushed. 'Surely it will do no harm if we just drink a little of it.'

'Regard it as the poison that will kill you.'

The heat troubled them as much as their thirst. Their exposed flesh was burned an angry red, pocked with white blisters, and the rubbing of their salt-encrusted flannel shirts was agonizing to their skin.

To cool themselves, Stephens suggested soaking their flannel shirts, wringing them out and putting them on again. He and Brooks tried the experiment, but they soaked them again too close to dusk and shivered uncontrollably in their wet clothes during the night.

On the following days they all stripped naked and took turns to hang from the gunwale and dip themselves once or twice in the water. They did it one at a time, for only a few seconds, while the others remained in the boat on watch, for every time they bathed in this way, sharks would soon circle the boat, as if able to sense the naked bodies in the water.

The cool water on their skins refreshed them and even slaked their thirst a little, but as the days went by, they became too weak even to undress themselves. They could only ladle a little water over their heads and the effort required even for that task left them exhausted.

As Tom took his turn on watch, he looked with horror on the bodies of his crew. Their ribs and hip-bones were already showing through their wasting flesh. There were angry, ulcerating sores on their elbows, knees and feet, their lips were cracked and their tongues blackened and swollen.

They had continued to live on the turtle-flesh for a week, even though some of the fat became putrid in the fierce heat. Tom cut out the worst parts and threw them overboard, but they devoured the rest and when the flesh was finished, they chewed the bones and leathery skin.

They ate the last rancid scraps of it on the evening of 17 July. When he had finished chewing on his piece, Tom looked at the others. 'If no boat comes soon, we shall have to draw lots.'

Richard darted him a nervous look, too scared to meet his eye. Neither of the others showed any surprise at the subject Tom had raised. There was a long silence. 'We would be better to die together,' Brooks said. After a moment, Stephens nodded.

'So let it be,' Tom said, 'but it is hard for four to die when perhaps one might save the rest.'

'A boat will come,' Brooks said.

'So it may, but if one does not, or if it passes us by . . .'

The boy gave him a frightened look. 'Why would a ship pass us by?'

'If they see four mouths to feed,' Brooks said, 'they may not stop.'

Richard turned towards Tom. 'Surely no Christian men would leave us to die for want of a scrap of their bread and water.'

Tom saw the plea in the boy's eyes, but knowing the truth of Brooks's words, he could only nod his head. 'If the seas are high or the wind strong, they may fear wrecking themselves if they come to our aid.'

Brooks interrupted him. 'But we have all heard tales enough of ships that have sailed by a wreck though the water was as flat and calm as the Itchen on a summer's day. Some look away and pretend they have not heard, though the poor wretches plead, cry, rail and curse against them. Others, more brazen . . .' His voice trailed away as Richard buried his face in his hands and began to sob, a terrible dry, rasping sound. No one moved to console him, each man too wrapped in his own dark thoughts.

As the boy's hoarse sobs still echoed through the boat, Stephens rounded on Brooks. 'What use was there in upsetting the boy with your foolish talk?'

'I spoke no more than the truth.'

They began a senseless, bitter argument. Fists clenched, they glared at each other and might have fought had Tom not interposed himself and cursed them both to silence.

Brooks retreated to his sanctuary in the bow. He lay down and wormed his way under the scrap of canvas covering it, hiding his head like a child burrowing under his bedsheets, and spoke no more to anyone that day.

'We were now in our worst straits,' Stephens later said. 'We used to sit and look at each other gradually wasting away, hunger and thirst in each face. The nights were the worst time. We used to dread them very much; they seemed never to end. We were so weak and cramped that we could hardly move. If we did get any sleep our dreams would be of eating and drinking.'

That night a rain squall passed over them and they caught some more water. Tom's hands were shaking so much that he spilled much of it as he tried to transfer some from his oilskin to the chronometer case, hoping to save it for a later moment.

There was no rain on the next day or the next, Sunday, 20 July, when Tom at last prevailed on them to give up their shirts. Stephens and the boy seemed past caring, lying listless in the bottom of the boat. Brooks began to argue again, then shrugged. 'What does it matter? We're doomed anyway. We'll die of sunstroke or thirst, but die we shall.' He took off his shirt and handed it to Tom.

Tom let Richard keep his shirt, but lashed the other three together, two above and one below, to form a triangular sail. They used an oar for a mast and split one of the boards for a yardarm. Tom hammered the back of his knife with the baler to open a crack in the wood, then forced it apart with the edge of the chronometer case until the board split along its length.

The shrouds and stays were fashioned out of the heart and outer strands of the boat's painter. With the makeshift sail rigged, the stern seats lashed up and a strong south-easterly blowing, they found the boat would run sternways before the wind, as long as there was not too much of a swell, and they made two or three knots.

Tom still had the burning determination within him to survive, but he could tell from the faces of the others that the faint hope of rescue to which they had clung was now extinguished.

The sting of salt on their skin added to the pain of their sunburn and together with the salt-water boils from which they were all suffering made even the slightest pressure unbearable. As they crawled about the cramped dinghy, taking their turns to steer and bale, it was impossible not to brush against each other, but the pain it caused was so agonizing that Stephens screamed aloud whenever he was touched.

When he asked to borrow Tom's knife and began scratching a further message in the lid of the sextant case, Tom knew that Stephens had given up his last hope of survival. Stephens scrawled his estimate of their position over the previous few days and then added:

> To whoever picks this up Sunday July 20th PM We Thomas Dudley, Edwin Stephens, Edmund Brooks and Richard Parker, the crew of the Yacht *Mignonette* which foundered on Saturday the 5th. of July, have been in our little dingy 15 days. We have neither food or water and are greatly reduced. We suppose our Latitude to be 25° South our Longitude 28° W May the Lord have mercy upon us Please forward this to Southampton.

That night the wind dropped and in the calmer conditions Richard took the night watch. Tom and Brooks were asleep but Stephens was only dozing when he heard an unfamiliar sound and opened his eyes. Richard was leaning over the side, scooping up sea-water in one of the empty tins. He drank some of it then looked round. He started as he saw the mate watching him.

Stephens put his finger to his lips, then worked his way back to the stern. He bent close to the boy's ear and whispered, 'How does it taste, Dick?'

'Not so bad.'

Stephens glanced behind him, then took the tin and swallowed a mouthful. He coughed and spluttered, then spat out the remainder. 'It burns my throat like fire. It's madness, Dick, you should not do that again.'

'Then what would you have me do – die of thirst instead?'

Stephens crawled back to his berth and huddled down in the bottom of the boat, but just before he closed his eyes, he again saw Richard lower the tin into the water.

Tom was woken by the sound of the boy retching and vomiting over the side. Brooks grabbed the steering oar and Richard fell back and lay on the bottom of the dinghy, gasping for breath.

Tom put his hand on the boy's forehead. It was burning hot. 'What ails you, boy?'

'I – I drank sea-water.'

'How much did you drink?'

'I don't know, perhaps three pints.'

'Then you're worse than a fool,' Brooks said.

Richard began to cry. No tears came from his matted eyes but his chest heaved with dry sobs. 'I had to drink something.'

Brooks hesitated, then put a hand on his shoulder. 'Cheer up, Dicky, it will all come right.'

He shook his head. 'We shall all die.'

They left him where he lay and over the next few hours his condition worsened. He began to suffer from violent diarrhoea and several times Tom and Brooks had to help him to squat over the gunwale as his body was shaken by spasms. Then he crawled back into the bottom of the boat and lay bent double from the pains in his stomach.

That night he became delirious, shouting and ranting, and he began slipping in and out of consciousness. Each time he woke, he said the same thing, 'I want a ship to get on board.'

The ship was all they ever heard him speak about. Whatever the frictions between them from time to time, the three others all shared an affection for the boy and did their best to lift his spirits, but he seemed barely to recognize them or hear their cracked voices. In one of his rare intervals of lucidity, he tried to drink some of his urine but was unable to do so, gagging and choking on it instead. He slumped down again.

There was a question in Tom's eyes as he glanced at the others, but neither man would meet his gaze. 'Something must be done,' he said.

Brooks looked up. 'Let us not talk of that further. Another ship will come.'

Tom shook his head and looked away. He pressed his fingers into the swollen flesh of his legs. The impressed marks turned white and remained visible for a long time after he released his grip. As he stared at them he felt something loose in his mouth. One of his teeth had dropped out. He spat it into his hand and threw it into the sea. He tested each of his other teeth with his fingers. All of them were loose in their sockets, barely held by his soft, pulpy gums.

Despite the positive face he took care to present to his crew, he was now beginning to despair. He took out the note he had begun writing to Philippa the morning after the shipwreck and scrawled a few more lines with the stub of his pencil.

9th picked up turtle. 21st July we have been here 17 days and have no food. We are all four living hoping to get passing ship if not dear we must soon die. Mr Thomson will put everything right if you go to him and I am sorry dear I ever started such a trip but I was doing it for our best. Thought so at the time. You know dear I should so much like to be spared you would find I should lead a Christian life for the remainder of my days. If ever this note reaches your hands dear you know the last of your Tom and loving husband. I am sorry things are gone against us thus far but hope to meet you and all our dear children in heaven. Do love them for my sake dear bless them and you all. I love you all dearly you know but it is God's will if I am to part from you but have hopes of being saved. We were about 1300 miles from Cape Town when the affair happened. So goodbye and God bless you all and may He provide for you all. Your loving husband, Tom Dudley.

There was no rain again that day. They lay sprawled in the boat without speaking, neither awake nor asleep, their minds drifting. Tom was astonished at the breadth and depth of his recall. Long-forgotten events, some great, some small, returned to him with crystal clarity. He heard the voices of childhood in his head and saw the village children scrambling over the fields, marshes and saltings. He saw Philippa at the piano in their first house in Oreston and heard every note of the songs she sang.

When he fell asleep, he was tortured by the same constant recurring dreams – soft rainfall speckling the surface of the Blackwater, morning mist hanging over Woodrolfe Creek, the cool shade of the trees in the sunlit meadows where he and Philippa used to walk, and the lemonade, cold from the cellar, that she would bring to him as he sat in the garden at Sutton and the children played in the grass around his feet.

Then he would jerk awake, dragged back to the present by his thirst and the pains in his body. To move was agony, but to remain still for long was an impossibility, as the rough boards dug into him and his salt-encrusted clothes chafed at his sores.

Even the effort of swallowing his urine tortured him. It was thick, yellow and stained with blood, and his throat seemed so dry and constricted that he could barely force it down without choking. It gave him no relief from his thirst.

By the following morning the men's mouths had become so parched and their tongues so swollen, they could hardly speak at all. Richard still lay in the bottom of the boat drifting between consciousness and oblivion.

Tom looked down at him, then glanced at the others. 'Better for one to die than for all of us.' Even to speak was torture, the words seeming to tear at his dry, cracked throat. 'I am willing to take my chance with the rest, but we must draw lots.'

'No. We shall see a ship tomorrow,' Stephens said.

'And if we do not?'

No one replied.

The day passed without rain and when a shower did come just after midnight, it barely troubled their upturned mouths or dampened their capes.

Although he hardly slept at all, Tom's mind drifted constantly. Mirages began to appear to him. He saw lush islands and snow-capped mountains rising sheer from the sea, and a bank of haze lying on the water became the chalk cliffs of Kent. Sailing ships bore down on the dinghy and he was pulling himself upright, heart pounding with joy, when the vision faded again, leaving only the endless wastes of empty ocean.

Then he saw his father standing on the end of a jetty, beckoning to him. He felt drawn to the side of the dinghy and had to fight the urge to slip over the side into the water. He shook his head and shouted, 'No, I cannot do it,' in his cracked voice. The others barely stirred as he slumped down again.

Whenever he did lapse into unconsciousness, he dreamed of walking out of the dinghy across the sea to a beach or a waiting boat. Once he woke to find that his legs were already over the gunwale, his feet trailing in the water. The discovery barely shocked him; sometimes he saw himself slipping downwards as the green waters closed over him, and dreamed that he was already dead.

The next morning dawned hot and leaden once more. Tom leaned forward and laid his hand on the boy's forehead. It was still burning hot and his breathing was shallow and erratic. 'Dick? Do you hear me, boy?' he said, his voice a cracked whisper.

There was no reply.

Tom sat back on his haunches and looked at the others. 'You both know what must be done.'

'Better for us all to die than for that,' Brooks said.

'Even when the death of one might save the lives of the rest? You are a bachelor, but Stephens and I are family men. It is not just our own lives, we have the fate of others to consider. Would you have us see our children cast into destitution, even the workhouse, when we have the means at hand to save ourselves and keep them from that fate?'

'I, too, have a—' Brooks began, then fell silent. 'At least wait for him to die,' he said. 'Let us not have the boy's murder on our consciences.'

'But if we wait for him to die, his blood will congeal in his veins. We must kill him if we are to drink the blood. And it must be done, it may save three lives.'

Brooks again shook his head. He lay down in the bow and hid his head under the canvas.

Stephens did not speak, but Tom read a different message in his eyes.

That night Brooks had the watch from midnight. While he steered, Tom and Stephens sat in the bow, talking in whispers.

'What's to be done?' Tom said. 'I believe the boy is dying. Brooks is a bachelor – or says he is – but you have a wife and five children, and I have a wife and three children. Human flesh has been eaten before.'

Stephens hesitated. 'See what daylight brings forth.'

'But if sunrise brings no rain and no sign of a sail?'

Stephens stared out over the dark water, then muttered, 'God forgive me,' and nodded his assent.

Soon after dawn Tom and Stephens hauled themselves up in turn on the improvised rigging and searched the horizon for a sail. There was none in sight under the cloudless sky. Richard still lay in the bottom of the boat, with his head on the starboard side and his feet on the port side, his arm across his face. He was rapidly sinking into unconsciousness.

'We shall have to draw lots,' Stephens said. 'It is the custom of the sea.'

Richard lay comatose in the bottom of the dinghy and gave no sign that he had heard Stephens's words. Brooks remained silent and Tom did not wait for a reply from him. He pulled out his knife and whittled four thin slivers of wood from the gunwale of the dinghy. He trimmed three to equal length and cut the other one a half-inch shorter.

'We'll have to draw Dick's lot for him,' Stephens said.

The three men exchanged looks between themselves. Tom laid the pieces of wood across his palm, the ends protruding beyond his index finger. The shortest lot was on the right. Palm open, he showed them to Stephens and Brooks. Then, without changing their positions, he closed his hand over the bottom ends of the slivers and held them out.

Brooks licked his blackened lips and, as Stephens hesitated, he reached past him and took the left-hand lot. Stephens took the next. Tom was about to complete the ritual by taking the next when he paused, looked the others in the eye and then threw the remaining slivers into the sea.

'Why go through this charade?' he said. 'What is to be gained when one lies dying anyway? We all know what must be done. Let us be honest men about it, at least.'

No further word was exchanged, but Stephens looked down at the boy and nodded. Both then turned towards Brooks. He hesitated, then bowed his head.

'Who is to do it?'

'I cannot,' Brooks said.

Stephens shook his head. 'Nor I.'

'Then I shall have to,' Tom said.

He stared at Brooks. 'You had better go forward and have a rest. Stephens, take over the watch.'

Stephens took the steering oar, while Brooks moved towards the bow and lay down, once more hiding his face under the canvas sheet.

Shading his eyes against the glare of the burning sun, Tom took hold of the shrouds and pulled himself up to search the horizon all around them for any trace of a ship. Nothing broke the glassy surface of the sea.

He remained motionless for a moment, offering a prayer for the boy's soul, and asking forgiveness of his Maker. Then he placed the chronometer case next to Richard's head, took out his knife and opened the blade. The sunlight glinted from the blue steel.

He glanced towards Stephens. 'Hold the boy's legs if he struggles.'

Richard had appeared to be unconscious but his eyes flickered open at the words. His pupils had lost almost all their pigment and were the colour of skimmed milk. Tom doubted whether he could even still see.

'What – me, sir?' he said.

Tom made no reply. He placed the knife against the boy's neck. Trying to close his mind to what he was about to do, he began reciting under his breath the instructions in *The Steward's Handbook* that he had been forced to learn years before on his first voyage as cook-steward. ' "Proceed immediately to bleed the beast. This is done by cutting up the gullet and severing the arteries and veins on each side of the neck, near to the head. The blood will now flow out quite freely." '

He took a handful of the boy's hair in his left hand, holding his head still against the boards, then plunged the knife into his neck. He jerked the blade sideways, severing an artery and slicing into the windpipe, then dropped the knife and held the metal bowl against Richard's neck.

The boy did not even cry out, but as blood began to pump from the wound in a slow, palsied beat, his arms flailed and a terrible, wet sucking sound came from his torn windpipe. His white eyes stared sightlessly up at Tom.

He tried to shut his ears to the sound of the boy's death throes, but they echoed in his mind long after the noises had at last ceased and the twitching body lay still. Only a dribble of blood still flowed from the wound.

The blood he had collected in the chronometer case was thick and viscous and already beginning to congeal. They began to drink it in turn. Brooks scrambled from under his canvas cover. 'Give me a drop of that,' he said, and they shared it with him.

As soon as they had finished the blood, Tom and Stephens stripped the clothes from the boy's body. Tom then pushed the knife into the stomach just below the breastbone and forced it downwards, opening a deep slit in Richard's belly. Even strengthened a little by the blood, he was so weak and slow that the cut seemed to take minutes to complete.

He paused, his breath coming in hoarse gasps. '"Now make a slit in the stomach and run the knife right up to the tail. Remove the fat from round the intestines and then pull out the intestines, paunch, and liver. Cut the gall bladder off the liver right away. Turn the kidney fat over and remove the kidneys. Now cut through the diaphragm, commonly called the skirt, which separates the organs within the chest from the intestines, and remove the lungs, heart, and thorax."'

He reached into the still warm chest cavity and pulled out the heart and liver. He put them in the chronometer case and cut them up. The three men ate them ravenously, squabbling over the pieces like dogs.

When they had eaten the last scrap, Tom raised his gaze from the bloodstained bowl and stared at the others. Their faces were smeared with blood and their eyes were wild. He shuddered, knowing that his own visage was no different, but he could already feel strength flowing back into his body. '"When this has all been done, get some warm water and wash out the carcass, and any blood that may be on it must be washed off."'

He leaned over the gunwale and rinsed the blood from his face, then sent Brooks aft to steer the boat while Stephens helped him to butcher the body. Not wanting to see the dead boy's face in front of him as he worked, Tom first cut off the head and threw it overboard. His fingers slippery with blood, he worked as fast as he could, hacking off strips of flesh, which Stephens washed in the sea and laid across the cross-beams to dry.

At first Tom used the wooden cross-member as a butcher's block, but fearing that he might further damage the boat's thin planking as he hacked and sawed at the body with his knife, he did the heavier cutting – parting the joints and severing the tendons – against the brass crutches of the oars. It took three hours to complete the grisly task.

The larger bones, and Richard's feet, genitals and intestines, were also thrown overboard. They looked on in horror as, astern of the boat, sharks thrashed the water into a pink froth, fighting over the bloody fragments. One was bitten in the head by a larger shark as they fought over some part of the body. In an instant, every one of the pack of sharks circling the remains had turned on the wounded creature. It was ripped apart in little more than a minute.

Even when the blood and entrails had been consumed or dissipated by the waves, sharks continued to track the dinghy. A fin showed above the water from time to time and there was a grinding thud as one broke surface right alongside the dinghy, sending it crabbing sideways. Tom tried to drive it off by hitting it with an oar, but already weak and further exhausted by his struggle to butcher the carcass, he barely had the strength to raise it above his head.

Brooks took over, and though he did not manage to hit the shark, the noise of the oar banging on the water was enough to scare it off. From time to time they glimpsed the sharks astern of the dinghy, and even when unseen, all of them continued to fear their presence.

CHAPTER 10

Survival cannibalism has occurred throughout human history. Some skeletons of Peking man and Neanderthal man show evidence of it in the gnawed and split bones, and the cerebral cortices on the skulls, artificially enlarged to enable the brains to be extracted.

The Greek historian Herodotus wrote of *anthropophagi* among the people beyond the Caspian Sea, and an Egyptian physician, Abd al-Latif, witnessed widespread cannibalism around Misr and Cairo during the great famine of AD 1201:

> The poor, under the pressure of ever-growing want, ate carrion, corpses, dogs, excrement and animal dung. They went further and reached the stage of eating little children ... The commandant of the city guard ordered that those who committed this crime should be burned alive ... The corpse was always found to have been devoured by the following morning. People ate it the more willingly, for the flesh, being fully roasted, did not need to be cooked ...
>
> The custom being once introduced, spread in the provinces so that there was no part of Egypt where one did not see examples of it. Then it no longer caused surprise. The horror people had felt at first entirely vanished; one spoke of it, and heard it spoken of, as a matter of everyday indifference.

Ritual cannibalism was also widely practised across the globe until the nineteenth and even twentieth centuries. Human flesh was usually eaten not from physical necessity but to absorb the courage and intelligence of an opponent – the heart and brains were the most frequently consumed body parts – or as the last act in the humiliation of an enemy, though some Australian Aborigines ate dead relatives as a mark of respect.

Aztec rituals included large-scale cannibalism and it was also widespread on the Gulf and Pacific coasts of America, in parts of Africa, in New Guinea and throughout Melanesia and Polynesia. In Fiji, separate cooking pots and implements were reserved for human flesh, and the New Zealand Maori regarded it as one of the prime rewards of war.

In sixteenth- and seventeenth-century Europe, a form of cannibalism even had state backing. Human blood was believed to have therapeutic properties, particularly for epileptics. As a result, hanged criminals were often cut down while still alive, and bled to death by doctors. They distributed the blood among their patients in the crowd who brought their own cups to be sure of receiving a share.

A few notorious individuals apart, Europeans showed little taste for ritual cannibalism, but survival cannibalism was practised on a wide scale. Desperate populations were often forced to resort to it in times of famine and war. The inhabitants of castles and cities under prolonged siege ate whatever was to hand – cats, rats, leather and straw – but once even these were exhausted, the bodies of the dead and dying were often the only available food.

Soldiers of Napoleon's army on the long retreat from Moscow turned to cannibalism, and the standard practice adopted by all armies of laying waste to a country as they withdrew, slaughtering or stealing the livestock and burning every crop, forced the survivors into a desperate search for food that could and did include human flesh.

There are several recorded instances of cannibalism among escaped convicts from the penal colonies of Australia and explorers in remote areas were often driven to the same desperate remedy. A number of cases were recorded in the exploration of the American West, and Arctic explorers were particularly vulnerable.

There were no survivors from Sir John Franklin's expedition to the Arctic in 1845, but when rescuers finally reached the site, cannibalism was obvious, as a famous letter to the Admiralty stated, 'from the mutilated state of many of the corpses and the contents of the kettles.'

In the early spring of 1829, a party of explorers chanced upon a crude hut on an uninhabited island in the Gulf of St Lawrence. Inside were 'the carcasses of four human beings with their heads, legs, and arms cut off and their bowels extracted'.

A cooking pot over the long extinct ashes of a fire contained more human flesh. The blood-spattered walls and ceiling suggested that the victims had not gone quietly to their deaths. There were no survivors, for the body of another man lay in his hammock. The dead men were not explorers but the remnants of the twenty-man crew of the British ship the *Granicus*, which had wrecked on the island the previous autumn.

Seamen in dire straits had been resorting to cannibalism as long as ships had been wrecking, and the congenital instability of square-rigged ships, the difficulties of establishing longitude, inaccurate charts, the dangerous practice of carrying deck cargo, and the large numbers of overloaded, poorly constructed or maintained and incompetently crewed or captained vessels on the high seas ensured that shipwreck was a common occurrence.

Losses of ships were so frequent that *The Times* recorded only the most significant in its daily reports of 'Disasters at Sea'. In the same year as the *Mignonette* was lost, another 560 British-registered ships went to the bottom, 397 of which were sailing vessels; 4,259 lives were lost – 1,490 passengers and 2,769 crew. Terrible as these figures were, 1884 was far from a bad year: three years earlier, no fewer than 838 sailing ships had sunk.

Some ship-owners provided so few stores that starvation and cannibalism were possible even without a wreck. Sir James Bisset recounted in his memoirs that, as a young man, he and the crew of the barque *County of Pembroke* had almost starved to death on a voyage from Callao to Falmouth.

Cannibalism occurred so often among sailors that it became a customary practice, complete with its own rituals. As surely as they knew that drinking sea-water would send them mad and kill them, all seamen were also aware that if they were starving, one of their number must be killed and eaten.

The victim was to be selected by casting lots. He was then bled to death so that his blood might be drunk, for thirst rather than hunger was usually the greater peril. The heart and liver – which were full of blood and the most perishable meats – were eaten at once. The rest of the body was then butchered.

Every experienced seaman knew of the custom of the sea, and the course that was to be followed in similar dire straits, for survivors felt that it legitimized what they did and saw no reason for concealment. The custom of the sea was known not only from the tales of actual cannibal ships circulating among seamen, but also from the popular ballads, broadsheets and novels that circulated far beyond the forecastles and the dockside taverns.

W. S. Gilbert wrote a poem, 'The Yarn of the Nancy Bell', in which the ten survivors of a shipwreck were steadily reduced to one. It was turned down by *Punch* on the grounds of poor taste, but appeared in *Fun* magazine in March 1866.

> *. . . For a month we'd neither wittles nor drink,*
> *Till a-hungry we did feel,*
> *So we drawed a lot, and accordin' shot*
> *The captain for our meal.*
>
> *The next lot fell to the Nancy's mate,*
> *And a delicate dish he made;*
> *Then our appetite with the midshipmite*
> *We seven survivors stayed.*
>
> *And then we murdered the bo'sun tight,*
> *And he much resembled pig;*
> *Then we wittled free, did the cook and me*
> *On the crew of the captain's gig.*
>
> *Then only the cook and me was left,*
> *And the delicate question, 'Which*
> *Of us two goes to the kettle?' arose*
> *And we argued it out as sich . . .*

Walt Whitman also referred to the custom of the sea in 'I Sit and Look Out', written in 1860.

I observe a famine at sea, I observe sailors casting lots
who shall be kill'd to preserve the lives of the rest,
... All the meanness and agony without end I sitting
Look out upon,
See, hear and am silent.

There was a near endless tally of actual wrecks whose survivors had practised the custom of the sea: the *Peggy*, the *Essex*, the *George*, the *Euxine*, the *Jane Black*, the *Cospatrick*, the *Sallie M. Steelman*, the *Caledonia*, the *Frances Mary*, the *Lady Frances*, the *Granicus*, the *Tiger*, the *Nottingham Galley*, the *Dolphin*, the *Mary*, the *Dalusia*, the *Lucy*, the *Earl Kellie*, the *Leader*, the *Blake*, the *Anna Maria*, the *Earl Moira*, the *Jane Lowdon*, the *Polly*, the *Turley*, the *Elizabeth Rashleigh*, the *Hannah*, the *Earnmoor*, the *Home* and the *Nautilus* is by no means an exhaustive list.

The most celebrated of all was the inspiration of Géricault's famous painting, *The Wreck of the Medusa*. The finished painting shows no sign of the cannibalism that took place, but it is depicted in many of Géricault's preliminary studies.

In July 1816, the *Medusa* ran aground off the African coast, on the Arguin Bank, near Cape Blanco. She was carrying 400 passengers and crew. A huge raft, some twenty yards by seven was constructed and 157 survivors boarded it. They had five barrels of wine, two of water and twenty-five pounds of ship's biscuits, though these were contaminated by sea-water.

They set off towards the distant shore, towed by the ships' boats, but after a short distance the officers in the boats cut the raft adrift and rowed away, leaving the survivors to their fate. The raft was so heavy-laden that the survivors were waist deep in water, and so overcrowded that the rough seas were continually washing people overboard. Mutiny broke out and wholesale killings began.

One of the eventual survivors recorded that,

Those whom death had spared during the night fell upon the dead bodies with which the raft was covered, and cut off pieces which some instantly devoured ... Those of us who had firmness enough to abstain from it, took a larger quantity of wine.

We tried to eat sword-belts and cartouche-boxes, and succeeded in swallowing some little morsels. Some ate linen, others pieces of leather from the hats, on which there was a little grease, or rather dirt. A sailor attempted to eat excrement, but could not succeed.

On the following nights, a further mutiny and more acts of violence reduced the raft's complement to thirty men, half of them wounded. Rather than waste rations on men who were likely to die anyway, the other fifteen decided to throw the wounded into the sea, retaining a few dead bodies as food. The fifteen survived to be rescued on the seventeenth day adrift, but five died soon afterwards.

If the *Medusa* was the most celebrated incident, there was no shortage of others. A Dutch physician, Nicholaus Tulpius, published a seventeenth-century account of a ship carrying seven Englishmen which set out from St Christopher – now St Kitts – in the Caribbean for a journey expected to last one day. However, a storm drove the ship out to sea and the crew were lost for seventeen days. They drew lots to see who should die to feed the rest and also cast lots for the executioner.

When the lots were drawn, the man who had suggested the idea was the victim. He was killed, his blood drunk and his body eaten. The survivors were eventually washed ashore on the island of St Martin. When they returned to St Christopher, they were put on trial for murder, but all were acquitted, on the grounds of 'inevitable necessity'.

In an eighteenth-century case, the *Peggy* sailed for New York on 24 October 1765, carrying a cargo of wine and brandy. Five days later the ship was hit by violent storms. Over the course of the following month of incessant gales, the sails were torn away one by one.

The food and water soon ran out altogether. The starving crew, working desperately by day and night to keep their ship afloat, began to plunder the cargo of liquor. On Christmas morning they seemed to have found salvation when a ship appeared to leeward of them. The captain of the *Peggy*, David Harrison, spoke to the other ship's captain, explained their plight and asked him to take them on board.

The man refused, even though Harrison swore that none of his crew would touch a scrap of the other ship's provisions. All the other captain would do, he said, was to give them some hard-tack, once he had finished taking his noon sun-sight. Harrison went below to rest, but a few moments later some of his crewmen burst in on him. The other ship had made sail without throwing them so much as a crumb.

As long as my poor fellows could retain the least trace of him they hung about the shrouds or ran in a state of absolute frenzy from one part of the ship to the other. They pierced the air with their cries, increasing in their lamentations as she lessened upon their view.

Two pigeons and the ship's cat still remained on the *Peggy*. The two birds were eaten that day and the cat the next. The crewmen cast lots for portions of it, Harrison drawing the head.

I never feasted on anything which appeared so delicious to my appetite. The piercing sharpness of necessity had entirely conquered my aversion to such food, and the rage of an incredible hunger rendered that an exquisite regale which on any other occasion, I must have loathed with the most insuperable might.

The crew continued to drink the liquor from the cargo and ate their tobacco and candles, the bone buttons from their jackets and every scrap of leather they could find, even taking the ship's pumps apart to get at the leather washers inside.

They then told the captain that they had drawn lots and the short straw had fallen on a slave, 'a poor Ethiopian', who was part of the cargo. He was shot dead, cooked and eaten. One crewman, too impatient to wait for the body to be cooked, tore out the dead man's liver and ate it raw. He went insane and died three days later, but his body was thrown overboard untouched lest his madness be ingested by his fellows along with his flesh.

When lots were again cast, the short straw was drawn by a popular crewman and some hours elapsed while they decided whether to eat him. The mental strain on him was more than he could bear, however, and he became deaf and then insane. The next morning, a ship appeared on the horizon. When the crew rushed in to tell Harrison they were saved, he almost shot them, fearing that it was his turn to be eaten.

Even after his rescue, Harrison ate virtually nothing for four days, except a little broth. When at last he ate some solid food he was shortly afterwards gripped by

> an occasion for a particular indulgence of nature. I thought I should have expired performing it. The pain it gave me was excruciating to the last degree and the parts were so contracted, having never once been employed for a space of thirty-six or thirty-seven days, that I almost began to despair restoring them to their necessary operations. I was, however, at last relieved by the discharge of a callous lump about the size of a hen's egg.

An even more famous and terrible case than the *Peggy* involved the *Cospatrick*, a 1,200-ton, teak-hulled ship launched in 1856. It saw many years' service as a troop-carrier, and had also carried out the less respectable trade of 'blackbirding' – kidnapping men to be sold to slave traders.

On 8 September 1874, it sailed from Gravesend under Captain Elmslie, on a voyage to Auckland. It carried 433 passengers, including 127 children and 42 crew. By 18 November the ship was well past the Cape in the roaring forties, running east towards New Zealand through a heavy swell, when at one in the morning a fire broke out in the boatswain's store in the forepeak.

Fanned by the headwind, the flames raced through the ship and ignited the cargo, including 1,700 gallons of linseed oil and almost 6,000 gallons of spirits. There were only enough boats for half the people on board and most of them could not be launched. There was no hoisting gear for the lifeboats, the planking of the cutter was rotten and it also had a large hole in its hull. The longboat caught fire before it could be launched.

Only two small boats were safely launched, carrying only eighty-one passengers and crew. Faced with being burned alive, many of those left on the *Cospatrick* had already chosen to throw themselves into the sea and drown. Captain Elmslie threw his wife and child overboard then drowned himself as the flames started to sweep the stern. Only when at last it disappeared beneath the waves were the fires finally extinguished.

The two small boats stayed together until the night of 21 November, when they were separated by a gale. The port lifeboat containing forty-two people was never seen again.

In these deep southern latitudes, with only one usable oar, no food or water and with many of the occupants dressed only in their night clothes, the situation in the other boat remained desperate. People began dying from thirst and exposure. The first few were thrown overboard to reduce the dangerous overcrowding, but then the living 'started to feast on the flesh and blood of the dead. First the blood was drunk and then the flesh was eaten, and having done that, we committed the remains to the deep. The biggest, fattest and healthiest-looking went off first. It was not from them that the blood was obtained but from the other men,' one of the eventual survivors, Edward Cotter, said. 'I only ate twice. I drank whenever a vein was opened.'

On 26 November a ship passed within fifty yards of them but ignored their cries for help, and when they were at last rescued by the *British Sceptre* out of Liverpool, after ten days adrift, only five remained alive – Henry MacDonald, Edward Cotter, two other seamen and a single passenger who had gone insane. Two, a seaman and the insane passenger, died within a couple of days of their rescue.

For three days, Cotter was gripped by an insatiable thirst, constantly crawling across the deck to help himself to water from a cask lashed to the mainmast. His ravenous hunger lasted several months and he took to bribing a steward on the ship that eventually took him home to provide him with extra food.

Claiming to be the only survivor of 475 people, he was celebrated as a hero and,

> taken about by a music-hall artist named Charles Williams, who worked me into a topical song. I had a seat in a stall near the stage and when Williams called attention to me there were storms of cheering. When we went from hall to hall in his brougham, there was such a rush to get a sight of me and shake me by the hand that more than once the windows were smashed.

Many starving castaways endured the unimaginable distress of being passed by ships whose captains either ignored them altogether or refused to rescue them because they had no spare provisions. The survivors of the wreck of the *Frances Mary*, whose tale Brooks had recounted to Richard Parker, had a similar experience. Ann Saunders later related how an English brig had sailed close to the hulk but refused to stop despite fine weather and calm seas.

> Our longing eyes followed her until she was out of sight, leaving us in a situation doubly calamitous from our disappointment in not receiving the relief which appeared so near.

The surviving members of the crew of the American brig *Polly* had an even more terrible tale to tell. She sailed from Boston on 12 December 1811 with a crew of nine. Three days later she sprang a leak during a gale and capsized. The crew chopped down her mast and cut away her rigging to right the ship, but they were now adrift with few supplies in the depths of winter. They drifted two thousand miles over the following 191 days before the only two survivors were finally rescued by the *Fame*.

> It is natural to inquire how they could float such a vast distance upon the most frequented part of the Atlantic and not be discovered all this time. They were passed by more than a dozen sail, one of which came so nigh them that they could distinctly see the people on deck and on the rigging looking at them; but to the inexpressible disappointment of the starving and freezing men, they stifled the dictates of compassion, hoisted sail, and cruelly abandoned them to their fate.

Not all captains who refused to give aid in such circumstances were black-hearted. To rescue men from a dinghy or a derelict ship was a delicate and dangerous operation, particularly in merchant vessels that had few spare men, or often none. The sails had to be taken in and the vessel hove to, then a boat put overboard and the ship manoeuvred to leeward of the dinghy or wrecked ship. In heavy seas it could easily be further damaged or sunk during this operation and the undermanned rescuing vessel was also in peril. Many captains would only take the risk in flat, calm conditions.

Certain features recurred in almost every instance of cannibalism among seamen. Not only was the custom of drawing lots almost univerally practised, but the way the lots fell also revealed a curious consistency. The American whaling ship, the *Essex*, was true to type. She sank in the South Pacific on 20 November 1820 after being rammed repeatedly by a whale – the incident that inspired Melville to write *Moby Dick*. The crew took to three whaleboats and all of them were forced to resort to the custom of the sea. In one, only one man was eaten, though another two died of starvation before the three survivors were rescued.

The occupants of the other two boats fared even worse, and as many as eight people were eaten by their starving crewmates.

> On the 14th January, the whole stock of provisions belonging to the second mate's boat was entirely exhausted. On the 25th, the black man, Lawson Thomas, died and was eaten by his surviving companions . . . The Captain and his crew were in the like dreadful situation . . . Another coloured man, Charles Shorter, died and his body was shared for food between the crews of both boats. On the 27th, Isaiah Shepherd, a black man, died in the second mate's boat and on the 28th another black man named Samuel Reed died out of the Captain's boat. The bodies of these men constituted their only food.

Only two men remained alive in the second mate's boat when it lost contact with the other one. It was never seen again. The captain, George Pollard, was one of only two survivors from the remaining boat.

> On the 1st of February, having consumed their last morsel, the Captain and the three other men that remained with him were reduced to the necessity of casting lots. It fell upon Owen Coffin to die . . . On the 11th, Braxilla Ray died. The Captain and Charles Ramsdell, the only two that were then left, subsisted on the bodies until the morning of the 23rd of February, when they fell in with the ship Dauphin.

That account, based solely on the captain's version of events, once more exposes but does not comment upon one of the more revealing

131

facts about the vast majority of incidents in which the custom of the sea was practised. The people who, according to the later accounts of the survivors, either died of natural causes and were then eaten, or who were the unlucky ones when lots were drawn, were almost invariably the weakest, most vulnerable, disliked or isolated individuals. Slaves were eaten first, black men before white, women before men, passengers before crew, unpopular crew members before the rest.

The hierarchy of the ship's complement was also followed: cabin boys or apprentices were eaten first, 'idlers' – carpenters, cooks, sailmakers and boatswains, who because of their specialist tasks, did not keep watches and received higher pay – came next, and ordinary seamen before officers.

It stretches credulity to breaking point to believe that natural causes or the random drawing of lots can always have produced such fortunate results ... for those who survived. It is clear that many deaths from natural causes were actually murder and that many – the majority of – instances of lots being drawn were rigged or fabricated afterwards to conceal the murder of a disliked or disposable member of the company.

If the custom of the sea was accepted without comment among seafaring communities, the reaction of the Victorian establishment was very different. Many of the horrors of the Victorian underworld, such as child prostitution, passed largely unnoticed, but the very openness and honesty of seamen who had resorted to the custom of the sea forced it to public attention.

Polite society abhorred the idea of Englishmen practising cannibalism like savages, in defiance of the law and Christian morality. Under the selfless Victorian ideal of service to society and to God, men were expected to die nobly for others, not kill them that they might themselves survive.

There was one famous example of such sacrifice. The iron-hulled troopship the *Birkenhead* sailed from the naval base of Simonstown in South Africa for Port Elizabeth on 25 February 1852, with 648 people on board. In addition to a full complement of fighting men, there were also many wives and children. At two the following morning the ship hit a reef in shark-infested waters off Danger Point.

The women and children were helped into one of the ship's two cutters. The second with about thirty men and a gig holding a few more were also lowered. The boats had barely got clear when the funnel crashed on to the deck, crushing the men who were trying to launch the remainder of the boats.

The captain, Robert Salmond, ordered the ship to be abandoned but the troop commander, Major Alexander Seton of the 74th Highlanders, countermanded the order at once, afraid that the men would swamp the boats that had already been launched. The soldiers were ordered to stay where they were, and only three made a move from the stationary ranks, jumping over the rail into the sea. All three were drowned or eaten by sharks as the ship's boats moved away.

Shortly afterwards the *Birkenhead* split in half and sank. Most of the troops could not swim and even those who could struggled to fight their way through the dense seaweed under constant attack from the packs of marauding sharks.

Sixty-nine men eventually reached the shore. Another fifty clung to the rigging of the mainmast, which was still protruding above the water. Many, exhausted, fell to their death during the remainder of the night, but thirty were still there when they were rescued by a passing schooner the next morning.

Of the 648 people on board the *Birkenhead*, only 193 were saved, including all the women and children. Seton and Salmond were among those lost. The official report by one of the survivors, Captain Wright, said,

> The order and regularity that prevailed on board from the time the ship struck until she totally disappeared far exceeded anything that I thought could be effected by the best discipline, and is more to be wondered at seeing that most of the soldiers had been but a short time in the Service. Everyone did as he was directed and there was not a murmur or cry among them until the vessel made her final plunge.

The example of the *Birkenhead*, 'To stand and be still in the *Birkenhead* drill,' in Kipling's words, was henceforth held up as the model others should follow.

The less exalted circles in which seamen moved preferred to hold to the custom of the sea, and despite the hostility of polite society to the practice few attempts had been made to test its legality. Since the unsuccessful trial of the men wrecked off St Christopher in the early seventeenth century, only two cases had been brought. The survivors of the *Euxine* faced only cursory court proceedings in Singapore and were released without facing trial in London.

The other case involved Alexander William Holmes, an able seaman on an American ship, the *William Brown*. The 550-ton ship had left Liverpool for Philadelphia with a crew of eighteen under Captain George Harris, sixty-five passengers and a full cargo of general goods.

Late in the evening of Monday, 19 April 1841, the ship was running before a south-westerly gale about 250 miles from Newfoundland when she struck ice floes. The impacts stove in the bows and the ship began to sink almost at once.

There were only two boats. Captain Harris, the second mate, six sailors and the cabin boy got into the jollyboat with one passenger, Eliza Lafferty, whose preferential treatment can only have been based on intimacy with Harris. Even her sister was turned away from the boat.

The first mate, Francis Rhodes, got into the longboat with Holmes, seven other sailors and a further thirty-three passengers. Holmes had already helped several people into the longboat and then climbed back on board to rescue a child of one of them, returning with her clinging to his back. A woman on deck offered him a year's wages to rescue her too, but he refused, saying he was 'not after money but saving lives'.

Holmes was 'the last person to leave the sinking ship'. Despite their entreaties, the remaining thirty people were left on board. They all drowned when she went down at eleven twenty that night.

Conditions in the desperately overcrowded longboat were appalling. It had to be baled continuously, and it rode so low in the water that it was at constant risk of foundering in the heavy swell.

The captain and his fortunate company sailed away. The sailors in the longboat manned the oars and began to row south, towards the main shipping lanes, but by evening they were surrounded once more by ice.

According to his later testimony, Rhodes 'thought it improbable that she could hold out, unless relieved of some of her weight. I then consulted the sailors, and we were all of the opinion that it was necessary to throw overboard those who were nearly dead.' Some time later, Rhodes threw down the baler, and said to the crew, 'This work won't do. Help me, God. Men, go to work.'

He had to repeat the instruction – he later claimed it was not an order, but merely a statement of their predicament – before the crew began their grisly task. By the time the crew had finished their work, only two male passengers remained alive.

Holmes had been one of the ringleaders in the early stages of the killing, but he later relented and tried without success to prevent two other crewmen from murdering the last two victims. 'No more shall be thrown over. If any others are lost, we shall be lost together.'

By a cruel irony, not long after the last two men had been thrown overboard, a ship, the *Crescent*, was sighted. Holmes forced the surviving passengers to hide in the bottom of the boat. 'Lie down every soul of you, and lie still. If they make out so many of us on board, they will steer off another way and pretend they have not seen us.'

The *Crescent* stopped and picked them up just in time; the longboat was crushed by the ice shortly afterwards. The crew were arrested when they reached Le Havre but each of the survivors' curiously similar statements exonerated the crew, and they were released from jail and took ship for America on the next available boat, while *The Times* remarked, 'The frightful necessity of sacrificing part of the passengers for the safety of the rest is fully proved.'

It did not appear so to Lord Palmerston, who excoriated the British consul in a series of telegrams, claiming that he had gone out of his way to justify 'a transaction which was revolting in its character . . . in which so many British Subjects were violently put to death by Foreigners . . . The perpetrators cannot be absolved from great apparent guilt except by the result of a legal tribunal.'

The anger of the survivors burned much more fiercely on their return to America than it had in Le Havre. Their complaints to the authorities in Philadelphia eventually led to the arrest of Alexander William Holmes. Neither the captain, nor the mate, nor any of the other crew was ever charged.

A grand jury threw out indictments of murder and left Holmes to face a single charge of manslaughter. US versus Holmes eventually opened on 13 April 1842. In the face of half a dozen sworn statements by eyewitnesses, counsel for the defence made no attempt to deny that

Holmes had been involved in killing the passengers. Instead he claimed that the act had been justified by necessity. Had the few not been killed, all would have perished, or such was the reasonable belief of the defendant at the time.

The judge did not rule out necessity as a possible defence but stated that it could only operate in cases where a man 'must owe no duty to the victim, be under no obligation of law to make his own safety a secondary object, and if in any of these particulars his case is defective, he is answerable by the law of the land'.

In his even-handed summing up, the judge pointed out that even if the mate had ordered Holmes to kill the passengers, an unlawful order did not justify his actions. He also drew the jury's attention to the normal custom of the sea – the drawing of lots – but pointed out that the necessity of keeping seamen rather than passengers alive in order to row and steer the boat might count against it.

He gave the jury no direction, leaving to them alone the decision on whether it had been necessary to kill anyone. They returned a guilty verdict and Holmes was sentenced to six months' imprisonment.

The case was both a prohibition and an endorsement of the custom of the sea. Although there had been a conviction for manslaughter, the judge had accepted that extreme necessity could justify acts that in other circumstances would be criminal. Holmes was guilty only because of the special duty of care owed to passengers by crew. The implication was that crewmen who practised the custom of the sea among themselves, and sacrificed some to save others, were guilty of no crime at all.

CHAPTER 11

Once dry, the meat that had once been Richard Parker was stored under the canvas in the bow, and twice more that day, they feasted on the boy's flesh. The next morning, a heavy storm passed over and they each caught and drank a good pint of water. No further rain fell over the next four days and the men were once again forced to drink their own urine.

Stephens's legs were so swollen that he could hardly move and he was now also suffering from stomach cramps that made him cry out with pain. That night he was so ill that Brooks thought he was going to die. He looked at Tom. 'Say a prayer for us, Captain.'

They took hold of Stephens's hands and began praying together, the words grating in their parched throats as they begged the Almighty to save them.

The next morning, their twenty-fourth adrift, Stephens's stomach pains had eased a little, though he was still able to move only by dragging himself along the bottom of the boat by his hands.

Tom and Brooks continued to feed on the body, even though it was getting rather high, but they cut out the bad parts and washed the rest with salt water.

Stephens ate much less. He was listless and considerably weaker than the other two and Tom was suspicious that he, too, had been drinking sea-water. When he charged him with it, Stephens shot him a terrified look and denied it violently.

Tom shrugged and turned away. He reached under the canvas cover and handed each of them a strip of dried meat. 'There's little enough left,' he said, his voice low and hoarse. 'And we've been four days without rain. If we are not all to perish . . .'

Stephens turned his head away as if ducking his captain's words, but Brooks shot him a warning look. 'Let's not talk of that again. A ship will come.'

'I pray you're right. But if one does not, or if it passes us by as the others have done—'

'I tell you, a ship will come.' Brooks moved back to the stern, cradling the steering oar under his arm as he gnawed at his scrap of meat.

Tom studied them both for a moment before beginning to eat his own piece.

Brooks finished his meal and pulled himself up by the mast to search the horizon. As he gazed towards the south-west, he froze and held out a shaking finger. 'A sail! Oh, my God, here's a ship coming straight towards us.'

Tom stumbled half upright, setting the dinghy rocking. Right on the horizon, a scrap of white was outlined against the sky.

'Let us pray to God that the ship is directed across our path,' Tom said. He bowed his head, his cracked lips moving, as he said a silent prayer. Then he glanced around him. 'He is to windward of us. Pull the sail down, we must not increase the distance between us. Brooks, steer for her. Stephens, bend to the oars with me.'

The wind was so light that the distant ship appeared to make almost no progress towards them. They rowed for over an hour as it crept over the sea, slowly closing the gap between them.

It was still some way off when the wind suddenly strengthened. A line of cloud scudded in over the sea and a squall struck them, whipping fine spray from the caps of the waves and blotting the ship from sight. Stephens dropped his oar with a cry of distress, burying his head in his arms.

Tom's expression merely hardened. 'Catch the rainwater, damn you. All's not lost yet.'

The three men sat motionless, holding out their oilskin capes like supplicants begging for alms, but the squall spurned them. Tom could see rain pocking the surface of the swell barely a hundred yards from the boat, but no more than a few fat drops stained the dark surface of his outspread cape. He cursed, then lowered his head to lick at the fast evaporating moisture with his parched, swollen tongue.

He threw aside the cape and hauled himself up again, clinging to the mast as he stared towards the south-west. For a few minutes he could see nothing but the wraiths of cloud scudding over the greasy water. Then a shape began to emerge from the mist. Vague and ghost-grey at first, the outline sharpened into the dirty white of a sail. It was larger and much closer now and beneath it he could make out the dark super-structure of the ship.

'Her course is still to the south of us. They may not see us. To the oars. We must row for our lives.'

Stephens barely seemed to hear him. Tom took his shoulder and shook him fiercely. 'Take an oar and row for your life.'

Stephens froze, then hauled himself on to the bench and took hold of one of the oars. He began a feeble, ragged stroke, his head lolling on his shoulders with each pull.

Tom heaved on the other oar, his mouth set in a thin, determined line. The boat crept through the water with a slow, dragging rhythm, punctuated by their grunts of effort, the laboured rasp of their breathing, the creak of the oars in the brass crutches and the soft splash as the blades entered the water.

Tom did not dare to look over his shoulder, terrified that the ship might already be sailing past them. He could feel his strength ebbing and fought against the deadly lethargy creeping over him.

With no oars to spare, Brooks used one of the bottom boards to steer. As he rowed, Tom searched Brooks's face for some clue to their fate. Their eyes met for a moment. 'If the ship doesn't stop . . .' He left the sentence unfinished but Brooks glanced towards Stephens, then gave a slow nod.

He cut through the rope binding the shirts and began to wave one over his head as the other men again bent to the oars. He struggled to hold a straight course as Stephens's stroke became even more shallow and ragged. Finally his oar broke surface in mid-stroke, throwing spray into the air. He slumped back and lay still, his chest heaving.

Tom did not spare him a glance, but pushed him aside and took both oars. The rough, salt-encrusted wood of the oars rasped against his swollen hands, but he used the pain to drown the agony of his wasted muscles, closing his mind to everything but the next stroke.

Stephens tried to hold up a shirt on the stick they had been using as a yard, but he had barely enough strength left to raise it above his head.

Tom's breath rattled in his chest like a dead man's, but he forced himself to count off a hundred strokes. With each one, the roaring in his ears grew louder until it drowned every other sound. He raised his eyes and again searched Brooks's expression.

He shook his head.

Tom glanced over his shoulder. The ship was now almost level with them, and still holding its course. He hauled on the oars in a frenzy for a few more seconds, then threw them down and bowed his head.

'Wait.' Brooks said something else, but his swollen tongue and cracked lips made it unintelligible.

'What?' Tom said. 'What is it?'

'He's changing course. He's seen us.'

He continued to wave the shirt, but Tom simply stared as the ship, a triple-masted sailing barque, began to bear down on them. It was flying a German flag and he could make out the name *Moctezuma* on the bow. He saw the figures of sailors climbing aloft to reef the sails. Others lined the rail, peering down at the tiny dinghy as it came alongside.

Brooks took the oars and Tom stood up. A rope thrown from the ship hit the water with a slap. It lay just out of reach as Tom scrabbled for it. The end of the rope sank from sight, but it was hauled back and thrown again. This time he caught it as it snaked across the gunwale. He winced as it bit into his torn hands but held on and made it fast.

The captain called down to him from the rail of the upper deck. 'Captain Simonsen of the *Moctezuma*, out of Port Andemer, Punta Arenas, bound for Hamburg. Who are you and what was your ship?'

Tom opened his mouth to speak but no words would come and he stared at the other man in a mute plea. He tried again and found his voice, but it was so weak and cracked, and his words so faint, that they barely carried over the water separating the two ships. 'Tom Dudley of the *Mignonette*, bound for New South Wales. For God's sake, help us. We have been twenty-four days adrift with nothing to eat or drink. We have wives and children depending on us. Please help us on board.'

He waited, not daring to breathe as the captain exchanged a few words with the woman at his side. Then he gave a curt nod and shouted for more ropes to be lowered. Tom's knees buckled as relief flooded through him.

Brooks glanced at him, then nodded towards the canvas sheet across the bow. 'What of the rest of our food?'

'What of it?'

'I could throw it overboard.'

Tom shook his head. 'Leave it be.'

Brooks began to argue, but Tom cut him off. 'I said, leave it be.'

Brooks hesitated, then turned away. He had enough strength remaining to clamber on to the ship by the chain plates, but then collapsed. Picking him up as easily as a child, the ship's carpenter took him on his back and carried him on deck. Tom and Stephens were too weak to climb even the few feet to the chain plates. Ropes were passed around them and they were hauled up by the crew.

They lay on the deck, huddled in the foetal position, croaking for water. The bony hands they held out in supplication were more like claws.

The captain's wife ladled water from a barrel lashed to the foot of the mainmast. She mixed it with a little wine and gave each of them a ladleful. They drank it greedily.

'Wait a few moments before you drink more,' she said, 'or it may make you ill.'

The captain called down to them from the upper deck. 'What of your dinghy?'

Brooks again shot a glance at Tom. 'Cast it loose. We have no need of it.'

Tom ignored him and called out, 'Please bring it aboard.'

Brooks stared at him. 'For God's sake, why?'

'As a reminder.'

'Do you think we could forget? I beg you, Captain, let it rest with our ship at the bottom of the ocean.'

'And I say no. The dinghy comes with us.'

They were carried down the companionway below decks to the crew's quarters. There was a feeling of safety and familiarity in the smells that filled Tom's nostrils: damp timber and tar from the ship's caulking, blending with the more exotic scents of the cargo – the warm smell of cedarwood and the musty odour of fustic.

Mrs Simonsen gave them more water, a little food and a tot of brandy, then the crewmen stripped them of their tattered, salt-encrusted rags. As the last of his clothes were removed Tom made a feeble attempt to cover himself with his hands, then lay back and closed his eyes.

'Please,' the captain's wife said, 'I must bathe your sores.' She gasped as she saw his wasted body. Purple, ulcerating sores covered his legs, hips and shoulders. His yellowing, waxy skin was tight-drawn over his ribs and the split nails of his hands and feet were the colour of tanned leather. While the rest of his body was stick thin, his legs were grotesquely swollen.

She wrung out a cloth in water and Tom felt its cool touch on his burning skin. She dried him gently with a soft towel, bandaged the worst of his sores and the crew then dressed him in clean clothes.

He opened his eyes and looked up at her. 'Thank you for saving us.'

'The Lord led us to you and we could not leave you to die. You are safe now and you must rest.'

Tom sipped some more water, then lay back on the bunk and closed his eyes. He heard the familiar sounds of a sailing ship at sea – the creak of the boom and the snap of canvas as the wind filled the sails, the greasy slop of water in the bilges and the scuttling and scratching of a rat behind the planking. Then there was a thud on the deck above his head as the dinghy was hauled on board.

Still leaning on the rail overlooking the main deck, Captain Simonsen ordered two seamen, Julius Wiese and Christopher Drewe, to clear out the boat. Wiese picked up the chronometer case and stared at its stained surface, then ran his fingers over the striations on the wooden cross-member of the dinghy and the marks on the brass crutches for the oars.

Under the canvas cover across the bow he found a small piece of rib bone and the remaining strips of the rancid, stinking meat. He held them up towards the captain. 'What are we to do with these?'

Simonsen shuddered. 'Throw them overboard.' He turned on his heel and went below.

Every few hours the captain's wife brought the men food and water mixed with wine. Between her visits Tom drifted in and out of consciousness. His sleep was broken by constant nightmares and several times he jerked upright, terrified that he was once more sprawled in the dinghy beneath the burning sun. He reached out to touch the re-assuringly solid timbers of the deck above him then lay back once more and closed his eyes.

Although Mrs Simonsen had been careful to limit the food and drink they took, Tom awoke early the next morning with a fierce griping in his guts. He crawled from the bunk and squatted on the earthenware chamber-pot as a violent spasm shook him, his first bowel movement in twenty-five days. As he attempted to stand up, his strength deserted him and he slumped back on to the pot. It broke beneath him and he felt stabbing pains as shards of the pot were driven into his buttocks.

He cried out as he sprawled on the deck and warm blood trickled down his thighs. He heard footsteps and the rustle of skirts. He closed his eyes and cried in shame, his humiliation complete.

Mrs Simonsen called out for help and a few moments later strong hands lifted Tom and laid him face down on the bunk. She picked out the broken fragments of earthenware embedded in his wasted flesh, cleaned his wounds and staunched the bleeding. She bandaged him as well as she could, then cleaned the mess from the deck.

By nightfall Tom was shivering with a fever and his cuts rapidly became infected. Each morning and evening, Mrs Simonsen dressed his wounds and bathed his sores, and every afternoon he, Brooks and Stephens were helped on deck to breathe the fresh air and take a few hesitant steps. None of them could yet stand upright or even lie flat, their limbs still contorted by the weeks on the cramped dinghy.

For days they did little but eat and sleep. The food was spartan but sufficient, and they began to regain a little strength. Brooks and Stephens remained forward in the crew's quarters of the 140-foot, 440-ton barque, but mindful of Tom's status as captain of the *Mignonette*, Simonsen invited him to use his day-cabin at the stern.

On the Sunday after their rescue, Mrs Simonsen judged the three men well enough to attend the divine service conducted by her husband. They stood bare-headed as the captain led his men in prayers and sang a Lutheran hymn.

Tom then touched the captain's arm and asked permission to say a prayer on behalf of himself and his men. 'Almighty Father, bless those who have rescued us from our peril and grant them Godspeed and a fair wind to bring them safe to home. We commend to you the soul of our shipmate Richard Parker, who did not live to be restored to his loved ones.' He broke off as tears tracked down his cheeks. 'God grant us forgiveness for our sins. Amen.'

The captain left him alone for a few minutes to compose himself, then invited him to share their meal. After they had eaten, they leaned against the stern rail on the upper deck, taking the sun as the ship cleaved through the waves, driven on by the wind on its quarter.

Tom stared at the line of the wake across the waves behind them. 'Where were we when you rescued us?' he said.

Simonsen went below for his log. 'You were twenty-four degrees twenty-eight minutes south, and twenty-seven degrees twenty-two minutes west, about a thousand miles east of Rio. You're lucky we spotted you at all. I was the first one to sight your dinghy. I thought I saw a small speck on the horizon and looked at it through my glasses. I saw something floating on the waters but at that distance I could not at first distinguish it as a boat; I thought it a piece of wreckage. As we neared it, I was astonished to find it was a dinghy with human beings in it. It was a frightful spectacle. You looked like living skeletons. I never saw men in such a state in my life.'

He suppressed a shudder at the memory. 'If your mate's dead reckoning of the position of the wreck was accurate, you had drifted over a thousand miles. At that rate of progress it would have taken you at least another twenty-five days to reach land. By that time, I think none of you would have been alive.'

Tom glanced at him, searching the words for malice, but there was only sympathy in Simonsen's face. 'You have examined the dinghy?'

He nodded.

'And you know to what straits we were driven?'

'I know. Desperate straits require desperate measures.'

He watched Tom for a moment. 'You're already a little stronger, I think, and we have five or six weeks yet before we make port, time for your body to heal and your memories to fade a little.' He paused. 'But if it is not too distressing for you, I would like to hear the story of your voyage. It is none of my concern, of course, and if you wish to remain silent I shall respect that, but I would be most interested to hear it. The cause of a sinking is always of interest to another ship's captain.'

Tom glanced towards Mrs Simonsen, standing close by. 'I think there are parts of my story that would not be suitable for the ears of a lady.'

She smiled. 'There is little enough that these ears have not heard during five years' voyaging with my husband, Captain Dudley, but in any event I have work to do below deck.' She walked towards the companionway and disappeared.

Tom still hesitated, reluctant to put himself back into that dark place again. He stood in silence, staring down at his calloused hands grasping the stern rail as if it was the dock of a court. At last, he began to speak. Slow and hesitant at first, words started to pour from him as he unburdened himself. Several times he stopped, racked by sobs at the memories he had unlocked. Simonsen stood silent at his side, neither judging nor condemning, and Tom resumed his narrative, watching the wake unfurling behind them, a signpost to the past.

By Tom's schedule, the *Mignonette* should have arrived in Cape Town on 15 July, and as the weeks went by without a cable, Philippa had been growing increasingly desperate for news of her husband.

She waited another fortnight, hurrying to answer each knock at the door in case it was a messenger boy with a telegram, but on 29 July, the day the *Moctezuma* rescued them from the dinghy, she could contain her impatience no longer. She went to the telegraph office and asked them to check their files, but there was no record of any cable for her from the Cape. Then she caught the train into London and walked to the Strand to see Andrew Thompson at the Thames Yacht Agency.

He did his best to allay her fears, stressing how often adverse weather could delay a sailing ship for days or even weeks, but he could not completely mask his own anxieties from her. He had already cabled an agency at the Cape, asking if any other ships had news of the *Mignonette*, but there had been no reports of any sightings in the six weeks since Tom had handed letters for home to the captain of the *Bride of Larne*.

As the weeks dragged by, Philippa's concern deepened. When Lloyds posted the ship missing, Andrew Thompson travelled out to Sutton to tell her in person, confirming her worst fears.

Philippa had been paying the crew's wages during the voyage, sending Brooks's to his lodgings and Stephens's and Parker's to their families, but Thompson now advised her to suspend their payments at once. It was a standard, if harsh, practice once a ship was lost, and it was worse for many seamen, who fell foul of the hoary old saying, 'Cargo is the mother of wages.' If a merchant ship and its cargo were lost, the crew were not paid for any part of the voyage.

Philippa hesitated, knowing how hard things would now be for Stephens's family, but then she acceded. Even if she had wanted to keep paying them, she had no money to do so other than her own wages from the school. If the *Mignonette* was lost, there would be no payment for her safe delivery to Sydney.

Philippa clung to the belief, fading to a hope, that her husband was still alive, but every day that passed without word made it harder to sustain. She was also beset with worry about their younger daughter, Winifred. She was a frail child and constantly ill, with wheezing breath and a cough that, even at the height of summer, rattled in her lungs like a consumptive's. As Philippa's anxieties ate into her and disturbed her sleep, she became ill herself.

Ann Stephens, too, was in torment. She had received her husband's letter from Madeira asking her to emigrate with him, and had sent a reply to the Cape saying that she and the children would follow him as soon as he sent word of his arrival in New South Wales. Since then she had heard nothing.

The letter from Philippa, telling her that the ship was missing and that Stephens's wages would now be stopped, offered reassurances that neither woman believed. It concluded, 'All we can do now is wait and pray.'

CHAPTER 12

Tom awoke one morning to a flurry of activity from the ship's crew and knew that they were not many days' sailing from home. Captain Simonsen had as much pride in his ship as any sea-captain and he had set his men to work to restore his ship to prime condition before it made port.

The crew swarmed over the rigging, tarring the ropes, shrouds and stays. The mast and yardarms were scraped and painted, the decks holy-stoned and even the cable and anchor were banged with hammers to remove the rust.

As they neared the approaches to the Channel, the ship was stopped to take soundings at every change of the watch. The sails were taken down and as the barque lost headway a man on the bowsprit swung the lead. Three others at intervals back along the deck held coils of the line, which they released in turn until bottom was found.

'Seventy fathoms. Shell and sand.'

'Make sail.'

Later that day, Friday, 5 September 1884, they were hailed by a pilot boat. Gustavus Lowry, Falmouth pilot first-class, was cruising the western approaches to the Channel in Pilot Boat 13, looking for trade. It was a cut-throat business and pilots often tried to steal a march on their rivals by meeting vessels making for the Channel as far to the west as possible.

Lowry had one of the fastest pilot cutters in the area. It gave him an advantage over his rivals, for he would often find himself racing as many as three other pilots towards a sail sighted on the horizon, but he had had no luck that day. Every ship he had hailed was bound for a port further up the coast.

He was beginning to resign himself to a fruitless day when he hailed a triple-masted German sailing barque heading up Channel. '*Moctezuma*, where are you bound?'

Captain Simonsen came to the rail and called down to him. 'We're bound for Hamburg, but we've three English castaways to discharge.'

'Then you'll be needing a pilot. I'll take you in to Falmouth. Carrick Roads is the best harbour in England, a mile wide and almost as deep. You can enter in any sea conditions, whatever quarter a gale may blow from.'

Simonsen smiled. 'Then why do we need a pilot?'

'Because it's the law. You can't enter the Roads without one.'

'Then come aboard.'

Once the *Moctezuma* was again under way, Simonsen invited Lowry to his cabin. 'You'll take a drink?' He poured him a tot, then gestured to Tom. 'This is one of our castaways. We rescued them thirty-eight days ago in the South Atlantic.'

Tom shook the pilot's hand. 'Tom Dudley, formerly captain of the yacht *Mignonette*, lost in a storm on a voyage to New South Wales.'

'And how long were you adrift?'

'Twenty-four days in an open boat.'

The pilot's gaze took in Tom's gaunt, ravaged face and the scarred, lath-thin forearms poking from his sleeves. 'Your sufferings must have been terrible. How many were there of you?'

Tom's gaze flickered to Captain Simonsen, then back to Lowry. 'Four.'

'And what became of the other one? Was he drowned?'

'He was killed.'

'When the ship was lost?'

'No.'

Lowry studied him in silence for a moment. 'And who killed him?'

'I did.'

The pilot nodded, impassive. There was not a seafaring man afloat who had not heard such grisly tales, nor one who doubted that he would take the same measures in the same dire need.

'It's the custom of the sea,' Lowry said. 'You drew lots?'

There was the faintest hesitation before Tom's reply. 'No.'

For the first time the pilot's face showed shock.

'I wanted to,' Tom said, 'but the others would not agree. A few days later the boy drank sea-water. He was nearly dead. It would have been folly to have drawn lots then.'

Lowry gave a slow nod, though his expression remained thoughtful.

The *Moctezuma* was driven up the Channel by a stiff south-westerly breeze. More and more sails appeared on the horizon and soon boats were thick on the water – coasters and tramp steamers, fishing smacks heading in with the day's catch, pleasurecraft and racing yachts hugging the shores, barques and frigates outward bound, beating against the wind.

In the early hours of the following morning they rounded Lizard Point and Lowry guided the ship north along the coast of the peninsula. As they passed the Manacles reef, Tom saw the light on St Anthony Head in the distance ahead of the ship, a sight he had never thought to see again. Beyond it lay Falmouth.

As the pre-dawn light began to strengthen, he saw the towers of tin mines rising from the clifftops above the jagged coastline and smoke drifting upwards from houses clustered around the sheltered coves. The steep cliffs of Nare Point and Rosemullion Head, flanking the Helford river, appeared on the port beam.

As the *Moctezuma* glided into Falmouth Bay, Tom glanced up at a familiar landmark, the arsenic works with its tall chimneystack high on an exposed clifftop above Pennance Point, where the prevailing westerlies blew the poisonous fumes away from the town.

Lowry set the ship's course for the broad channel between the head-lands, steering west of Black Rock, its marker-buoy jutting from the middle of the channel like the broken spire of some drowned church. The *Moctezuma* passed below the rusting, silent guns of the Tudor forts on Pendennis Point and St Mawes, and entered Carrick Roads.

As Lowry had boasted, it was the finest natural harbour in England and one of the largest in the world. Fed by seven rivers, it was deep enough for the largest ocean-going ship to find anchorage, but accidents of geography and climate had prevented it from becoming one of the great ports. There was no large agricultural or industrial hinterland to support it. The output of even the biggest tin mines was only a handful of tons a week, and was as likely to be shipped out by rail or through any of the multitude of small ports in every creek, river and inlet along the coast.

Its strategic position at the western approaches to the Channel should still have made it Britain's premier naval base, but while the harbour was shielded from every other direction, it was impossible for a square-rigged sailing ship to leave Carrick Roads in the teeth of a southerly gale. To make ground into the wind, a sailing ship has to be able to present the leading edge of a sail to it. The difference in air pressure between the two sides of the sail generates lift, and it is this that drives the boat forward.

A yacht like the *Mignonette*, with a sail attached to a boom that swung over to change tack, could be sailed far closer to the wind than the clumsy square-riggers. Their rigid yards at right angles to the mast made it impossible for them to make any progress in anything approaching a head-wind.

The prevailing westerlies in the Channel would often pin the French fleet in harbour at Brest, but such gales often backed southerly. Britannia's square-rigged ships-of-the-line could not rule the waves if the French were able to put to sea while the British fleet was trapped in harbour. As a result, Falmouth was passed over in favour of Plymouth.

The packet boats carrying mails brought some prosperity to the town but the trade was narrow in focus. To deter attacks by pirates, the fast, armed boats were forbidden to carry any other cargo than the mails. The only trade goods they carried were those hidden in the sea-chests of the crewmen, and the gemstones they smuggled attracted the largest Jewish population in England outside London and made Falmouth a temporary rival to Antwerp and Amsterdam.

Falmouth had held the mail contract since 1688, but it was lost to Southampton in 1852, and the port began to decline. There was still work for some yards repairing ships limping into port after a battering from gales on the Atlantic crossing. Ships loaded at other ports also continued to make a last call at Falmouth 'for orders' from the shipping agents who, gauging the current market conditions in a hundred overseas ports, would give them their destination. Falmouth's central wharves remained busy and bustling, but the days of the packet boats were now long past and an air of dilapidation and dereliction hung over the outlying docks.

As the *Moctezuma* nosed into the sheltered waters of the Roads, Lowry glanced at Simonsen. 'You'll not be allowed to tie up at the quay,' he said. 'There's a cholera scare and any foreign ship is suspect.'

Simonsen smiled. 'I've no intention of tying up there. I've crewmen aboard who would jump ship at the first whiff of a landfall. Let them swim for it.'

Under Lowry's instructions, the *Moctezuma* dropped anchor on Falmouth Bank, a mile from the town, early on the morning of Friday, 6 September. He took his payment, said his farewells, then sailed his pilot boat to shore, passing the flotilla of watermen's bumboats heading in the opposite direction. They were soon clustered around the hull of the ship, clamouring like costermongers as they offered water, beer, fresh meat, fruit, vegetables and passage to shore for any passengers. Grease-dealers climbed on board trying to buy the cook's 'slush' from the voyage and were as quickly repelled by Captain Simonsen.

Lowry tied up at the dock and headed for a waterfront tavern, where his tale of the castaways aboard the *Moctezuma* earned him a few free drinks. The story was circulating through the town well before one of the local watermen, Richard Hodge, brought the three men and Captain Simonsen ashore.

Beyond the breakwater surrounding the inner harbour, Tom saw the rear of the Georgian Customs House at the centre of the quay. Next to it was a taller granite building, housing the harbour master's office, with a top-floor balcony from which he could survey his domain.

Fishing smacks and coasters crowded the waters and half a dozen barques were tied up at the quayside. Another two lay in the repairers' yards further round the bay. Merchants and agents jostled for space on the quayside with crewmen and dock-workers loading and unloading cargo.

The watermen operated out of Barracks Ope Quay, a narrow wharf flanked by a tall warehouse, a quarter of a mile further along the waterfront. Hodge tied up near a fishwife taking crabs from a wicker basket and binding their claws with twine. She tossed them into another basket, where they landed with a clack of shells like the roll of dice on a tavern table.

Hodge helped Tom, Brooks and Stephens from the boat in turn. They stood staring, mouths agape, disoriented and intimidated by the colour, noise and bustle of activity around them as watermen loaded and unloaded their craft, porters touted for business and fishermen, coster-mongers and street hawkers shouted their wares.

Tom remained for a moment on the granite setts at the water's edge, offering a silent prayer of thanks for his deliverance as he explored the unfamiliar sensation of solid ground beneath his feet. He stumbled as he walked along the quay, struggling to readjust after four months of adaptation to the constantly shifting deck of a ship at sea.

Drawn by Gustavus Lowry's tavern tales, a large crowd had gathered at the end of the quay to greet the survivors from the *Mignonette*. Among the spectators was a local customs officer and a sergeant in the Falmouth Harbour Police, James Laverty.

Tom winced with pain as he was seized by the arms, hoisted on to an upturned barrel outside the tavern and forced to address the crowd. As he looked over the sea of faces, uncertain of his reception, he heard boos and jeers from one section of the crowd.

'Why did you not draw lots?' a voice shouted. 'It is the custom of the sea.'

'I offered to,' Tom said. 'My men refused. After a few more days had passed, the lad drank sea-water during the night. He was dying anyway. What, then, would have been the sense in drawing lots between still-living men with families and children depending on them, and a sick and dying orphan boy?'

Tom again scanned the circle of faces below him. There were mutterings, then nods and murmurs of assent. A moment later a voice shouted, 'Three cheers for Captain Dudley and his men, hip-hip—' There was a roar and hats were waved in the air to celebrate the men's survival.

The crowd detained them a little longer, pestering them with questions about the wreck and their ordeal, but finally they were allowed to leave. A precipitous flight of granite steps ran up the narrow alleyway leading to the street. All three men were still very weak and could walk only with difficulty on level ground. It took them almost half an hour to negotiate the steps.

Simonsen stayed with them for a while but then, at Tom's insistence, moved on ahead, making for the office of the German consul in Falmouth.

As the three men reached the street and paused for breath, they were confronted by the customs officer and Sergeant Laverty. 'You are aware that the three of you and the captain of the *Moctezuma* are required to make a deposition about the wreck before the shipping master?'

Tom nodded. 'We are, but may we first rest and eat?'

The customs officer hesitated, looking to Laverty for guidance. He said nothing at first, looking from Tom to the others with an expression of distaste.

'We are on our way to the Sailors' Home,' Tom said, after waiting in vain for some reply. 'We shall break our fast and rest for a while, but we shall appear before the shipping master not later than noon.'

'Be sure you do,' Laverty said, turning on his heel.

The customs officer gave a nervous glance after him, then turned back to Tom with an uncertain smile. 'The sooner you make your depositions, the sooner you will be able to continue your journey home.'

Brooks waited until the man was out of earshot, then looked at Tom. 'What is this statement?'

'It is a formality, but it must be done. It is required by law after the loss of any merchant ship.'

'And is that all the shipping master will wish to know about?'

'He must be told about the boy too.'

'And what will you tell him?'

Tom met his gaze. 'The truth.'

'But, Cap—'

Tom interrupted him: 'What have I to fear from the truth? There is no man walks this earth whose eye I cannot meet, nor one who can say I have wronged him.'

'There is one who no longer walks this earth.' Brooks hurried on as he saw the fury in Tom's expression. 'I beg you, Captain, think again, for all our sakes.'

'I know my mind on this matter. There is nothing to be gained by discussing it further.'

153

Brooks looked about to go on with the argument but then he shook his head and turned away.

The three men made their way to the Royal Cornwall Sailors' Home, where a doctor was at once called. He examined them in turn. 'You have been well nursed on your voyage back to England, gentlemen. You are fortunate indeed to have come through your ordeal so well. Your wounds have been slower to heal, Captain Dudley, and no doubt the humid air of the tropics and your weakened condition must share the blame for that. But I shall give you some salve to ease them and with rest, a proper diet and the good English air to aid you, I am sure they will soon be healed. The deep scars left by your salt-water boils are a different matter, however. I am afraid they will never heal. I have patients who still bear the marks of theirs twenty years after suffering them.'

They ate some breakfast in the wood-panelled dining room and rested for a while, watching the dust motes dance in the sunlight, their peace disturbed only by the slow tick of a grandfather clock, but as soon as the banks were open, Tom went to draw money so that the three of them could cable their families.

Just after nine that morning he sent a telegram to Philippa, in Surrey. '*MIGNONETTE* FOUNDERED 5 JULY, TWELVE HUNDRED MILES FROM THE CAPE. IN BOAT TWENTY-FOUR DAYS, SUFFERING FEARFUL. AM WELL NOW.'

A couple of hours later they passed between the Doric columns of the imposing façade of the Customs House to make the formal deposition for the Board of Trade, required by law after any serious damage, loss, abandonment, or casualty aboard a British-registered merchant ship.

Captain Simonsen had also been summoned to make a statement. In turn, each man was called into the Long Room of the Customs House, and questioned by Robert Cheesman, the local shipping master, receiver of wrecks, collector of customs and superintendent of the Mercantile Marine Office. A clerk laboriously recorded their statements.

Sergeant Laverty was also present, but though the statements were compulsory, their function was to help increase safety at sea, not to provide police evidence for criminal proceedings.

Asked about the loss of the *Mignonette*, Tom came close to an open admission that she had been too old for such a voyage. 'At the time of sailing, the ship was tight, staunch and in every way fit for the voyage. She had two pumps in good working order, worked by hand. The only

154

thing I can say to account for the accident is that the *Mignonette* was rather aged to make the passage. But we proved she was a good sea boat, and had she been a new boat, I feel sure we should have made the passage in perfect safety, if only putting up with a little discomfort.'

In another written statement prepared for the *Mignonette*'s owner, Jack Want, but later deleted by Tom after second thoughts, he appeared to blame the 'stiffness' of the *Mignonette*, caused by the tons of lead carried on its keel and the water butts and other cargo stowed amidships. 'I myself felt when the sea was on the quarter just as if the after end was being knocked away from the solid weight which would now allow the frames to spring as if something bound her amidships.'

Dick Fox, the shipwright at Fay's Yard, later confided to a young apprentice, Vernon Cole, that the *Mignonette* had sunk when the hood ends of the garboard strakes, which fitted into notches in the stern of the ship, had sprung.

Fox had repaired the *Mignonette* by screwing the garboard strakes into the stem, even though he had noticed that the deadwood of the stem had been 'a little sick'. He said that, ever since then, he always drilled right through from one side of a yacht's stem to the other and used copper rods flanged at both ends to secure the garboard strakes.

According to Vernon Cole, he repeated on several occasions, 'I'm sure I did everything right,' an assertion at least partly contradicted by his change of technique, but if blame is to be apportioned for the loss of the yacht, others must share it. Jack Want and Andrew Thompson recruited Tom Dudley to sail an elderly and infirm yacht through some of the most violent oceans on the planet, and Tom himself insisted that the repairs were carried out with recycled wood rather than new.

However, the freak wave remained the major cause of the sinking. Tom, Brooks and Stephens all said that they had never seen a bigger wave and far newer, larger and stronger ships than the *Mignonette* had been sent to the bottom by rogue waves.

The brief statements before the shipping master were soon concluded. The ship's loss was formally attributed to 'stress of weather' – the standard description for a loss caused by a storm or other natural hazard – and Richard Parker's death certificate recorded the cause of his demise as 'killed'.

Cheesman spent some time talking to Tom in the Long Room after he had given his statement. He showed a prurient curiosity in the death of Richard Parker, but his tone was friendly and his only apparent concern was the well-being of Tom and his crew.

'How did you kill the boy?' he said.

Tom described the events, even lying down on the floor to show how Richard had been curled up in the bottom of the boat. He then pulled the knife from his pocket and showed Cheesman how he had used it to cut Richard's throat.

Sergeant Laverty was still present, listening to the exchanges. He held out his hand. 'Be kind enough to give the knife to me.'

'I should not want to lose it,' Tom said. 'I want it as a keepsake.'

Laverty nodded, his hand still extended. 'And you will have it back on some future occasion.'

Tom handed it over and Laverty immediately left the Customs House. After he had gone, Tom passed Cheesman a sheaf of papers, written in his cramped, painstaking hand. 'While I was aboard the *Moctezuma*, I also made a record of the sinking of the *Mignonette*, and of our time aboard the dinghy. I thought to forward it to the ship's owner, Mr Want, in Sydney, but perhaps you first wish to examine it?'

'I shall send it to the Board of Trade with the other documents,' Cheesman said, 'with the request that it be returned to you once the formalities are completed. As you may know, I am required to file a report to the board after any death at sea, but it is usually a matter of routine.

'The board has the power to hold a formal wreck inquiry and even strip an errant ship's officers of their certificates of competence, but such a course of action is usually followed only if passengers have died. I imagine that they will not regard the loss of one seaman aboard a small vessel like the *Mignonette* as worthy of any official comment.

'I will cable the Board of Trade for instructions at once. You can return to the Sailors' Home, but do not leave Falmouth until I have had some reply from London. I hope that you will be free to return to your homes later today.' He shook their hands in turn. 'You have my sympathy, you have endured a terrible ordeal.'

They bade an emotional farewell to Captain Simonsen outside the Customs House. 'Captain,' Tom said, 'without the gentle care of yourself and your wife we should surely have perished, even after our rescue.

Words are not enough to thank you.' His eyes filled with tears as he spoke. 'The only thing that troubles me now is how we can repay you for the kindnesses you have given us. In due course we will present you with something that will ever keep the sufferers of the *Mignonette* in your memory, but we owe you our lives, and that is a debt that can never be repaid. I hope we may meet again one day and may God forbid that either you or any of our brother seamen ever have to go through the hardships we poor souls did.'

The two men embraced, then Simonsen turned and walked away towards the waterfront.

On their way back across Falmouth to the Sailor's Home, Tom stopped to cable his wife again. 'AM HERE AND AS WELL AS CAN BE EXPECTED. HOPE TO BE ENABLED TO FINISH WORK AND LEAVE FOR HOME TONIGHT.'

At twelve fifty-six, a few minutes after Tom had left the Customs House, Cheesman sent a telegram to the Marine Department of the Board of Trade, copied to the Registrar-General of Shipping:

SURVIVORS OF WRECK OF YACHT *MIGNONETTE* OF SOUTH-AMPTON BROUGHT HERE BY GERMAN BARQUE *MOCTEZUMA*, PICKED UP IN LATITUDE 24.28 SOUTH AND LONGITUDE 27.22 WEST. AFTER HAVING BEEN IN OPEN BOAT FOR TWENTY FOUR DAYS AND ONLY TWO ONE POUND TINS OF TURNIPS, NO WATER, RICHARD PARKER, BOY, KILLED ON TWENTIETH DAY BY THOMAS DUDLEY, MASTER, WHO HOLDS MATE'S CERTIFICATE, TO SUSTAIN SURVIVORS' LIVES. I AM TAKING STATEMENTS FOR BOARD OF TRADE. NUMBER OF CAPTAIN DUDLEY'S CERTIFICATE UNKNOWN. BOY WAS KILLED 25TH JULY. A COPY OF THIS TELEGRAM SENT TO THE ASSISTANT SECRETARY, MARINE DEPARTMENT, BOARD OF TRADE. SHOULD THE SURVIVORS BE DETAINED FOR INQUIRY? PLEASE TELEGRAPH IF I MUST APPLY TO POLICE.

Having fulfilled his statutory duty, Cheesman strode off to his club for his customary hearty lunch. James Laverty had no appetite for his own more frugal repast. He had gone straight from the Customs House

157

to the clerk to the justices, John Genn, to obtain a warrant for the three men's arrest, but Genn would not act without the authority of Henry Liddicoat, the chairman of the borough magistrates, and Liddicoat, who was also mayor of Falmouth and a local shopkeeper, was politically astute enough to know where sympathies lay in the town.

He stalled and stonewalled Laverty, then promised to consider his request over lunch and left for his club. When he returned, ninety minutes later, Laverty was still waiting. He had watched Cheesman's interview with the men with a dismay bordering on contempt. The shipping master might have been willing to turn an indulgent or blind eye to some of the lawless ways of the seafaring community – it was even whispered that he took a share of the proceeds of smuggling and wrecking – but Laverty was made of sterner stuff. He had learned to live with the opprobrium of his fellow men. Brought up to a stern and unbending Wesleyan creed in a small community on Bodmin Moor, he saw Falmouth as a sink into which all the depravity, licentiousness and criminality of the county drained as surely as the streams and rivers flowed into Carrick Roads.

Cheesman might look out from his window overlooking the harbour with the proud, paternal gaze of one who saw profit for his community – and himself – in the ships dotting the water, and the agents, traders, watermen and stevedores crowding the wharves, but Laverty's baleful gaze saw only a miasma of corruption emanating from the harbour he policed, like the mist hanging over the water. Footpads, cutpurses, whores, smugglers, river pirates and thieves, they would steal the goods from the wharves, the cargo from ships' holds, and even the ropes and rigging from the masts. When there were no outsiders to rob, they preyed on each other.

Small wonder, then, that even murderers convicted out of their own mouths should be treated like heroes, while those who sought to bring them to justice were reviled. But if Cheesman and that other over-stuffed member of his club, Liddicoat, showed any reluctance to do their duty, Laverty would compel them.

After another hour of fruitless argument with Liddicoat, Laverty switched his attack and returned to the Customs House. There he pressured Cheesman into sending a further cable to the Board of Trade and the registrar-general of shipping: 'PLEASE REPLY TO MY TELEGRAM

RESPECTING *MIGNONETTE* AS SOON AS POSSIBLE AS THE MASTER AND CREW ARE ANXIOUS TO LEAVE FALMOUTH.'

The replies were swift but contradictory. The registrar-general of shipping cabled back at once: 'SURVIVORS SHOULD ALL BE DETAINED, BUT YOU WILL NO DOUBT RECEIVE INSTRUCTIONS FROM THE BOARD OF TRADE.'

When it replied a few minutes later, the Board of Trade counselled that no action should be taken, though they also sent a copy of Cheesman's cable to the Home Office, the ultimate authority in matters of law and order. By the time it arrived there, it was mid-afternoon, and the thoughts of the Home Office civil servants were already turning to the weekend.

No reply was sent that day, but the indefatigable Sergeant Laverty had already returned to Henry Liddicoat. After being hectored for a further hour, he finally secured his own departure for the weekend by signing a warrant for the arrest of Tom Dudley, Edwin Stephens and Edmund Brooks.

In celebration of their safe return from their ordeal, the superintendent of the Sailors' Home, Captain Jose, had cooked a substantial meal for the three men. 'The finest dinner we have had for many a long day,' Brooks said, refilling his plate. 'I never thought to eat such food again.'

Captain Jose had lit a fire against the chill of the September afternoon and the men sat around it drinking strong, sweetened tea as they waited with increasing impatience for permission to leave Falmouth. Late that afternoon, as the setting sun was casting the harbour front into shadow, they heard loud voices and the pounding of heavy boots on the cobbles outside.

'At last,' Tom said. He paused with his cup half-way to his mouth and turned towards the door. Sergeant Laverty strode in, followed by two special constables. Their ruddy faces, calloused hands and ill-fitting uniforms suggested that they had been pulled from the quayside or the farmyard to do their duty.

Laverty stood in front of the three men and drew himself up to his full height. 'Thomas Dudley, Edwin Stephens, Edmund Brooks, you are under arrest.'

159

Tom's cup fell from his fingers and shattered on the floor. 'Arrest? On what charge? What have we done?'

Laverty's moustache seemed to bristle with indignation. 'The charge is murder, the murder of Richard Parker.'

'But we are innocent,' Tom said. 'We have done nothing wrong.'

'That is for the justices to decide.'

They were hustled down the steps and marched through the streets in the gathering dusk. As they passed the telegraph office, Tom held up a hand. 'At least let me send word to my wife, I beg of you. She is expecting me at home tonight.'

Laverty hesitated, as if suspecting a trick. 'Very well, then. Be sharp.'

Tom sent a final terse telegram to his wife. 'SHALL NOT BE ABLE TO COME HOME TONIGHT UNTIL THINGS ARE SETTLED HERE.'

Tom, Brooks and Stephens stood in a line before the high counter of the borough police station as their meagre possessions were taken from them and recorded in the ledger in a clerk's spidery copperplate.

The constables took them down a steep flight of stone steps into the dank cellars of the building. The walls glistened with damp. A row of six oak doors opened off the central corridor. The three men were pushed into a cell and the door banged shut behind them with a thud that reverberated from the bare stone walls.

Four plank beds, little more than shelves, protruded from the walls. There were no mattresses, only a single coarse blanket for each man. A rusty bucket covered with a piece of torn sacking stood in a corner. There was no other furniture and the only light was the dim glow of a lantern burning in the corridor, seeping through the barred grating in the door.

'Why have they arrested us?' Tom said. 'We have done nothing wrong.'

'We should have kept our mouths shut as I warned you,' Brooks said. 'We could still change our story.'

'You would have me lie on oath?' Tom said.

'There are worse crimes. And who would know?'

'God would know. I will not lie.'

Brooks narrowed his eyes as he stared at him, as if squinting into the sun. 'If the truth would hang you and a lie would save your neck, would you still tell the truth?'

'We have nothing to fear from the truth,' Tom said.

Brooks swung away from him. 'And what say you, Stephens?'

The mate was silent for a moment. 'The captain is right. We have done nothing wrong. All we have done is to follow the custom of the sea, like many men before us.' Hesitant at first, his voice grew in conviction as he spoke. 'If we speak the truth and stand together, we have nothing to fear.'

Brooks spat on the floor, walked across the cell and threw himself down on a bunk.

Tom remained motionless, his gaze fixed on him. 'Are you persuaded of this, Brooks? Are we of one mind?'

Brooks did not reply.

'I ask you again. Do we stand together?'

Brooks raised himself on one elbow and stared back at him. 'Aye, we stand together. Damn fools, all of us.'

A few moments later they heard Laverty's voice as he ran down the steps, cursing his constables. 'Have you learned nothing? Do you have straw between those ears?'

The cell door was thrown open again. 'Two of you, out,' Laverty said.

Tom and Stephens were led out and pushed into different cells. For over four months the three men had lived so close they smelt each other's sweat, heard the faintest whisper, saw each other at their lowest ebb. Now they were alone, separated by stone walls and stout oak doors.

Tom paced the cell for some time, hobbling backwards and forwards over the cold stone flags. Only twelve hours before he had blessed the feel of English earth under his feet and thanked God that their ordeal was at an end. He sank to his knees beside the bunk and offered up a prayer for himself and his family. Then he hauled himself upright, holding on to the bunk for support, lay down and closed his eyes. The only sound in the darkness was the drip of water from the slimy walls.

161

PART 2

CHAPTER 13

Tom spent the next thirty-six hours in a dark void. No daylight reached his cell and the passing hours were punctuated only by the arrival of his meals – stale bread and water, and a bowl of thin, watery gruel – and the slopping out of the stinking bucket that served as his toilet.

He saw and heard nothing of the others. Only a warder entered his cell, who neither met his eye nor spoke a word to him as he laid down a platter of food and took away the previous one.

Early on the Monday morning Tom was taken up the stairs to an iron-barred room on the ground floor. Shielding his eyes from the strong sunlight, he studied the other occupants of the room. They sat at a table covered with scrolls of paper, bound with ribbon.

One man was thin and bony, with the high collar and ink-stained suit of a clerk. The other was middle-aged, stout and ruddy-complexioned, with thick sideburns and a bushy moustache. His suit was crumpled and shiny with wear and his waistcoat gaped open between the buttons straining to contain his paunch. He had a jovial look and a warm smile, and looked more like a farmer in town for market-day than a lawyer.

'Captain Dudley, I'm Arthur Tilly.' He spoke with a broad Cornish accent. 'I'm a solicitor here, a partner in Fox and Tilly, and am to defend you in court.'

'Why would I want a lawyer? Is God's truth not defence enough?'

Tilly paused, as if uncertain how to reply. 'Perhaps, but I shall have even greater trust in the Lord if we for our part have first done everything that is humanly possible in your defence.'

'I mean you no offence, Mr Tilly, but I'm sure that once the court has heard the narrative of our sufferings, they will not detain us further. I would prefer to put my trust in the unvarnished truth than in the fine words of a lawyer, no matter how eminent.'

Tilly chuckled. 'Oh, I am far from eminent, Captain Dudley, though I like to think I have served the people of Falmouth well enough over the years. They have great sympathy for your plight and I owe it to them as much as to yourself to see that you are properly represented in court.' He paused. 'It is, after all, a murder charge that you are facing.'

Tom remained silent for some time. 'I am not a wealthy man, Mr Tilly.'

'Nor I, Mr Dudley, and I have no intention of enriching myself at your expense. I am not a celebrated criminal lawyer, but I am an honest man and a hard-working one, and if you will have me as your lawyer, I will defend you to the best of my abilities.'

Tom still remained silent and Tilly paused, searching his expression. He checked his fob watch. 'You are to appear before the magistrates at eleven, and there is no time for another lawyer to acquaint himself with the facts of the case. I shall appear for you this morning, and if you then decide to retain another lawyer to act for you, you are quite at liberty to do so, and you shall not pay me a penny piece. Is this acceptable to you?'

Tom hesitated, then nodded. 'I thank you, Mr Tilly. If I seem doubtful, it is nothing to your discredit, but I have always preferred to stand my ground and fight my own battles.'

Tilly inclined his head. 'And that is your right, but let me represent you before the magistrates this morning and then we shall talk again.'

He paused, seeking Tom's nod of approval before he continued. 'It will be a brief hearing. I expect the prosecution will apply for a remand in custody pending instructions from London, but I shall endeavour to persuade the magistrates to set you at liberty on bail, so that you may return to your family.'

Tears started to Tom's eyes at the thought, but the lawyer laid a hand on his arm. 'Please do not raise your hopes too high. It is almost unheard-of for defendants in a murder case to be released on bail, but I shall do my best for you. Even if I fail I shall, I hope, succeed in persuading the authorities to have you moved from the cells to a room where you may at least get some air and sunlight.'

He paused, his gaze travelling from Tom's sunken eyes to the wasted flesh on his hands. 'What is your state of health?'

Tom shrugged. 'As you would expect. Stephens is the worst of us. He is able to get but little sleep and his head aches very severely. He says he gets so "dazy" at times that if he sits down to write a letter he sometimes forgets the way to spell. We all suffer great pains in our limbs and joints and the muscles of our arms are so tender they will scarcely bear a finger touch. Our feet and legs are also very much swollen. It increases as night comes on and is painfully acute in the tread of the feet.'

He pulled back his sleeve to show the lawyer his arm. 'The whole skin of our bodies is peeling off; when we were picked up we were as yellow as a gold picture frame. We've also noticed that the whites of our nails have started and are growing out. The doctor says it has often been known to supervene upon a severe shock.'

Tilly nodded. 'I shall do my best for you in court, Captain Dudley. That is all I can promise. Now I must speak to your crewmates.'

Just after ten o'clock that morning, Tom, Brooks and Stephens were brought out of their cells and led up the steps. They formed up into a column just inside the doors of the police station with Sergeant Laverty in the van and two burly policemen on either side of each of them. When Laverty pushed open the door, the crowd gathered outside let out a great cheer.

His face white with anger, Laverty began to elbow his way through the crowd. 'You treat common murderers as if they were heroes,' he said. 'Clear a path or you'll try the inside of the lock-up yourselves.'

A hand reached out of the crowd and knocked off his helmet, to another burst of cheering.

Still weak and tired, Tom struggled to maintain the pace that the policemen were setting. They half pushed, half dragged him through the jostling mass of people. Many reached past the police to slap him on the back, but each well-meaning blow caused him to wince in pain.

The procession made its slow way up the steep, cobbled street to the Guildhall, a hundred yards from the quay where they had landed. The tall arched windows flanking the entrance were secured with thick iron bars.

Pale and sweating, Tom was helped up the steps. He had no more than a glimpse of the courtroom before the three of them were hustled down into the holding cell in the cellars.

'Stay with them,' Laverty said to one of his constables. 'Make sure there is no talking between them.'

They waited in silence, listening to the tread of feet and the scrape of chairs on the wooden floor above their heads. Half an hour later they were summoned, and began to climb the steep flight of stone steps. The murmur of the spectators grew to a rumble as Tom and the others entered the dock.

The courtroom, no more than forty feet by twenty, was densely packed. Tom could see even more people blocking the street outside and fighting to press their noses against the windows.

Brooks sat down, but Tom's wounds made it impossible for him to sit on the hard wooden bench and he took his stand at the front of the dock, gripping the rail. Stephens hesitated for a moment, then stood alongside him. He nudged Tom and gestured to the dog-collars on several of the spectators. 'It seems as if every parson for fifty miles around is here.'

'Let's hope they're here to pray for us.'

The justices' clerk, John Genn, called for silence and the eight borough magistrates filed in, led by the chairman, Henry Liddicoat. Genn rose to his feet and read out the charge. Only one witness was called, James Laverty. His face reddened as every eye turned towards him. He bowed his head and began to read from his notebook in a slow West Country burr. He recounted what he had heard in the Long Room of the Customs House as Tom talked to Cheesman, then produced the knife from his pocket. There was a gasp from one or two of the spectators at the sight of the murder weapon.

Laverty placed his bony finger against the side of his neck. 'Dudley told me he put the knife in there and the boy never moved,' he said.

Mr Tilly rose to cross-examine. 'Have you heard the captain say how long they were in the open boat?'

'No, sir, I cannot say I did.'

'Then do you know for a fact that they were in the boat for over twenty days?'

'I never heard them say that,' Laverty said. 'I never had any personal intercourse with them.'

'They voluntarily went to the collector of customs?'

'Yes.'

'And did you hear the collector examining them?'

Laverty paused, as if examining the question for traps. 'No, sir, all I heard was an ordinary conversation between Dudley and the collector in the Long Room.'

'I have nothing further to ask,' Tilly said.

Genn turned to address the bench. 'The solicitor to the Treasury has been instructed to carry on the prosecution,' he said. 'He has applied for a remand in custody.'

Tilly again rose to his feet. 'May it please the bench,' he said, mopping his brow, 'I wish to ask you to allow bail for the prisoners.'

Liddicoat's face showed his surprise. 'And are you prepared to produce bail?'

'I am informed by Captain Dudley that any reasonable bail should be given.' He paused. 'The reasons I make the application are on the grounds that what evidence has been adduced has been volunteered by the prisoners themselves. There has been no attempt in any way to conceal the facts of the case. Further, I would point out that these poor fellows had been twenty days in an open boat without food and without water before they did what they did.

'There is no wish on their part to shirk inquiry. They have been actuated with no other idea than that of having the facts of the case brought before the tribunal of their country. On all these grounds I would ask you to admit them to bail.'

Liddicoat and his fellow magistrates consulted together for some time. As Tom stood there watching them, gripping the rail of the dock, he again felt tears welling up in his eyes. Although he felt foolish and embarrassed at weeping in front of this courtroom full of people, still he could not prevent the tears from rolling down his face.

Liddicoat rapped the bench with his gavel. 'We have given the point serious consideration, but we regret that the circumstances of the case prevent us from granting the request for bail. The case is adjourned until Thursday of this week.'

There were mutterings from the public section and then a woman shouted, 'Shame on you, Henry Liddicoat. Have they not suffered enough?'

The cry was taken up by the crowd outside. The mayor flushed and spread his hands, then directed a venomous look at Sergeant Laverty.

Tears still running down his face, Tom and the others were marched back through the streets to the borough lock-up. Tilly accompanied them. 'If we are not to be allowed bail, Captain Dudley, the least we can do is ensure that your accommodation is rather more comfortable than the stinking cellars of this building.'

He raised his voice. 'Superintendent Bourne?'

Rolling like a ship on the ocean as he walked, the rotund police superintendent had ambled over from the courtroom just in front of them, deep in conversation with the reporter from the *Western Morning News*.

'Mr Tilly?' His speech was as ponderous as his gait.

'Superintendent, it is quite intolerable that after all the privations that these men have endured on the high seas, they are now incarcerated in your foul dungeons.'

'They are charged with murder, Mr Tilly.'

'That is a mere technicality, Superintendent. Would you throw them in gaol with common criminals?'

The superintendent hesitated. 'What other accommodation would you propose?'

'You have an apartment within this building, do you not?'

'I do, but I hardly see—'

'Then surely these men can be accommodated in one of the rooms there.'

'I – I suppose they can.'

'And the three of them will be accommodated together?'

As the superintendent again hesitated, Sergeant Laverty intervened, his face reddening with anger. 'I cannot allow that. These men could then concoct whatever story they wished.'

Tom's fists clenched in anger, but Tilly laid a restraining hand on his arm. 'Really, Sergeant,' he said. 'These men have been at sea for almost six weeks since their rescue. If it had been their wish to concoct a story, surely that would have been time enough? Yet even you must admit they have exhibited no desire to do anything other than utter the plain, unvarnished truth.'

He held Laverty's gaze and eventually the policeman muttered something indistinct and turned away.

Tilly touched the tips of his index fingers together as if ticking off the first point on a list. 'And then there is the matter of food. These men were starved to the point of death. Look at them now. They are still little more than walking skeletons. They need decent food, not prison slops.' He turned to Tom. 'Do you have the means to pay for meals?'

'I have enough to pay for meals for all three of us.'

'You have no objection to food being sent in for them, Superintendent? Mr Dudley will pay for it.'

The police chief raised his shoulders in a faint shrug. 'I have no objection.'

Tilly swung back to face Tom again. 'I bid you good-day, Captain Dudley. I shall call on you in the morning when we shall begin preparations for your defence.'

'Thank you for what you have done for us today, Mr Tilly, but God's truth is the only preparation I need.'

The lawyer smiled. 'I envy you, Captain Dudley. I shall need considerably more than that. Until the morning, then.'

The superintendent's apartments were on the first floor of the building. If cramped, the room into which Tom, Brooks and Stephens were ushered was at least dry and airy, but the iron bars on the window were a constant reminder of their plight.

Whatever doubts there had been in Falmouth about the failure of the men to draw lots had now been forgotten. Collections were already being taken in the streets and taverns to pay Tilly's fees for their defence, and there was only sympathy and support for the three men, coupled with hostility to those responsible for keeping them behind bars. But whatever a seafaring community might have thought, they were soon made aware that metropolitan opinion would be very different.

Along with the meals Tom had ordered, supplied by a neighbouring inn, the turnkey brought them the local newspaper. In addition to reporting their appearance before the bench in minute detail, it also reprinted the editorials on the case in the London papers.

If Tom was surprised that the case of the *Mignonette* should command national coverage, he was horrified by its nature. The *London Standard* set the tone.

171

The mere outlines of the tragedy are so revolting that we might under other circumstances have set it down as the ravings of a brain disordered by hunger and hardship, but we fear that this last comfort is denied us.

The picked bones of the cabin boy were lying by the side of those who had devoured him when the *Moctezuma* came alongside the boat, and the men have told the story with such circumstantiality that they will find it difficult to modify their cold-blooded narrative in any of its most damning features when they appear in the dock to stand their trial for the murder of Richard Parker.

Evidently they expected no such episode at the end of their voyage and until the law has decided whether three men are justified, in order to save their own lives, in taking that of a fourth, we may forbear to discuss the ethics of a tragedy the callousness of which it is hard to redeem by any casuistry.

The *Spectator* was no more sympathetic.

The magistrates of Falmouth have done a public service in arresting Captain Dudley of the yacht *Mignonette* upon the charge of murder, and in insisting upon an open inquiry. It is high time that the hideous tradition of the sea which authorizes starving sailors to kill and eat their comrades, should be exposed in a Court of Justice and sailors be taught once for all that the special dangers of their profession furnish no excuse for a practice as directly opposed to human as it is to divine law.

Nobody doubts that shipwrecked sailors left without food in open boats have in certain instances killed each other and have sustained life for various periods on human flesh, and nothing would be gained by calling attention once more to incidents so horrible. The case of the *Mignonette* is, however, peculiar in this, that it reveals in a special way and past all question, the hold which the diabolical tradition has upon all sailors and, as we discover with surprise, even upon landsmen.

The sole authority for the shocking stories that have incriminated them is the yachtsmen themselves. So complete is the belief of sailors in their right to eat their comrades that Captain Dudley, believed to be a most respectable man and certainly with an excellent record, who spoke most kindly to his victim and asked God's pardon before he took his life, without any compulsion voluntarily related the whole story to the Custom House officers at Falmouth in all its details, some of which are worse than any we have given, and subsequently signed his narrative as a formal deposition.

He did not, be it understood, make a confession as one who committed a crime and was full of remorse, but simply narrated with the straightforward truthfulness with which a sailor usually describes any noteworthy incident of a voyage. He had apparently had no idea whatever that he was liable to legal proceedings and when arrested expressed nothing but astonishment.

Before the magistrates he denied nothing, but broke repeatedly into tears. He was in fact obviously originally a decent man of the ordinary type under the influence of the traditional feeling of his profession that cannibalism is excusable in a starving sailor and that even killing a man in order to eat him is, if all alike perishing in an open boat, not an act amenable to human justice.

That is the belief of all seamen and even of Arctic voyagers, and of course tends directly to induce them when in extremity to resort to the traditionary means. To our amazement, we find at least half the journalists who have mentioned the case are of the same opinion. The public in the port is on the same side and the Falmouth magistrates are blamed for breach of the un-written law which compels or, it is argued, should compel us to condone or pass over such offences.

We have little patience, we confess, with a modern tolerance of cannibalism which came out so strongly in the discussion of the recent case in the Arctic regions. It is excusable on the ground of insanity caused by suffering but on no other grounds whatever.

There are things which man has no right to do, not by reason of their consequences but because they are forbidden by the most direct command, the inner conscience, which is the same in all races and all regions. There is no good race of cannibals and never will be and no race which when it has once risen to the possession of full consciousness is not instinctively ashamed at the practice and debased by having resort to it.

In its origin cannibalism springs from an enthusiasm for murder from the spirit of brutal destruction carried to its last, extreme expression, and is as little to be excused as any other crime against the inherent instinct.

The Times took much the same line, expressing surprise that, 'The common people received them with every mark of sympathy and regard, and treat them as if they had performed some meritorious and praiseworthy act.' It also approvingly quoted a British precedent in 1836 when the dead were cast overboard, 'lest the living should be tempted to forget themselves and seek relief from their misery in a horrible repast'.

The only consolation that Tom and Stephens could draw from the paper was that reporters had also interviewed both Philippa and Ann at their homes. The accounts gave them their first news of their wives since they had set sail.

Philippa was,

in frail health and very concerned for her husband. She was continuing to teach at the Newtown Board School where she had received a large number of letters from friends and former subordinates and superiors of Captain Dudley. All expressed their highest admiration of him. One person wrote to him: 'I have thought of you many times since you left and tell you candidly I was afraid you would not get by with the yacht.'

'I believe my husband has told everything as it happened,' Mrs Dudley said. 'He was always candid and I don't think he means to contradict the main incident but I cannot believe they were in their right minds. There must be something else. Put yourself in his place. Would not any man with a wife at home and children dependent upon him have acted similarly? I have heard that it was he who went back for food while the others entreated him not to risk his life. He must be a brave man to have done that. And he is a Christian man.'

Tom immediately wrote Philippa a letter, which she received the following morning.

> No harm can come to me or any of us dear, be sure and trust in God to give you strength to bear the horrid lies that are in the papers. They say it was my statement that has caused the inquiry. I have told the truth. If I had told a lie I should be sharing the comforts of home instead of being here. Don't think about coming down; it would only make you ill, the journey and seeing me here.

He took it for granted that she had already read the details of their ordeal in the press reports but she had refused to read any of them, preferring to await Tom's own version of events. The little knowledge she had gleaned of 'the thrilling and harrowing story', as she called it, had come only from what friends had told her and the brief references in Tom's letters.

Stephens wept as he read the newspaper interview with his wife. She was,

> in a state of great mental distress and burst into tears at the mere mention of the troubles of her husband. She has received several affectionate letters from him since his detention at Falmouth. He says he is still so ill that he has had the attendance of the doctor every day since landing. He begged her not to believe all that had been said about him in the papers and to bear up until she hears from his own lips the story of the fearful trials he had gone through.
>
> At Madeira he wrote saying he would stop in Australia if she would join him as there seemed to be no luck for him in England. She had replied that with her five little children she would come out as soon as possible. The letter never reached him. She declared he was one of the kindest and noblest of husbands who would not harm a living creature willingly.

Tom had only just finished reading the reports when the turnkey opened the door and led him downstairs to the ground floor, where the lawyer and his clerk were waiting for him.

'You are up betimes, Mr Tilly.'

'There is much to do, Captain Dudley, and I cannot deny that I will take a certain pleasure—' He paused. 'Forgive me for saying that about so grave a misfortune for you and your crew, but for forty years I have attempted to settle squabbles between neighbours, husbands and wives, or farmers arguing over grazing rights. I have drawn up wills, conveyanced properties, and defended drunkards, smugglers and petty thieves. It is a rare pleasure, and again I apologize for the use of the word, for me to be involved in a case of such great import as this.' He flushed. 'That is not to say I have not the skills and experience to defend you, of course.'

Tom was forced to smile. 'Of course, of course.'

'I promise you that we shall not fail for the want of effort on my part. May I take it, then, that you are content for me to continue as your lawyer?'

'For the moment, yes, but I am yet to be fully convinced of its necessity.'

Tilly inclined his head in acknowledgement. 'In due course I shall need from you a list of those gentlemen who might testify to your good and Christian character, but first I would wish you to tell me in your own words the story of the voyage of the *Mignonette*. Omit no detail germane to the charge you face.'

He poured Tom a glass of water from an earthenware jug. The clerk dipped his pen in the inkwell, then waited with an expectant look, his pen poised over a sheaf of blank paper.

Tom gazed out of the window. Through the gap between the buildings on the opposite side of the street he could see a flight of steps running down towards the waterfront. Ships jostled for space at the quay and beyond them he glimpsed a three-master sailing on the morning tide, making for the open water beyond the Roads.

'You are a sailing master?' Tilly prompted.

'Latterly, yes. I've been a sailing master these last ten years, like my father before me. But I've served my time on fishing smacks, coasters and cargo ships, as cabin boy, able seaman, cook-steward, boatswain and mate.'

'So you had to learn to butcher animals?'

Tom turned a cool gaze on the lawyer. 'I learned that knack, yes.'

'And the *Mignonette* was your ship?'

Tom shook his head. 'It is a rich man's sport and I am far from a rich man. A few yacht-owners skipper their own vessels, but most hire a master and crew for the yachting season. I hire myself as sailing master to one of them from March to September and in winter I take whatever work I can find – on fishing boats, oyster dredgers, or as a merchant seaman. Sailing master is a safer and better living than any of those. It's a good wage and there's a share of the prize money too. I've known owners give the whole purse to their captain and crew.'

'A good wage, yes,' Tilly said. 'But safer?'

Tom gave a rueful smile. 'If you stay in inshore waters. Racing yachts don't even put to sea in storm conditions. They carry too much canvas.' As he spoke, his gaze travelled upwards, as if he expected to see the sails and rigging of a yacht rather than a plaster ceiling.

'Yet you were sailing a yacht to Australia.'

'The *Mignonette* was built as a cruiser and fishing-boat. Only later was she turned into a racing-yacht.' His eyes strayed back to the window, following the three-master as it approached the mouth of the Roads. As he began to recount the story of the voyage, he could almost hear the creak of wood and crack of canvas as the sails filled with wind and the ship picked up speed, passing out of sight down the Channel towards the open sea.

CHAPTER 14

When Tom had finished his tale, Tilly sat in thought for some time. 'Why did you stop Brooks from throwing the fragments of the boy's flesh overboard when you were rescued?'

'Because it had been my intention from the first to retain them if we should fall in with a vessel, so that we could state the circumstances under which we acted.'

Tilly gave a slow nod, then began searching through the papers in front of him. 'And after you landed you went with Brooks and Stephens to the Customs House and made the statement before the shipping master, of which I have a copy here? "On the twentieth day the lad, Richard Parker, was very weak through drinking salt water. Deponent with the assistance of the Mate, Stephens, killed him to sustain the existence of those remaining, they being all agreed the act was absolutely necessary."

'Stephens's statement was equally candid. "On the twentieth day deponent agreed with the Master that it was absolutely necessary that one should be sacrificed to save the rest and the Master selected Richard Parker, boy, as being the weakest. Deponent agreed to this and the Master accordingly killed the lad."'

He sat back and studied Tom for a moment. 'What do you know of Brooks?'

'He's an Essex man, like me. I'd never sailed with him but I'd known him for a dozen years or so. He's sailed on some of the best racing yachts and is a first-class hand. He worked as a rigger at Fay's Yard on the Itchen during the winter. That's where he heard I was looking for hands.

'He'd been offered a berth on a new yacht, the *Irex*, but he told me he was thinking about emigrating. There were rumours that he had deserted a wife and children. I charged him with it, but he denied it on his oath. I cannot speak to the truth of it.'

'A copy of Brooks's statement to Mr Cheesman is not yet to hand,' Tilly said. 'Do you have any idea what he said?'

Tom shook his head. 'Neither myself nor Stephens was in the room when Brooks made his statement, but he would have said the same.'

'Are you sure of this?'

For the first time a shadow of doubt crossed Tom's face. 'I'm sure. Why?'

'No matter.'

Tom gave him an uncertain look. 'Mr Cheesman seemed most sympathetic to our plight.'

'No doubt he was,' Tilly said. 'As shipping master, he had a legal duty to report any death at sea, but he also knows how often shipwrecked seamen have been forced to resort to the custom of the sea. Had it been left in his hands, or had you claimed that the boy had drowned with the wreck or died of natural causes while adrift in the dinghy, I'm sure the incident would have been quietly buried in the files of the Board of Trade.

'Unfortunately your determination and even eagerness to tell the whole truth, while it does you great credit, did alert Sergeant Laverty, who was much less sympathetic. According to Mr Cheesman, Laverty said he had no intention of allowing officials in Whitehall to decide whether you should be prosecuted. He had witnessed your full confession to the crime of murder, corroborated by Stephens, and you had handed him the murder weapon.

'He immediately left the Customs House to obtain a warrant for your arrest. The chairman of the justices of the peace was very aware of the widespread sympathy for you in the town and I know that he showed a marked reluctance to sign a warrant, but I'm afraid Laverty was not to be denied.'

'But the charges will be dropped? It will go no further?'

Tilly hesitated, selecting his words with care. 'News of your arrest is already widespread and there is great public sympathy for you, not just in seafaring communities like Falmouth but throughout the country. But it is not shared by the Home Office.'

'But we were simply following the custom of the sea.'

Tilly pressed the tips of his fingers together and studied them in silence before raising his eyes to meet Tom's gaze. 'I'm afraid you should not put your trust in the custom of the sea. No matter how many shipwrecked men have had resort to it, it has no legal status whatsoever.'

Tom's expression darkened, but when he spoke, his voice remained strong and certain. 'Then I'll put my faith in God's truth and English justice. We have committed no crime and no jury of Englishmen will convict us.'

Tilly pursed his lips and looked away from Tom's unwavering gaze. 'I hope your trust is not misplaced.'

While Tilly was preparing Tom's defence, the Home Office civil servants had turned their attention to the cables from the Board of Trade. The notes written on the Home Office file as it passed up the official pyramid reflect the uncertainty and ambivalence felt – at low levels at least – about a prosecution.

The first annotation, made on the morning of Monday, 8 September, as Tom, Brooks and Stephens were appearing before the Falmouth magistrates, read: 'It does not appear to me a case in which any action should be taken. They had been nineteen days without food or drink, were driven mad with thirst and the only question was whether they should kill the boy or all of them die.'

Later the same day, a second official added: 'If they are committed on a capital charge the case will in ordinary course come into the hands of the Treasury Solicitors.'

The attorney general, Sir Henry James, also saw the file and wrote at once to the home secretary, Sir William Harcourt. 'The *Mignonette* people ought to be properly prosecuted. They certainly ought to be convicted, for if the principle of these proceedings be admitted as correct and justifiable I shall decline for the future to sit near any men with a large appetite.'

When the file reached the home secretary, any doubts about the proper course of action were removed. 'This is a very dreadful case. The law must decide what is the character of this terrible act. I presume the men will be committed. In any case I should wish the Public Prosecutor to take charge of the case so that it may be properly dealt with.'

His instruction to the Board of Trade was even more specific: 'If these men are not tried for murder, we are giving carte blanche to every ship's captain, whenever he runs low on provisions, to eat his cabin boy.'

The Crown already possessed the self-incriminating statements given to the collector of customs and the murder weapon, but other evidence was also secured. Richard Hodge was sent back to the *Moctezuma*, which was still in port awaiting orders to sail, and towed the *Mignonette*'s dinghy into the harbour. It was locked up in a private warehouse, Mr Buckingham's store at Upton Slip, where it was examined by officials from the Customs House.

Hodge also brought ashore the other items from the dinghy: two paddles, the brass crutches for the oars, the chronometer and its metal case, the sextant and a bundle of clothing. A packet of papers fell out of the clothes as they were being unloaded and Sergeant Laverty examined them. They were drafts in Tom's hand describing the sinking of the *Mignonette* and the fate of Richard Parker. They did not deviate significantly from the one that Tom had already handed to Cheesman, but Laverty added them to the now-bulging file of evidence and witness statements.

When he was handed the clothes later that day, Tom searched through them. 'Did you not find any papers?'

'I did,' Laverty said.

'Please give them to me. They are my private property.'

'They were. They are Crown exhibits now.'

On the Tuesday evening, 10 September, Tom heard a commotion from Superintendent Bourne's apartment. Richard Parker's eldest brother, Daniel, who bore a strong likeness in both looks and voice to his brother, had been working as a hand on the yacht *Marguerite*. It was at anchor in Torquay when he heard of the death of his brother and the arrest of Tom, Brooks and Stephens. 'I only heard a little bit about the news on Sunday afternoon and I could not believe it was true, but on

Monday morning the skipper of the yacht read it out from the papers to all hands and we were, of course, much shocked.'

Daniel at once asked the captain for leave to go to Falmouth for the hearing at the magistrates' court. As soon as he arrived, he went straight to the police station and was shown upstairs into Superintendent Bourne's apartment. Tom had never met Daniel and had not seen him arrive, but when he overheard the two men talking, he cried out, 'Why, that's Richard's voice.'

Daniel at once asked to see the three defendants, and persisted until he had overcome the initial opposition of the superintendent and the vociferous protests of Sergeant Laverty.

As he entered their room, Tom stood up and extended his hand. After a momentary hesitation, Daniel shook hands with each man in turn, first Tom, then Brooks, then Stephens.

'You are so like your brother,' Tom said. 'He was a fine lad and a credit to you.'

Daniel nodded. 'He was always a smart little chap. He knocked about on the boats and got his own living almost as soon as he could crawl. He had it a little bit rough like the rest of us, but I can tell you there was not a healthier young fellow in the place.' He paused. 'I was filling out my vessel at Lymington at the time he went away. I saw him after he had shipped on the *Mignonette* but if I had seen him before he signed articles I might have persuaded him not to go.'

He looked away from them, gazing out of the window, then swung back to meet Tom's steady gaze. 'Why did you not draw lots, as the custom of the sea requires?'

'My men refused to,' Tom said, his voice matter-of-fact. 'I would have taken my chance with the rest, but they would not do so. Then, the poor boy drank sea-water one night. He was dying anyway and we had wives and children depending on us. To save the lives of three, I hastened his end.' He held Daniel's gaze. 'Had I my time over again, I would do no different.'

Daniel remained with them for another forty minutes. The talk was friendly, ranging from the voyage of the *Mignonette* and the causes of its sinking, to their mutual acquaintances in the small world of professional yacht-racing.

At length, he stood up. 'My object in coming here was to let people know that someone owned Dick, and I am very glad I did so, because it has set my mind at rest a little. I shall be at the courts on Thursday.'

He shook hands with them all again, then rapped on the door. Laverty opened it so quickly he must have been waiting outside. Once more, his expression showed his displeasure.

The next morning Tilly called to see Tom. 'A retired gentleman, Captain Douglas, has expressed a desire to talk with you. He is waiting outside.'

Tom's expression did not change and after a moment, Tilly added, 'He has travelled some distance.'

'And why would I wish to meet him?'

'He would give you valuable counsel.'

'Then let us see this gentleman.'

Captain Douglas was white-haired and stoop-shouldered, but he had a seaman's weather-beaten face and his hazel eyes were clear and sharp. His grip was firm as he shook Tom's hand. 'Captain Dudley, thank you for seeing me. I have come at Mr Tilly's request . . .'

Tom gave the lawyer a sharp look.

'. . . to offer you some advice, if you will have it. I was the police magistrate in Singapore when the survivors of the *Euxine* were landed there. You know of the ship?'

Tom nodded, his unblinking stare fixed on Douglas. 'I know of it.'

'Ten years ago, Sir William Harcourt's predecessor as home secretary tried to set a legal precedent by prosecuting the men involved for murder. Like you, the survivors from the *Euxine* had neither denied the killing nor hidden the evidence.

'They were taken from Batavia to Singapore, where the shipping master sought the opinion of the attorney general. He notified the Board of Trade in London that there was no necessity for any judicial inquiry and that the men were "free to engage themselves on any vessel requiring their services".

'However, a letter from a former sea-captain to the *Singapore Daily Times* forced the hand of the governor.' Douglas passed Tom a yellowing newspaper clipping and sat in silence as he read it.

This story is told from their own lips, and horrifying to relate, they seem to consider that they were justified in committing the atrocious murder for the sake of appeasing their own wants . . .

I trust that for humanity's sake and for the credit of my brother seamen to whatever nationality they may belong, that steps be taken to bring these man-eaters to justice, and that from Singapore may go forth the decision that under no circumstances, however great the sufferings may be, are seamen allowed to sacrifice one of their number that others may live.

I am fully aware, after having some forty years' experience of a sailor's life, that during the dull night watches they are in the habit of relating such horrible stories of suffering which may have come to their ears, and by recounting them they may imperceptibly come to the conclusion that they are justified under certain emergencies in sacrificing one of their number. The sooner they are disabused of the idea the better. I recommend prayer not cannibalism in such emergencies.

Tom refolded the clipping and passed it back, and Douglas told him the remainder of the tale of the *Euxine*, holding his gaze as if determined to impress on him the importance of what he said.

The paper had followed up the publication of the letter with a leader demanding a judicial inquiry to establish the law once and for all. The governor felt any trial should take place in a British court, not in a remote dependency, but the Colonial Office ordered him to proceed with an inquiry in Singapore.

Two of the survivors were persuaded to appear as witnesses for the prosecution, on the promise of a free pardon providing they gave their evidence in 'an unexceptionable manner'. The remainder were charged with murder. The committal proceedings began before Captain Douglas on 30 January. They reflected the attorney general's lack of enthusiasm. The Crown called only one witness, the shipping master, Captain Ellis.

He had copies of the depositions made in Batavia made by the accused men, but the originals had been sent to London and the copies were inadmissible as evidence. All that Captain Ellis could say was that the second mate of the *Euxine*, James Archer, had voluntarily confessed that a crewman had killed the cabin boy. It was neither a confession by Archer nor admissible as evidence of a confession by the crewman.

Captain Ellis's own testimony was no more helpful to the Crown. During cross-examination it emerged that he had once been shipwrecked himself and cast adrift in an open boat. Asked if the men were responsible for their actions, he replied, 'Certainly not. I feel sure they were not in a position to know right from wrong.'

He was then asked as a matter of naval history whether there were other instances of shipwrecked men drawing lots as to who should die for the rest and replied, 'Yes, twenty or twenty-five years ago these cases were most common. I have never heard of men being punished for doing so.'

The hearing was adjourned indefinitely to enable the prosecution to collect further evidence, but the *Java Packet* had long since sailed without leaving more than a barely useful affidavit from the captain. The only other admissible evidence – the originals of the men's confessions – was in London. The authorities in Singapore were also concerned that an acquittal or conviction for the minor offence of culpable homicide, where the person killed consents to his own death or takes the risk of death with his own consent, would send an undesirable message to seamen that it was acceptable to eat their fellows.

The attorney general favoured a trial in London.

> The law as laid down in an English court would have more weight in all parts of the world and would probably be considered binding in all parts of the British dominions, whereas the law as laid down by the courts here would not be binding even upon the court itself, and this being the first case of its kind which has ever been proposed to be tried it is important that the principles that govern cases of this sort in future should be authoritatively upheld.

Officials at the Board of Trade in London were much less enthusiastic about a prosecution. As one noted,

> I suppose we should send this to the Home Office, but no steps will be taken by that department. There is a horrible sanity

about all these proceedings but the men were not, I believe, responsible for their actions. No social advantage can be derived from prosecution or punishment. To live must be sufficient punishment.

The assistant secretary at the Marine Department of the board concurred. 'It is not likely that any jury would convict and if a Court of Law were to stamp this custom with clear authority it might be made a pretext for getting rid of troublesome people. I should be inclined to leave it alone, the details are too disgusting to take to court.'

The permanent under-secretary called it,

One of the very saddest and most disgusting incidents that I have known. The act was done under the direct pressures of necessity and it is too abhorrent to all the feelings of human nature to be repeated, except under similar circumstances. Punishment if practical or exposure are not needed and would have no effect in future cases.

The ship's articles were annotated by a clerk, who wrote 'Killed by the crew for food', after the name of the boy, and the papers were sent to the Home Office as a formality. Officials there showed considerably more appetite for a prosecution, but there were considerable legal problems in trying in London a case concerning murder on the high seas, and involving men detained first in Singapore, and key witnesses who were Dutch nationals and currently at sea somewhere on the five oceans. The Home Office also shared the fear that an acquittal would send a wrong signal to seamen.

The attorney general wanted the men sent back to England on the warship HMS *Adventure*. In fact, they returned on a merchant ship, the *Nestor*. It had already sailed with the men on board when the Colonial Office, alarmed at the illegality of returning them to England, sent a cable telling the Singapore authorities not to do so.

The five survivors arrived in London, aboard the *Nestor*, on 9 July and were held in custody for five days while civil servants dithered over what to do. The Home Office remained very eager for a prosecution to establish a leading case defining the law. Two factors weighed against them.

The first was the lack of evidence. The witnesses were in Batavia, Singapore and, in the case of the *Java Packet*, on the high seas. The only admissible evidence was the depositions of the men involved which were vague and contradictory. Detaining the men without charge and shipping them half-way round the world was also plainly illegal.

Douglas paused. 'There was also a political dimension to the case of the *Euxine*. You have heard of Sir Edward Bates?'

'The ship-owner? I've heard of him, and nothing but bad at that. They say he overloads his ships and starves the men who crew them.'

Douglas nodded. 'He was also a Conservative Member of Parliament. When the men of the *Euxine* arrived in Britain, Mr Disraeli's government was under great pressure from "the seaman's friend", Samuel Plimsoll.

'In July of that year Mr Plimsoll addressed the House of Commons. He spoke of thousands of living beings consigned to undeserved and miserable death in coffin-ships. He described the murderous tendencies of ship-owners and before he was shouted down, he pronounced himself determined to unmask the villains who sent thousands to death and destruction. He named Edward Bates as one of them, "a ship-knacker", who owned three ships sunk the previous year with the loss of eighty-seven lives.

'Amongst the ships Bates owned was the *Euxine*. It would have been a political catastrophe for the Government if the trial had gone ahead. Here was a prominent member of the Conservative Party already accused of starving the men who served on his ships. The men of the *Euxine*, forced to resort to cannibalism to survive, would have been seen as living proof of that.

'Much against their own wishes, Home Office officials were persuaded to drop the prosecution. The home secretary, R. A. Cross, made his decision on the thirteenth of July, and the parliamentary under-secretary of state then wrote to the Board of Trade.'

He referred to the papers on his lap. '"With reference to the Italian seaman who was killed and partially eaten on board a boat containing some of the survivors of the wrecked vessel *Euxine*, I am directed to acquaint you that, after careful consideration of all the circumstances, the Secretary of State does not consider that this is a case in which it would be advisable to institute proceedings against these men."'

'The defendants were released and allowed to return to sea, only after they had signed pledges not to seek legal redress from Edward Bates.' He paused again, studying Tom closely. 'I tell you all this, precisely because it is my belief that the Home Office has long been waiting for another opportunity to set the full weight of the law against the custom of the sea. Your own case has provided them with that opportunity, and by a cruel twist of fate, Samuel Plimsoll has, albeit unwittingly, been the instrument by which the home secretary, Sir William Harcourt, has been empowered to order your prosecution.'

Sir William George Granville Venables Vernon Harcourt was fifty-seven. Elected as Liberal MP for Oxford in 1868, he was Gladstone's solicitor general from 1873 to 1874 and had been home secretary since 1880. He was an extremely intelligent and erudite man – a former professor of international law at Cambridge and such a prolific correspondent with *The Times* under the pseudonym 'Historicus' that his collected letters had been published in 1863 – but he was far from unworldly.

One contemporary, Augustine Birrell, described him as 'a good, old-fashioned parliamentary bruiser'. Sir Henry Campbell-Bannerman, less circumspect, compared him to a 'big salmon . . . lurking under his stone, and ready for occasional plunges which will not always be free from a sinister intention'.

Harcourt's tenure as home secretary had threatened to be over almost before it had begun, for he lost his seat at Oxford by fifty-four votes in the general election of May 1880. He began at once to cast around for another safe seat.

Samuel Plimsoll knew that his trusted friend Joseph Chamberlain was now installed as president of the Board of Trade, and he was concerned about the demands his own parliamentary duties were placing upon him at a time when his wife Eliza was in failing health. He was accordingly persuaded to stand down as MP for Derby in favour of Harcourt. In return he extracted a promise from the home secretary that he would champion Plimsoll's lifetime campaigns on behalf of seamen.

The electors of Derby showed some reservations about the move and Plimsoll wrote to Harcourt: 'There is greater reluctance than I expected. The nonconformists and radicals are sore but I am hopeful of success. If we succeed you had better appoint me your election agent. I am qualified and should of course act gratuitously.'

On 18 May 1880, Plimsoll stood on the balcony of the Midland Hotel in Derby and introduced Harcourt to the crowd as 'a gentleman who I hope will be your future member. Do not believe that I am abandoning the [seamen's] cause. I believe that by standing aside now and giving the post of honour to a stronger man, I am really helping the cause much more effectively than it has ever been in my power to advance it.'

Harcourt was returned unopposed a week later. A *Punch* cartoon showed Harcourt as 'A man overboard rescued by the Sailor's Friend' – Plimsoll, in seaman's uniform.

Eliza Plimsoll wrote to Harcourt:

> Thank you much for your good opinion of my dear husband. Those who know him best think most highly of him, and I am sure he will rejoice to have given up his seat, if by doing so he has secured for the sailors a more powerful friend than he was himself. A truer one they could not have ... I hope you will long continue Member for Derby as my husband has done, as the representative of the 'Working Men'.

Far from being a powerful friend to the sailors, however, the only time that Harcourt interested himself in nautical matters during his term as home secretary was when instigating the prosecution of Dudley, Brooks and Stephens for the murder of Richard Parker.

Douglas held up his hand as Tom started to speak. 'Captain Dudley, we are men of the sea and we know what a harsh mistress she can be. You and I and many others will feel that you have committed no wrong, but that is not the way it will appear to the gentlemen in Whitehall.' He held Tom's gaze. 'I most strongly urge you to avail yourself to the full of the legal advice being offered to you. It is my belief you will have full need of it.' He got to his feet. 'I bid you goodbye and good fortune.'

For some time after Douglas had left Tom sat in silence. When he raised his head, he found Tilly's eyes upon him. 'Very well, Mr Tilly, I am convinced. I shall be grateful for all the legal advice you can offer me.'

The lawyer broke into a broad smile.

Tom received one more visitor that morning, a florid-faced West Countryman by the name of John Burton, proprietor of a noted Falmouth attraction, the Old Curiosity Shop. Its contents were not dissimilar to those described by Dickens in the book of the same name:

> ... one of those receptacles for old and curious things which seem to crouch in odd corners of this town ... suits of mail standing like ghosts in armour, here and there; fantastic carvings brought from monkish cloisters; rusty weapons of various kinds; distorted figures in china, and wood, and iron, and ivory; tapestry, and strange furniture that might have been designed in dreams.

A West Country P. T. Barnum, Burton had even made an unsuccessful attempt to buy the Eddystone lighthouse and have it re-erected in Falmouth as an attraction.

After a visit from the Duke and Duchess of Edinburgh, who 'spent upwards of an hour at Mr Burton's Old Curiosity Shop' in March 1882, the proprietor, an economical man, had his original Gothic script notepaper overprinted in strident block capitals. From then on, it was always

ROYAL
"𝔅urton's / 𝔄uriosity 𝔖hop, 𝔉almouth."

The notepaper also proudly proclaimed visits from the home secretary, Sir William Harcourt, in April 1882, and Sir Garnet Wolseley in May of that year, and boasted of Burton's 'Direct Communications with Buyers in Constantinople, Nagasaki, Zanzibar, Shanghai, Trincomalee, Rangoon, Akyab, Moulmain, Poonah, Singapore', and a host of other exotic ports.

After some thought, Tom accepted Burton's offer to stand bail and help to raise money for the costs of the three men's defence in return for access to those papers and artefacts from the *Mignonette* that had not been impounded by Sergeant Laverty.

190

Tilly was hovering outside the door when Burton had left. Tom raised an eyebrow. 'What a curious coincidence, Mr Tilly, that I should be visited in the space of two hours first by a gentleman urging me to avail myself of every offer of legal assistance and then by a man promising me the means to pay for it.' He smiled. 'I thank you for it.'

CHAPTER 15

On the Thursday morning, 12 September 1884, Superintendent Bourne had marshalled every available policeman around the borough lock-up and the Guildhall, but another huge crowd had gathered and the three men were mobbed as they were led across town. They were taken into court through the magistrates' entrance at the back and sat on a bench at the side of the courtroom, waiting for the proceedings to begin.

The eight magistrates took their seats before the doors were opened to admit the public just after eleven o'clock. The crowd had jammed the street outside and the court was at once overrun with men and women fighting for seats and even pushing out those who had already occupied them. Within minutes every seat was filled and large numbers of people crowded the aisles at the sides and back of the room.

It took the efforts of several police and court officials to secure Richard's brother a seat in the front row. He was dressed in a yachtsman's jersey with the name *Marguerite* sewn in red on the breast. Tom's eyes strayed to him frequently during the proceedings.

Despite the press of people in the room there was an unnerving silence as Mr Genn rose to read out the charge. 'The defendants are charged before Her Majesty's Justices of the Peace that on or about the twenty-fifth day of July in this year of our Lord eighteen eighty-four, being subjects of Our Lady the Queen on the High Seas, feloniously, wilfully and of their malice aforethought, did kill and murder one Richard Parker against the Peace of Our Lady the Queen, her Crown and Dignity.'

He turned to face Tom. 'How do you plead?'

On Tilly's instructions, each man in turn made the same response: 'I reserve my defence.'

Genn then turned back to the bench. 'An application for a further remand has been received from the Treasury. I wrote to them asking for clarification and more definite instructions.' He paused. 'I have today received a reply that the solicitors of the Treasury will take charge of the case henceforth and they have requested me to ask for a week's remand from today.'

Tilly was on his feet almost before Genn had stopped speaking. 'May it please Your Worships, in consenting to the application made by the Treasury for a further remand, I feel it my duty again to apply to Your Worships that these unfortunate men may be admitted to bail.

'The small room in which they are at present confined is ill adapted to their health. They have not recovered, and probably never will, from the privations and sufferings undergone. They are in a wretched state of health, and in addition to all that, the difficulties of properly preparing and conducting their defence under the circumstances of their confinement are very great indeed. Therefore, I still hope, after some further consideration of the point, that Your Worships will reconsider the question and grant my request.'

Liddicoat gave a grave nod. 'We understand your application and will retire to consider it.'

Tilly remained on his feet. 'There is only one point upon which I should like to address an observation or two,' he said. 'That would be the amount of bail, because it must occur to you that these men are by no means wealthy and have to get their living by the sweat of their brow. If you are led to fix an impossible bail, that would really not be granting my application at all. You would only be trifling with their feelings.'

Tilly paused and a smile tugged the corners of his mouth as he heard a rumble of agreement from the public seats. 'That, I am sure, would be very far from any of Your Worships' minds. Probably it will occur to you that this is a very serious case. So it is, but I must tell you as a lawyer who has practised before you a great number of years, that these men are only technically charged with the highest offence a man can commit against the law of England.'

Again he paused for emphasis. 'It is merely a technical charge of murder which is alleged against them. I therefore think it is my duty at this early stage of the case just to record in your minds what the text books bearing on the criminal law of England have to say relating to offences of this kind. There is no abler commentator on the criminal law of this country than Mr Justice Stephen and he says there is one species of justifiable homicide where the party who is to blame is equally innocent as he whose death he occasions. This homicide is also justifiable from the great universal principle of self-preservation which, where one of them must inevitably perish, prompts every man to save his own life rather than that of another.

'In pondering this question of bail, I wish you to consider the great universal principle of self-preservation. Admitting everything said about this case, it is not one in which there is the slightest possibility that the charge alleged against these men can hold. Therefore you should not consider it as if it were an ordinary allegation of murder but as one in which the charges are of a purely technical nature.'

He sat down to a round of applause from the public sections, quickly silenced by the bench. The magistrates retired for a considerable time, and Tom gnawed at his knuckles and dug his fingernails into his palms as he tried to hold back the tears he once more felt welling up. He searched the faces of the magistrates as they returned but their impassive expressions revealed nothing.

'On the application of the Treasury,' Liddicoat said, 'this case will be remanded until Thursday next. The bench have carefully considered the application of Mr Tilly and grant it. The Captain to find sureties for two hundred pounds and—' His words were drowned in a burst of cheering. He banged his gavel until the applause subsided. 'Sureties for two hundred pounds and the other two for a hundred pounds each.'

There were more cheers and Liddicoat acknowledged them as if they were directed at him. He was a shrewd enough politician to know how strong local feeling had been against the incarceration of the three men, and the arrival of an anonymous letter, postmarked Sheffield, can only have further concentrated his mind.

He had passed it to the local paper which revealed that it contained,

A series of disgusting oaths, calling the Mayor by the most outrageous names for having issued the warrant for the

194

apprehension of the survivors of the *Mignonette*. He had no right to take such a course as the men had not committed murder and the writer concluded by saying he intended to come to Falmouth the next week to shoot the Mayor for having issued the warrant and thereby entailed more suffering upon men who had already gone through so much. The letter was evidently written in a disguised hand and was upon two half sheets of paper, the style being incoherent.

As he had promised Tom, John Burton offered to stand surety for him. His offer was greeted with yet more cheers and shouts of 'Good old Burton' from the crowd.

Both Stephens and Brooks named people in Southampton as their guarantors. J. H. Cocksey, the chairman of the Southampton magistrates, was one of those named as ready to stand bail for Stephens, but although anxious not to have the public mood swing back against him, Liddicoat could not grant bail simply on the strength of names unknown to the bench, no matter how respectable they might be. 'Is there no Falmouth man who will stand bail for these men?' he said.

After a brief silence, John Burton again stood up. 'I'll go bail for fifty pounds for each of them if any other person will stand surety for the other half.'

There were no volunteers. Liddicoat then allowed Stephens and Brooks to leave the dock and cross the courtroom to where Burton was standing. After a brief, muttered conversation, he told the bench, 'I'll stand surety for all of them in the full amount.'

The cheers rose to a crescendo as Daniel Parker walked over and shook hands with each of the defendants in turn. It was a very public exoneration from the dead boy's closest relative.

To Tom's infinite relief, the majority of the back-slapping crowd did not pursue them far down the street once they left the court. By the time they reached the market square, the group following them had dwindled to a handful of people.

Tom hailed a hansom cab, then shook Tilly's hand. 'Thank you for what you have done for us.'

'I've done little enough yet,' Tilly said, though his face was flushed with pride. 'The true test will come in a week's time when we shall have to try and persuade the bench not to commit you for trial. That will not be so easily done. But I'm glad that you can at least now return to your loved ones.' He walked away down the hill with his clerk.

Tom turned to the others. For five months they had been confined together – on a ship, a dinghy and in a jail. Even if only temporarily, they were now at last free to go their separate ways. Once more he struggled to contain his tears. He had cried more times since his rescue than in his whole life beforehand, often for the most trivial of reasons. He could find no apposite words to say to them and after muttering, 'Until next Thursday, then,' he climbed into the cab and was driven away.

Cheesman was waiting at the station to see him off. He shook Tom's hand and expressed the hope that his temporary release would soon be made permanent. He had also brought two valuable items with him, Tom's sextant and chronometer, which were not required as evidence and had been released by the police.

Tom arrived at Paddington by the mail train at four the next morning. He shuffled along the platform, wearing slippers because his legs were still so swollen that he was unable to bear the pressure of shoes. Although she had been ill all week, Philippa was there to meet him, accompanied by two friends. They crossed London by hansom cab and caught the five-fifty train from Victoria to Sutton.

A few people were waiting at Sutton station to welcome him home and show their support for him. He shook each hand that was offered to him and managed a few words of thanks, but his thoughts were focused only on reaching his house and seeing his children.

At the sound of the gate-latch, the two elder children, Philippa and Winifred, came running from the house. Julian tottered after them; he had taken his first steps while Tom was at sea. As he hugged them to him, Tom cried as if his heart would break.

Philippa's first action was to pack him off to bed and send for their doctor to examine him and dress his wounds. While they waited for the doctor, Tom gave her the letter he had written to her in the dinghy.

She read and reread it, then laid the letter down. Their tears mingled as they wept on each other's shoulders, while the children clustered around them, crying too, without knowing why.

Later, while Philippa plied him with food and drink, Tom told her the story of the sinking and the ordeal in the dinghy. By the time the doctor arrived, a group of reporters was waiting outside the house. Despite his weariness, Tom spoke to them at length, repeating his account of the voyage and the death of Richard Parker.

Philippa added her own trenchant defence of her husband, pointing out his role in saving Richard's life when he was drowning, and in keeping the crew alive by risking his own life to search for provisions before abandoning the *Mignonette*. He had plugged the hole in the side of the dinghy, made the sea-anchor that stopped it from foundering, had insisted on raising a sail against the objections of the others, and time and again had 'stopped them from committing suicide' by drinking sea-water.

When the reporters had at last departed, Philippa led Tom inside and closed and barred the door. As he settled into his wing-chair with the children playing on the rug at his feet, Tom felt at peace for the first time in all the months since the *Mignonette* had sailed.

Stephens and Brooks had taken longer to reach home. After Tom had left them, Brooks insisted on heading for a tavern to celebrate their release. Although Stephens was desperate to see his family, the thought of travelling alone filled him with an illogical but undeniable fear, and he clung to his shipmate's side.

In his wasted condition, two mugs of ale were enough to make Brooks drunk, and by the time they staggered down to the station, they had missed the through mail train to Southampton. They did not arrive there until Friday lunchtime.

A number of reporters were among the crowd of family, friends and curious onlookers waiting for them at the station. Those who knew them were shocked at their haggard appearance. As the local paper reported, 'Both men bore on their features the impress of privation.'

Stephens appeared daunted by the crowd. His eyes darted from side to side seeking his wife, and he seemed unable to understand the questions shouted at them by reporters and bystanders. Ann stepped out of the crowd, embraced him, and led him away.

Brooks proved more willing to speak. 'We had not the least idea that we should be apprehended in Falmouth,' he said. 'If people would only imagine for a moment what our sufferings were in the boat, such charges made against us would be about the last thing that would be thought of.'

There were some shouts of support, but also a number of boos and hostile questions. Just as in Falmouth, most of them centred on the men's failure to draw lots before killing Richard Parker. Brooks looked around, very aware that he was merely a lodger in the dead boy's home area.

'I am very, very sorry that our poor little friend Parker did not come back with us,' he said, 'but we should none of us have returned if we had not done what we did. As to offending myself, if there is a trial I have got no money. Everything I had was lost in the *Mignonette* and our wages were stopped from the moment she went down.'

Among the onlookers as Brooks was speaking was a woman holding a ragged bundle of possessions. Two children clung to her skirts. When the reporters and the crowd had heard enough from him, Brooks took her to one side, exchanged increasingly heated words with her then handed her a handful of coins. When his friends hailed a hansom cab to take them to the County Tavern at Northam, she and her children were left standing alone at the side of the road. They cut a forlorn picture as they turned and plodded away.

The following day Daniel Parker also arrived back in Southampton. He had returned to Torquay to rejoin his yacht, only to find that the *Marguerite* had already left for the Channel Islands. That evening a reporter from the *Southampton Times* tracked him down at his home in Itchen Ferry. Daniel's comments to him reflected the ambivalence of the local people. They had known and liked Richard, but as a seafaring community, they also understood the custom of the sea.

'As regards the feeling among the fishermen here,' Daniel said, 'I may say that, of course, we don't know who is best and who is worst but all I have spoken to seem to think that the Captain ought "to get into it" – answer for his actions – but they say that Brooks and Stephens refused to draw lots.

'I know it may be argued that three lives are better than one, but the lad was an orphan and we seemed to think that advantage was taken of him. As to whether any punishment should be awarded, we say there should be a little in case others might go to sea, get into trouble and be killed because people might say nothing was done in this case.'

The same reporter also won the confidence of Richard's adoptive mother, Mrs Matthews. 'Dick was a fine young fellow for his age; he would have been eighteen next February. I had charge of him over three years and always found him a very good lad. He was always a rough and ready boy and was not afraid to go to sea, although he had never been right away from home before.

'On the nineteenth of May, the day they left England, he got up very early and was downstairs by five o'clock in the morning. I and my husband came down to see he was all right and as he said goodbye he kissed us both and hung upon both our necks for several minutes. He seemed then sorry that he was going to leave us and this was the first time that he had shown any sort of regret for the resolve that he had taken. That was the last I saw of him as I did not see the *Mignonette* leave the river though she was towed down the Itchen the same afternoon.

'I had one letter from Dick from Madeira. It was written by himself. I heard nothing more about him until Sunday morning last when I was told the ship was lost. When I heard of his dreadful death I could not believe it; it was a hard death indeed for him to die. It has almost broken my heart because he was as dear to me and to my husband as if he were our own son.

'I don't think there is any really strong feeling in the Ferry against these poor unfortunate men and all I have to say about it is that I really don't think they should have killed him. I can seem to see him now looking up to Captain Dudley and saying, "What – me, sir?"'

The editorial in the *Southampton Times* reflected the prevailing view among its readers.

> While many of the briny fraternity complain that an equality of chance was not given to the four exhausted survivors by the casting of lots, others regard with more charity the unparalleled extremity to which they were driven and contend that it would have been equally a crime to have sacrificed one of the other three, when it was evident that the boy could not have survived.

Faced with such generous views from those closest to the victim, the treatment of the case by some sections of the metropolitan press was also beginning to soften.

There was even a sympathetic editorial in the *Standard*, in stark contrast to its earlier outright condemnation.

> It is hardly possible for those enjoying the comforts of a life on shore to form a just opinion as to the state to which men must have come before they adopted this terrible alternative. It is, we believe, the first time that the law has taken cognisance of one of these awful tragedies at sea and the interest in the trial especially among seafaring men cannot fail to be very great.

The *Daily Telegraph* was even more understanding of the men's position.

> For humanity's sake, we must regret that such confessions as have fallen from these rescued men ever came to the light of day. It would be better perhaps that it had never been told at all. Repulsive as the last resource of this boat's crew appears, it is but just to remember that it was arrived at only through and after an anguish of suffering which would dethrone reason and reduce manhood to a raving craving for food and drink, utterly beyond the limits and wholly unimaginable to any save the victims.
>
> During the rest of their lives the shadow of this awful memory must of necessity darken their days and often trouble their nightly slumber. But it is for their fellows to be compassionate rather than condemn them and to hear this piteous story of the sea with the assurance that, despite their unspeakable grief, even the friends of the poor lost sailor lad will pronounce no other judgement against them than one of sorrowful silence.

Public sympathy for the three men was heightened still further by the publication of Tom's moving last letter to Philippa, written while in the dinghy. John Burton was responsible for that, beginning to collect on his *quid pro quo* with Tom, Brooks and Stephens by hawking copies of the creased, folded and waterstained letter to the newspapers.

The letter and the interviews with the survivors and Richard's relatives served only to fuel an already insatiable public appetite for news of the *Mignonette* case. It had been reported worldwide and continued to dominate the British press, even relegating to second place the daily bulletins on the progress of Sir Garnet Wolseley's expedition up the Nile to relieve the besieged General Gordon at Khartoum.

Reporters continued to pursue Tom, Brooks and Stephens, and interviewed everyone with even the most tangential connection to the men. A flood of correspondence from members of the public – the vast majority supportive of the men's actions – filled the letters columns of the papers and many others wrote directly to the three men, whose addresses had been published in the press.

A ship's captain from Perth wrote to Tom:

> I feel I must give vent to my feelings by sending a letter. How glad your dear wife must have been to get you back safe and how deep must be your gratitude to Him who has so signally blessed and delivered you. I have to assure you of the sympathy of our entire ship's company, as we all feel sure you acted for the best in all things.
>
> I have not the slightest conception of what you have undergone in your late dreadful trial but I do feel grateful that your lives have been spared. May God bless you yet further and may He instruct the hearts before whom you will stand next week. You have all our prayers.

There were too many letters for Tom to respond individually and he instead replied through the correspondence columns:

> May I express my thanks for numerous favours of sympathy to myself and companions for our past unparalleled sufferings and privations on the ocean and our present torture under the ban of the law, being charged with an act which certainly was not accompanied by either premeditation or malice in the true sense of the words as my conscience can confirm.

There can have been few, if any, other instances where a man accused of murder was able to plead his innocence in *The Times*.

Stephens also received several letters, including one, congratulating him on,

> Your remarkable and providential escape from a watery grave. The great privations you and your noble companions have undergone and the great skill with which you handled your frail craft under such exceptional circumstances and under a tropical sun, have placed you at the first rank of England's heroes.

Other individuals, some rich and powerful men associated with yachting, petitioned the home secretary. The owner of one of Tom's former yachts, Iain MacNab, wrote to Harcourt:

> Sir, May I venture to approach you with a brief appeal on behalf of one of the three unfortunate men in that terrible tale of the sea which is thrilling the whole land?
>
> Tom Dudley was at one time Captain of my yacht and while in my service I conceived the highest regard for him in every way. He was skilful and brave in his calling, upright, truthful and honest as a man and kind to a degree to all under his command. He was generous too, and gave freely of his small store to his less fortunate friends. In all the relations of life his conduct was such as commanded respect; he was emphatically an honest man. All this is within my personal knowledge.
>
> It passes my understanding to conceive the horror of the extremity that could induce so good and brave a man to do wrong. I am sure of this, that whatever view the law may take of the act, Dudley could not have thought it unjustifiable. Neither selfishness nor cruelty had any part in his character.
>
> I apologize for intruding on your valuable time by placing these facts before you. But human life and happiness are at stake and I feel it my duty to state what I knew of poor Dudley, for whose sad position I feel deeply, and I think I am sure of your forgiveness when I crave your kind intervention on his behalf.

The letter was noted and filed, but Harcourt had no intention of being swayed into making any 'kind intervention' on Tom's behalf. He remained determined that the full weight of the law should fall on the *Mignonette* case.

Not all legal opinion agreed with him, however, and the correspondence columns of *The Times* and the *Telegraph* carried a series of letters from barristers and solicitors arguing the procedural merits and demerits of prosecuting the men. 'A Barrister' wrote:

> To judge these men from a severely legal standpoint for what they have done would be most unjust. After nearly twenty days of such fearful privations they can hardly be accounted responsible creatures. The longing for the dying boy's blood was a phrensy, induced by physical and mental suffering. No doubt the youth would have shortly perished from want of stamina and from the draughts of sea water which he had imbibed.
>
> The rough arguments with which the Captain and Stephens justified the action of killing to themselves because they were married men with families and the boy had nobody dependent upon him for support, are good arguments as far as they go.
>
> It must also be remembered that it was on their own confession that they stand indicted; they did not conceal the offence that they had committed although it would probably have been perfectly easy to do so.
>
> The Falmouth Magistrates were perfectly right in ordering their arrest on the charge of murder. Every taking of a human life is presumed to be murder. It would be for the accused themselves to disprove their guilt or to adduce such extenuating circumstances as will ensure their escaping with slight punishment.
>
> What is interesting to notice in this case is that we have here got beyond the boundaries of law. We have touched the lowest strata of practical ethics and have come to a question of primary morality which everybody will answer according to his own moral feeling. To dogmatize is absurd.

Another correspondent to *The Times* drew attention to the eerie parallels between the case and a short story written by Edgar Allen Poe in 1837. 'The Narrative of Arthur Gordon Pym of Nantucket' told the tale of four shipwrecked men who having earlier killed and eaten a turtle, killed one of their number, the cabin boy named Richard Parker, and drank his blood and ate his flesh:

> Our chief sufferings were now those of hunger and thirst, and, when we looked forward to the means of relief in this respect, our hearts sunk within us, and we were induced to regret that we had escaped the less dreadful perils of the sea. We endeavoured, however, to encourage ourselves with the hope of being speedily picked up by some vessel, and encouraged each other to bear with fortitude the evils that might happen . . .
>
> I immediately saw by the countenance of Parker that I was safe and that it was he who had been doomed to suffer . . . I must not dwell upon the fearful repast which immediately ensued. Such things may be imagined, but words have no power to impress the mind with the exquisite horror of their reality. Let it suffice to say that, having in some measure appeased the raging thirst which consumed us by the blood of the victim, and having by common consent taken off the hands, feet, and head, throwing them together with the entrails into the sea, we devoured the rest of the body, piecemeal.

CHAPTER 16

The following Thursday, 18 September 1884, the three defendants returned to Falmouth to surrender to their bail at the magistrates' court. Stephens and Brooks had travelled back from Southampton on the Wednesday evening and spent the night at the Sailors' Home.

Tom arrived early on Thursday morning on the mail express from London to Truro, and took the train along the rattling, single-track line around the curve of the hills down into Falmouth. He disembarked at the station, but no hansom cabs were waiting for business at that early hour and he had to make his slow, painful way across town on foot.

He still needed daily treatment for the wounds to his buttocks he had suffered on the day after they were rescued, and Stephens also remained in a frail physical and mental state. Tom also noted with concern that Brooks, the only one strong enough to climb on to the ship when they were rescued, now seemed the weakest of the three. He sat quiet and listless as they ate their breakfast, avoiding Tom's eye and barely joining the conversation.

'Cheer up, Brooks,' Tom said. 'We'll see our homes again tonight and all this business will be behind us.'

Brooks gave a weak smile, then looked away.

When they had finished their breakfast, Captain Jose sent a boy for a cab to take the three of them up the hill to the Guildhall. It was almost an hour before the hearing was due to begin, but another huge crowd was already blocking the street, and the doors of the court were under

205

siege from people desperate even for standing room in the small space allotted to the public.

A shout went up as they alighted and the crowd pressed even more closely around them as they fought their way through to the magistrates' entrance. Hands trembling, Tom rested against the wall of the courtroom as the other two waited on a bench.

The magistrates entered the court just as the clock struck eleven and the three men took their places in the dock. When all was in readiness, the clerk to the justices signalled to the police to open the courtroom doors. There was another mêlée as people fought for a space, and many were locked out when the doors were forced shut again.

The small table in front of the dock was almost equally crowded with lawyers. Mr Tilly's ruddy face was topped by a bird's nest of dishevelled hair. Facing him across the table was the tall, patrician figure of William Otto Julius Danckwerts, QC. A barrister at the Inner Temple, a junior Treasury counsel and a specialist in wreck inquiries, he appeared for the prosecution with Mr G. Appleby-Jenkins, a solicitor who was also the town clerk of Penryn.

As Tom's gaze wandered around the courtroom, he found himself the object of scrutiny from the press bench, where the reporters were filling the time before the hearing by sketching pen-pictures of the defendants. Every national and all of the local and regional papers were represented, and the proceedings were punctuated by the sound of clogs clattering down the cobbled street as the local boys recruited as runners took each verbatim instalment to the telegraph office.

Tom would not have been offended by the description of him offered by the *Weekly Mercury*:

> A little under an average height, broad-shouldered and power-ful looking. His well-shaped head and pleasant features are indicative of a genial and generous nature and, to judge from appearances, the last man in the world who would be capable of a deed of cruelty. Although not a teetotaller, he has always been of very moderate habits in the matter of drink and diet, and his friends attribute his staying power in a great degree to this fact.
>
> Stephens is taller and of a more rugged aspect than the

Captain, a fine fellow in every respect and a good specimen of the British sailor as far as physique is concerned. Both Dudley and Stephens are florid and red-haired. Brooks is a little taller and bigger than the Captain with a dark complexion and almost jet-black hair.

Tom loosened his jacket. It was a warm morning and the closely packed courtroom was already unpleasantly hot. The murmurs of conversation died away as Liddicoat called the court to order and the clerk to the justices read the charge.

Danckwerts then got to his feet. 'Your Worships, I appear in this case to prosecute by direction of the Crown and the public prosecutor. It is my duty to lay the facts as shortly and as briefly as I can before you and it will then be for Your Worships to say whether the prisoners should be committed for trial.'

He paused and glanced towards the reporters, as if directing his remarks to them as much as to the bench. 'While the case has excited profound sentiments of sympathy, you and I and the duties we have to discharge must not allow ourselves to be turned to the right or to the left by any feeling of pain or pity, or any other sentiment but a sincere desire to further the public justice and nothing more.

'As you are aware, gentlemen, we are not attending here today to try the case. We do not meet here to convict or accuse the prisoners, but for the sole purpose of saying: "Is there any evidence for which these prisoners should be sent for trial by a jury of their countrymen?"'

He paused again and this time his gaze lingered on Tilly seated at the lawyers' table. The ghost of a smile crossed Danckwerts's face. 'There are some cases in which the law warrants you in taking the life of a fellow creature but I venture to submit to you in the greatest confidence that this is not one of those cases. We must not omit to recognize that the law regards this as murder and it requires to be satisfied.

'There is by the constitution of this country a power placed in one higher than any of us to mitigate the rigour of the law.' He raised his eyes to the portrait of Queen Victoria hanging high on the wall above the bench. 'And perhaps there are circumstances which will distinguish this case from others. When the law is satisfied, these circumstances will be taken into account and given their proper and due effect.

'The case lies within a very short compass indeed. The facts are few and I venture to say are beyond dispute. Upon one occasion when Brooks was lying in the bow of the boat the captain and Stephens between them killed the boy. The captain, it appears, told Stephens to stand by and hold his legs, then ran a penknife into the boy's throat, caught the blood and they drank it.

'At that moment they seemed to have been seen by Brooks and he claimed a share of the blood. As far as I can make out, Brooks, although he knew their purpose, never actually lent his assent, and I suppose one can hardly say a great degree of blame is to be attached to him when he saw others drinking the blood, remembering the dire necessities to which they were reduced.'

As Danckwerts spoke, Tilly turned to look first at Tom, and then at Brooks. Concern was etched on his face. Brooks remained head bowed, staring at his hands.

'Now the law of England regards it as nobler and worthier that they should all die rather than take the life of a fellow creature,' Danckwerts said. 'What right have you or I or anybody else to feel that in misfortune we can make one or another suffer other misfortunes by taking their life in order to preserve our own?

'By the law of England, there is no authority for such a course and I call upon you . . .' He paused, adding emphasis to his words. 'You have in fact no option but to commit these prisoners for trial. The captain did the deed and Stephens was the essential party. In their case there can be no doubt whatsoever.

'As to Brooks, I have carefully considered his position and I have come to the conclusion that he was in no way an actor or participator in the crime of his two companions. What I propose to do is to offer no evidence against him.

'I ask you to discharge Brooks and I will put him in the box and I will call him as a witness in order that he might give an account of what took place. It is fair to Brooks and fair to the other two prisoners, because they will then by independent testimony have an opportunity of eliciting such facts as they think it right to elicit.' Danckwerts made an exaggerated bow to the bench and sat down.

Liddicoat conferred with his fellow magistrates for a few seconds. 'The defendant Brooks is formally discharged and—'

There was a loud cheer from the public section.

Danckwerts was back on his feet at once. 'I must request that these manifestations of feelings be suppressed.' The considerable agitation he displayed was explicable in the light of his son's subsequent revelation that Danckwerts believed that a conviction would put his own life in danger in the West Country.

Liddicoat flushed at the curt reminder of his duties, then banged his gavel. 'If there are any more outbursts I shall have the court cleared.'

Tom glanced at Stephens. 'Did you know aught of this?'

The mate shook his head.

Tom looked to his left. Brooks had made a show of surprise, but now again sat motionless, eyes downcast, still staring at his hands. Tom's gaze continued to burn into him as a policeman took Brooks's elbow and led him out of the dock to a bench at the side of the court.

As he turned his attention back to the court, Tom met Tilly's eye. The lawyer jumped to his feet. 'Your Worships, I must ask that the statements given by the defendants to the collector of customs be proved as evidence.'

Danckwerts uncoiled himself from his seat. 'If Mr Tilly will only wait a little, that will be done.'

Tilly ignored him, repeating his request to the bench.

Danckwerts's air of amused tolerance evaporated at once. 'Your Worships, I wish to conduct the case with the greatest forbearance towards the unfortunate men, but I protest against the conduct of their solicitor.'

'Whatever my learned friend may say,' Tilly said, 'I am bound to take every objection, bearing in mind the serious nature of the case.'

'But you are not taking a proper course.'

The two lawyers faced each other across the table. 'I am taking a course which I think is only fair to the case. We need have no personal matters about it.'

'Mr Tilly, you had better be very careful and allow me to conduct the matter fairly.' Danckwerts thrust out his chin and hooked his thumbs into his waistcoat. It was the posture of a bantam cock preparing to fight a rival and there was ripple of laughter around the court. He continued to stare at Tilly. 'You are evidently taking the most silly objections. I propose to read the statements that Mr Cheesman sent to the Board of Trade and you must make no objection to them.'

'I will take what objection I like,' Tilly said. 'The statements were made for the specific purposes of the Merchant Shipping Act. The objection I take is that they would be admissible in an inquiry into the cause of a shipwreck, but not in a criminal court.'

It was not a point that was ever likely to have been lost on Danckwerts, but Tom had watched the heated argument with the same bemusement as the magistrates. He now understood the reason. The statements they had given at the Customs House had not been preceded by a caution, and it was also arguable that they had not been voluntary since there was a legal duty to report any loss of life at sea.

Tom felt uncomfortable. He wanted the court to acquit him because it recognized that he had told the truth and committed no crime, not because a lawyer's trick had freed him.

Without their self-incriminating statements, the prosecution had no evidence against them, except . . . He glanced across the courtroom. Brooks had been watching him and could not avoid meeting his eye for a second before he looked away. The look of guilt that Tom read there convinced him that Danckwerts's decision to offer no evidence against Brooks was anything but a surprise to him.

To Tilly's barely concealed fury, Liddicoat ruled in favour of the prosecution after the briefest of consultations with his colleagues. The statements made to the collector of customs by Tom and Stephens, though not Brooks's deposition, were then read, and Cheesman was called as a witness to swear to their authenticity. Danckwerts also questioned him about the conversation he had had with Tom in the Long Room after the statements had been made.

Tom listened with keen interest, and in his anxiety that the record should be accurate in every respect, he even interrupted when Cheesman was uncertain whether Tom had told him that he inserted the knife on the right or the left side of the neck. 'It was this side,' Tom said, putting his finger to his neck.

Stephens gave an involuntary shudder and covered his face with his hands.

Still fuming, Tilly rose to cross-examine Cheesman. 'This statement was made before you as receiver of wrecks and as principal officer of the customs, was it not? Before he signed the statement, did you caution him in any way?'

'No. I was not enquiring into a criminal case. The statements were taken as regards the casualty to the vessel.'

'Did you point out he was accusing himself of a serious crime and was not bound to incriminate himself?'

'No, I did not. I had not the remotest idea that a crime was to be alleged against them.' Cheesman looked up, appealing to the public section of the court. 'I did not know when putting the questions to them that they would be used in evidence against them. Had I done so, I would not have put them.'

'Did Dudley appear surprised when apprehended?'

'Yes.'

'And was he evidently up to that time of the impression he could return home that night?'

Cheesman mopped the sweat from his brow. 'Yes, he was. It was an impression I shared.'

Tom was unsure if he was telling the truth, or merely trying to appease his local audience. He had no time to ponder the question further, for he was then called into the witness box, to be cross-examined by Danckwerts on one aspect of his statement. 'Captain Dudley, when you were discussing killing the boy, did not Brooks say he would not have anything to do with it?'

Tom's gaze was level and his firm voice carried to the back of the court. 'No, he did not say that.'

Danckwerts frowned. He began to frame another question, then thought better of it and shook his head.

Those six words were the only ones that either Tom or Stephens were to be permitted to utter throughout the entire legal process. Under procedures that had ruled English courts since medieval times, no defendant was permitted to give sworn testimony on his own behalf. It was for the prosecution to prove the case and the defendant's evidence was regarded as irrelevant since, guilty or not, he would be bound to deny that he had committed the crime.

Earlier in the Victorian era, a Bill was put before the House of Commons to allow a defendant to testify, but it had provoked such a furious parliamentary battle that the proposal was dropped. The law was finally amended when the Criminal Evidence Act was passed in 1898, allowing a defendant either to give an unsworn statement and not be cross-examined, or speak under oath but be subject to cross-examination.

The next witness to be called was Brooks. There was a buzz of excitement around the courtroom as he made his way to the stand at the right-hand end of the bench, at a diagonal from the dock in the centre of the court.

Brooks remained in the box for well over an hour and in all that time, he never once met Tom's eye, staring straight ahead of him, down the side of the courtroom, looking neither at the bench, nor at Danckwerts as the lawyer led him through his testimony.

He spoke in a low voice, scarcely audible even to the reporters next to the witness box, and Liddicoat was obliged to intervene more than once. 'We understand that this is painful for you, but please make an effort to speak more distinctly.'

To one of the reporters on the press bench, 'The impression created by his manner was that he assumed the role of the witness rather reluctantly and that the recital of the sad scenes to which he had been to some extent a participant was painful and repugnant.'

Danckwerts took great care to confirm that impression. 'This morning when you came here, did you know you were going to be discharged?'

'No, sir, I did not.' He shook his head for emphasis.

'With the exception of the statements you have made to the collector of customs, or the newspapers, or your solicitor, have you made any statement to anyone connected with the prosecution?'

'No, sir.'

'Did you know you would be called here as a witness this morning?'

'No, sir.'

'Not until you were discharged?'

'Not then, sir.'

'Oh, not then,' Danckwerts said, as if sharing Brooks's surprise.

'No, not until just before I was called.'

Danckwerts nodded to himself. 'Now, while you were adrift in the dinghy, when was the subject of casting lots discussed?'

'Dudley mentioned it on several occasions, the first soon after we ate the last of the turtle.'

As if to confirm his desertion of his crewmates, Brooks was now calling Tom 'Dudley' rather than 'Captain'.

'We had nothing to eat for eight days after that,' Brooks said. 'It was not agreed to, though. I said, "Let us all die together."' He glanced towards Danckwerts as if seeking approval, then reverted to his fixed stare ahead of him.

'What did the boy say about it?'

'He didn't join in the conversation. He was pretty well at the time, but on the fifteenth day he got ill.'

'Now, turning to the nineteenth day, the day before Richard Parker died, can you remember any conversation which took place about lots that day?'

'Yes, Dudley said that there would have to be something done. I did not make any answer then. There was not much said that day, we were looking very black at each other.'

'Who first started the talk about killing Parker the next morning?'

Brooks hesitated, shifting uncomfortably in his seat before replying. 'We all three were saying that there would have to be something done. We never talked about killing the boy, but I understood what would have to be done by Stephens nodding to the boy and then to me.'

'What happened next?' Danckwerts said.

'The boy was lying in the bottom of the boat. I went and lay down in the bow with my head right forward and my feet under the thwarts. I had an oilskin coat over my head. I – I heard no words, just a little noise. I looked around and saw the boy's neck was cut. I could not tell how, I did not look enough.

'I fainted away just after then for a minute or two. When I looked round again I saw Dudley and Stephens drinking the blood. The boy's eyes were quite white. I asked Dudley for some.'

He fell silent and Danckwerts prompted him. 'And he did so?'

'Yes, quite congealed, but I sucked it down as well as I could. I saw the knife soon after. There was blood on it.' Again he hesitated.

'What happened next?'

'I went aft to steer the boat and Stephens and Dudley cut the boy's clothes off. We ate his heart and liver between us and lived on the body for a few days afterwards.'

Danckwerts allowed a silence to build as his gaze travelled along the faces of the magistrates, measuring the impact of Brooks's words. 'I thank you, Mr Brooks,' he said. 'I am grateful for your courage and honesty in recounting such a terrible tale.'

Tilly rose to begin his cross-examination. 'You were all in a terribly bad state when you were in the dinghy, thin and weak? You were getting sore in your bodies by sitting and your feet and hands were very much swollen?'

'Yes,' Brooks said, keeping his face averted.

'And the lad was in a great deal worse condition than any of you. He appeared to be dying?'

'To the best of my judgement. He was lying with his face on his arm, not speaking or taking any notice of anything for a great many hours.'

Tilly broke off and paced to and fro in front of the witness box, the sound of his boots on the worn wooden floor echoing through the courtroom. He waited until Brooks darted a nervous glance towards him, before speaking again. 'Did you really object to casting lots?'

'Y-yes, at all times.'

'And why did you object?'

'I thought it would be better for us to die all together.'

'Now, let me ask you as a sailor, assuming one has to die, is not the casting of lots the fairest way?'

Brooks hesitated. 'I would rather die than cast lots. I should not like to kill a man nor for anyone to kill me.'

'Did you not give as your reason at the time that you had a wife and family and the boy had none?'

'I did not.'

'Are you sure? You are on your oath.'

'I did not.'

'But you had conversations together that something would have to be done and you understood that to mean that someone – the lad – would have to die.'

'Yes, sir.'

'There was some conversation with you as to who should kill the boy, wasn't there?' the lawyer said, fixing him with his gaze. 'I remind you again that you are on your oath.'

Brooks looked away and muttered something.

'What?' Liddicoat said. 'Speak more clearly, please, Mr Brooks.'

'No, sir, there was no conversation.'

'But you knew he was going to be killed. Were you told to go forward or was there any sign made to you to go forward?'

'No, sir.'

Tilly rapped his knuckles against the edge of the witness box. The noise made Brooks start and his eyes flickered towards him. 'Did you by any act of yours try to prevent the lad being killed?'

'No, sir.'

'And after the boy was killed you shared his blood?'

'Yes.'

'Thank you, Mr Brooks,' Tilly said. 'That is all.'

'Sir.' Brooks hesitated, glancing towards Tom and Stephens in the dock. 'I – I should like to add that but for the death of the boy I believe we would have died from hunger and thirst. And if the boy had died we should not have any blood from him, and of course it was something to drink that we wanted. I felt quite strong afterwards. In fact we all made use of the expression that we were quite different men.

'I and the Captain fed on the body and so did Stephens occasionally but he had very little. We lived on it for four days and we ate a good deal – I should think quite half of the body before we were picked up, and I can say that we partook of it with quite as much relish as ordinary food.' His voice trailed away. 'That is all I have to say.'

Danckwerts was already on his feet, raising his voice to drown the buzz of conversation from the public. 'That is the evidence I have to lay before you for the prosecution and I submit it will be your duty to commit the prisoners for trial.'

Liddicoat glanced towards the defence. 'Mr Tilly?'

The lawyer stood up. 'I am uncertain if Your Worships are still open to legal argument on the committal of the defendants, but this I must say at all events.' He had been holding a sheaf of papers, but now paused, threw them on to the table behind him, and spoke without notes. 'In former times, when the survivors of a shipwreck related how they had been driven by their unspeakable anguish to cannibalism, it was usually the custom of our grandsires to feel deep pity for them, to shelter and comfort them, to furnish them with money and in many other ways to let them know how thoroughly they understood the fearful distress they had happily come through, and how great was their compassion.

'I know of no incident – though there are a thousand cases of man-slaying and man-eating by famine-stricken seamen and passengers in our own marine annals – of men who had killed a shipmate and drunk his blood and eaten his flesh for the preservation of their own lives, having been cast into gaol on their arrival home and left to languish there until the judge and jury had decided their fate.

'And why?' He paused before answering his own question. 'Not only because such tragical things were as frequent then as they are rare now, and because the necessity of them was accepted as a condition, the last indeed, but nevertheless a condition of man's terrible and maddening strife with the remorseless deep, but because the whole world felt that deeds of this kind were outside the sphere of human jurisdiction.

'The deprivation of instinct by exquisite suffering such as no healthy mind can bear to think of compels an action for which the doer, as part of the nature that incites him, must not and should not be arraigned.

'Who amongst us who are judging Captain Dudley and his mate, who that shall judge them when they are brought up to their trial can in the smallest possible degree understand what it is to be exposed for twenty-four days in mid-ocean in a small boat without food or drink?

'Think of it. These sailors are plain men like most of their kind. They can only depose in brief, unlettered terms what they have passed through. To tell the truth, the truth as it happened to them, they would need to be great artists capable of analysing and expressing their own lives as day after day passed, seizing upon and exhibiting all of those hundred subtle flights of fancy, of hope, of terror, of wild thoughts of maddening despair, of burning resolutions which went to swell some total of their time of agony.

'Unless we know the sea, unless we know what exposure to nights of wet and days of scorching sunshine is, unless we know how thirst breeds madness and how madness robs the heart of its manhood and the soul of its divinity, how, I say, can we imagine what these men endured? What went before to bring them to the path of slaying Parker and how, not being able to imagine, shall we be capable of judging them?

'The sailors will be with them, I'll vouch. For it needs a sailor to know what will be the feelings of four men afloat in a little dinghy upon a heavy sea with nothing to divide amongst them as food but two tins of

216

vegetables. Far out of the track of ships, presenting so small an object upon the heave of the surges of the dark blue ocean as to easily escape the observation of a vessel passing at a distance of a mile.

'Yet this is but the beginning. Follow on, until you come to the sunken eyes, already repulsive with the fires of famine, to the gaunt and haggard faces, to the voices which can but whisper hoarsely as they seek to cast their accent the length of the boat, and to the boat herself that, as she sails softly along, throws out sweet, fountain-like rippling sounds of water to torture the thirsty wretches in her.

'Her thwarts and insides dry and baked, and the sickening smell of paint rising with the heat from her blistered sides, yet only a week may have passed and more than a fortnight yet must elapse before those despairing, cadaverous, white-lipped men, should be lifted out of the jaws of death.

'And for what? To be brought home and flung into prison.

'Think of it. It is no question of imagination. A sailor will know how to trace these poor fellows, step by step, until the madness of Nature's irrepressible cravings seizes them and humanity drops from them as a garment.

'Is there no limit to endurance?' He threw his arm out towards Tom and Stephens in the dock. 'A healthy man dies hard. He cannot perish like a weaker man who comes quickly to privation. Nature insists upon the prolongation of the horrible struggle and his instincts leave him, whilst the clay of which he is formed still throbs with a dreadful vitality.

'Let us in the name of the sailor, in the name of this country that owes him so much, let us be merciful in our judgement of Captain Dudley and his comrades. Twenty-four days in an open boat, at sea with a thousand horrors of mind and body to preface the dreadful deed. And then the companionship of the remains to follow, to abide with them under bright sunshine and to be with them for another, and yet another intolerable night, as darkness comes down with starlight enough to make a mutilated thing thrice horrible as it stares up white from the gloom in the bottom of the boat.

'Think of it, I say, if the mind has power to bring true thought to bear on this most ghastly subject. Have they not suffered enough? Has memory failed them that penance must be imposed upon them in a prison cell and the expiation at the hands of a tribunal which, if it be not of Heaven, can never compass the significance of those weeks of anguish which forced them to the deed for which they are arraigned?'

He paused and wiped his eyes, as if moved by the power of his own oration. There was a deathly silence in the court, broken only by the sound of a woman sobbing. Then the people in the public seats began to applaud. Slow and hesitant at first, the sound grew in strength and volume. The police attempted to silence them, but men and women alike clapped their hands, stamped their feet on the wooden floor and raised their voices in shouts of support, the whole seafaring community finding its voice, united against outsiders in defence of its own.

Danckwerts was on his feet protesting and Liddicoat added to the clamour, pounding the bench with his gavel and calling for order, but the noise continued to swell. The applause was taken up by the crowds still waiting in the street outside. Tom turned his head and could see faces pressed against the window, yelling and cheering.

The demonstration continued for some minutes before Liddicoat finally made himself heard, shouting at the top of his voice and beating a tattoo with his gavel. 'Silence! Silence! I will have silence in this court or the public will be ejected.'

The noise slowly abated. Liddicoat then turned to Tilly. 'This is a magistrates' court, Mr Tilly. There is no jury to be swayed by your powers of oratory. Be so good as to confine any further remarks to topics that will assist us in our deliberations without further inflaming the passions of the public.'

Tilly bowed his head. 'If Your Worships are still open on the point as to whether you will commit the defendants to trial, I shall be pleased to address some further remarks. But if you are not, I would not presume to take up any more of the time of the court.'

Liddicoat nodded. 'Thank you, Mr Tilly, I think we will retire.'

Tilly turned to Tom and shook his head.

The magistrates returned within five minutes and resumed their seats. Liddicoat's face was grave. 'The bench have come to the decision that the charge against the prisoners is of too grave and important a character for us to decide upon. We have therefore agreed to commit the prisoners to be tried by a jury of their fellow countrymen.'

There was a growing rumble of dissent from the public section.

Tilly stood up. 'I ask that they should be liberated on bail. John Burton will again stand surety for them.'

Liddicoat began his answer before Tilly had finished speaking. 'The bench accedes to your request and admits them to the same bail as before.'

The chairman of the Southampton magistrates was again ready to stand bail for Stephens, but John Burton once more stood surety for both men.

The mutterings from the public benches turned to cheers, which the police made only a token attempt to silence. The clock outside struck the half-hour. It was five thirty: the committal proceedings had occupied six and a half hours.

Stephens had showed a great deal of emotion throughout the hearing, frequently leaning forward and burying his head in his hands, but Tom had kept his face impassive, though he had burned with anger when Brooks had walked to the witness box to testify against them. When he left the dock, however, he relaxed, lost control of himself and burst into tears.

Tilly put a hand on his shoulder and stood by him until he had controlled himself. 'I am sorry, Captain Dudley, I have done my best for you, but I am afraid that the magistrates knew their minds before they sat down this morning. It is always easier to duck a hard decision and let someone other than yourself take it, is it not?'

'What will—' Tom broke off as he caught sight of Brooks. He pushed his way through the crowd of people to reach him. He gave a start and flinched as Tom took his arm, and could not meet his eye.

'So, Brooks, you're a free man,' Tom said, his voice even, but his gaze fixed on him. 'Mr Danckwerts seemed at great pains to claim that there had been no agreement with you to testify against us.'

Brooks said nothing, his eyes darting over the throng of people around them. 'I did not kill him, Captain.'

He tried to pull away but Tom held him fast. 'You did not. You had not the stomach for that. But you were quick enough to seek your share while the boy's blood was still flowing, and you ate heartily enough of his body.' He paused. 'Did you not shake my hand a score of times that day, say that I had saved us all and that if we were ever fortunate enough to see our native land, you would not rest until you had repaid me?'

Brooks kept his head down.

'And this is the repayment? Will you sleep soundly in your bed tonight?' Tom stood looking at him a moment longer, then released his grip, turned on his heel and walked away.

Tilly was still waiting for him.

'What will happen now?' Tom said.

'You'll be tried at the Winter Assizes at Exeter in a fortnight's time.'

'And you will defend us there?'

Tilly shook his head. 'I cannot. A solicitor is permitted to appear before the magistrates, but not one of Her Majesty's justices. You will need a barrister, but I shall obtain you the best that we can find . . . and afford.'

'Then he will not be much of a barrister,' Tom said, 'for the money I had is already gone. I cannot go to sea and earn my living and as of today my wife is no longer in employment either.'

'The man I would recommend – and fearing today's decision, I have already taken the liberty of speaking to him on your behalf – is Arthur Collins. You will not, I think, find a more able advocate of your cause in the whole of the West of England. He was called to the bar at Gray's Inn twenty-four years ago and has been a Queen's Counsel these last seven years and the recorder of Exeter the last five.' He smiled. 'He has two other things to recommend him: he's a West Countryman and a keen yachtsman.'

'But the fees such an eminent gentleman must command would be well beyond our reach.'

'We shall see,' Tilly said. 'I know that moves are afoot to raise funds for your defence and Mr Collins is very eager to take the case. Meet him at least, and meanwhile we shall see what can be done to help meet your costs.'

'And your own bill?'

'A small matter and one that is far from pressing. The good folk of Falmouth have already contibuted a part of it. We will talk of it in good time. Let us first concentrate our minds on securing your acquittal.'

Tom again felt tears welling in his eyes. 'Mr Tilly, all three—' He checked himself. 'Stephens and I are more grateful to you than I can say. You have worked hard in our cause and it is through no failing of yours that we are not already free men.'

Tilly gestured with his hand as if to brush away Tom's words. 'I shall forward all the papers on the case to Arthur Collins. He has chambers in London and I shall instruct his clerk to arrange an appointment there later this week, if that is convenient?

'Then I shall bid you good-day and good luck, Captain Dudley. I trust this business will soon be behind you and please do me the honour of calling on me when next you put into Falmouth.' He shook Tom's hand and walked away.

The late conclusion to the court proceedings meant that both Tom and Stephens had to spend the night in Falmouth and leave for home the next morning. Stephens returned to Southampton by boat after being offered free passage home on the *Lady Wodehouse* by J. E. le Feuvre, another Southampton magistrate and a prominent member of Stephens's masonic lodge.

Tom left Falmouth on the first train the next morning. Despite the early hour, Cheesman was again there to see him off. Tom spent the night at home in Sutton, then travelled up to Tollesbury to see his sister. His father remained on his ship in the Americas, though he would almost certainly have heard of Tom's plight from reports in the American newspapers.

CHAPTER 17

Tom's financial situation was every bit as desperate as he had painted it to Tilly. The Newtown School Board had already told Philippa that she would be obliged to resign her post as mistress if he was committed for trial. The Dudleys now faced a rapidly rising legal bill with no income other than sporadic hardship grants from Andrew Thompson's Thames Yacht Agency.

The following week, Thompson wrote to *The Times*, announcing a public subscription to defray the expenses of the men's defence, pointing out that they were unable to earn their living while facing court proceedings and were unable to meet the costs.

At first Tom had refused to consider the idea, but the entreaties of his wife and the parlous state of his finances eventually persuaded him to accept, on the condition that any money over and above the cost of the defence should be used to pay for the education of Richard Parker's sister Edith.

Financial aid also began to arrive from other sources. Broadsheet ballads were published and sold on the streets to raise funds and several yacht clubs also launched appeals and took collections for Tom and Stephens.

The *Mignonette*'s dinghy was still in Mr Buckingham's warehouse at Upton Slip and the *Falmouth News Slip* urged readers to 'see the Boat of the Yacht *Mignonette* at Buckingham's and leave some coppers for the men'.

The *Falmouth & Penryn Weekly Times* also enlisted the support of its readers:

> It appears that the seamen castaways are destitute and our friend Mr John Buckingham who has charge of the boat is prepared to show her to all people who will pay a small contribution for the benefit of these unfortunate men.
>
> We are further gratified to find that Mr R. D. Patterson, a great New Zealand showman, will give a benefit night on Wednesday next at the Polytechnic Hall, so that the inhabitants of Falmouth will have an opportunity of showing their practical sympathy for distress, for which Falmouth has always been justly renowned. We have no doubt that an assembly of sympathizers will be present at the hall waiting to give ovation in the remembrance of the deliverance of these men whose sufferings are almost without a parallel and whose fortitude belongs to the men of the sea.

Mr Patterson's attraction was a 'Grand Diorama' containing fifty scenes of New Zealand life on a canvas two thousand yards long. The paper later revealed that the benefit night 'has resulted in a handsome donation for the benefit of the sufferers of the *Mignonette*'.

Another West Country paper reported:

> The small mahogany boat in which the men were drifting is still at Falmouth and during the last day or two has been visited by hundred of persons including many experienced mariners, all of whom expressed the greatest surprise that so many men could have existed at all in so frail a craft tossed about on the stormy billows, and how they could have lived at all in such weather as Captain Dudley and his companions experienced.
>
> The boat has been very minutely examined but no traces of blood are discoverable. There are plenty of indications however that the boat was sadly knocked about. The public feeling at Falmouth and indeed throughout the rest of England is one of deep sympathy for the unhappy men.

Jack Want, the *Mignonette*'s owner in Sydney, also sent a donation to the defence fund. Although unable to forward the report he had prepared, which had been impounded as evidence, Tom had written to him outlining the events and hinting at some suitable reward for Captain Simonsen.

> We were able to tell Captain Simonsen our sad tale but not before himself learning a little by his crew having the remainder of the body to throw out of the boat. I begged him to save the boat for me and am thankful he did so.
>
> We were on board *Moctezuma* 38 days during the passage to Falmouth during which time Captain Simonsen gave us every possible attention. We were nothing but skin and bone at the time we came on board, but thanks to the treatment and kindness we received from that gentleman, we all have him to thank so much for recovering so far to our general health and the kindness we received, no words can express. Nothing we could ever do and give could repay him for past kindness. However I trust something may be done to keep him in remembrance of the poor souls he saved.

In addition to sending Simonsen a token of his appreciation, Want also sent Tom the hundred pounds he would have received had the *Mignonette* been safely delivered to Sydney. Want had the yacht insured for more than he had paid for it and was not out of pocket by the gesture, but it was still a generous act.

Tom and Stephens also sought to take the first steps towards earning their own living again by applying for the renewal of their Board of Trade certificates of competence. They had been lost with the *Mignonette* and without them they could find employment on a ship only as ordinary seamen.

Two Board of Trade officials approved the request, noting on the file, 'I suppose they should have them,' and 'I see no reason for withholding them,' but the request was referred to the Home Office for a final decision,

> ... as it is understood that both Mr Dudley and Mr Stephens, now out on bail, are still lying under the charge of having

murdered one of the crew of the *Mignonette*, I am to request you to move Sir William Vernon Harcourt and cause them to be informed whether he sees any objection to the renewal of the certificates as requested.

Home Office officials feared that if the men had their certificates, it would give them an incentive to breach their bail and the home secretary decided the matter: 'I think their certificates might not be renewed at least until the court has decided whether the men are guilty of murder.'

Brooks had none of the financial problems of his former shipmates. Although required as a witness at the assizes, he was free to return to sea in the interim, or resume work as a rigger at Fay's Yard, but he preferred the offer of more remunerative employment in a travelling show. Several showmen had also approached Tom, offering him money to exhibit himself, but he turned them all down flat. Brooks had no such scruples. Billed as 'The Cannibal of the High Seas', he appeared all over the West Country and the south coast in a sideshow to a travelling fair amongst the bearded ladies and manacled 'Wild Men'.

Unshaven and dressed in suitably distressed rags, Brooks posed in front of a crudely painted backdrop of the *Mignonette*'s dinghy adrift on the ocean. For the further edification of the paying customers, he devoured scraps of raw meat in a gruesome simulacrum of the ordeal he had endured. In addition to his wages and his keep, he was allowed half the proceeds from the souvenir postcards of himself that he sold.

The *Mignonette*'s dinghy also became an attraction in its own right. After being exhibited in Falmouth it was later sold to an Exmouth showman for fifty pounds. Although it was the genuine article, the dinghy was enhanced before being put on show. The existing marks on the cross-members and brass crutches for the oars were deepened to give them more prominence and bloodstains were added to heighten the audience's vicarious thrill.

There was no shortage of paying customers wanting to see Brooks or the dinghy. The Victorians had a voracious appetite for the curious, ghoulish or criminal. Even after public hangings were outlawed, the Dead Houses, in which unidentifed bodies scavenged from the rivers or harbours were displayed until claimed or buried in paupers' graves, were always thronged with crowds eager for the macabre spectacle. Parties of members of polite Victorian society also amused themselves by touring the Bedlams – the hospitals for the insane – poking fun at the unfortunate occupants.

Penny ballads about natural and man-made disasters were hastily penned and hawked around the streets, and penny dreadful newspapers, such as the *Illustrated Police News*, achieved huge circulations on an uninterrupted diet of gruesome pictures and ghoulish copy celebrating crimes and disasters. The *Mignonette* case provided their illustrators with plentiful source material.

The proprietors of travelling freak shows were merely cashing in on this insatiable public appetite. They had evolved out of the annual country goose, horse and hiring fairs, held on holy days and holidays. Curiosities were often exhibited among the hucksters, whores, quack-medicine salesmen, travelling toothpullers, and the recruiters for King and country, pressing the King's shilling on drunken farm boys.

These travelling shows often attached themselves uninvited to attractions such as the Great Exhibition of 1851, but the urbanization of the population as a result of the Industrial Revolution provided a ready audience for larger, more permanent attractions – dime museums in the US and the English penny museums and curiosity shops characterized by Dickens.

At a time when theatres were regarded as little more than brothels with entertainment, the penny museums found a way to evade local by-laws that prohibited lewd or indecent displays by pretending to an educational status that few deserved. Some had a genuinely educative role, but in most cases, like John Burton's Falmouth shop, they were simply collections of animate or inanimate curiosities, described in pseudo-scientific terms such as 'The connecting link between man and brute creation'.

The largest museums, like Madame Tussaud's in London or P. T. Barnum's in New York, became true mass entertainments. Barnum's vast American Museum was the biggest public attraction in New York, so large that families would bring packed lunches and spend all day there.

Some attractions were recruited as adults, others – children and even babies – were bought from their parents. Annie Jones, 'the most marvellous specimen of hirsute development since the days of Esau, 3,700 years ago', was first exhibited as 'The infant Esau' at just twelve months old.

Attractions were advertised on huge painted banners, posters and handbills, and by barkers outside the entrance, using unequalled heights of hyperbole.

> The greatest, most astounding aggregation of marvels and monstrosities ... looted from the ends of the earth, from the wilds of darkest Africa, the miasmic jungles of Brazil, the mystic headwaters of the Yan-tse Kiang, the cannibal isle of the Antipodes, the frosty slopes of the Himalayas, and the barren steppes of the Caucasus ... a refined exhibition for cultured ladies and gentlemen ... The most prodigious paragon of all prodigies in over fifty years. The crowning mystery of Nature's contradictions, the incarnate Paradox before which Science stands confounded and blindly wonders.

Every aspect of their lives was also fictionalized. Kings, queens, princes and princesses abounded, and wives and children of normal appearance were invented to emphasize the abnormality of the attraction. 'Darkest Africa' and 'The Cannibal Islands' were frequently cited origins, but some freaks were given an even more ludicrous provenance. Two albino brothers were presented at one freak show as 'Ambassadors from the Planet Mars'.

By the middle of the century most museums and freak shows also incorporated live shows, in which the attractions would perform either in *tableaux vivants* or full-scale productions, even including song-and-dance routines. Like Ned Brooks, most attractions were required to produce some performance. Wild Men paced up and down, growled at the audience, gnawed on bones, ate raw meat or bit the heads off live chickens or rats, but the crowds would also be entertained by fire-eaters, sword-swallowers and snake-handlers – invariably scantily clad women.

Cannibals had been standard freak-show fare for half a century before the *Mignonette*'s sinking, but the attractions had almost always been exotic, primitive peoples. Mrs Fraser, who survived the sinking of the *Stirling Castle* off the Queensland coast, was an exception, an exhibit in a London freak show in 1837 whose tales of life amongst 'the cannibal savages' of Australia were recounted in a popular broadsheet.

In the eighteenth century, South Sea islanders were regarded as 'noble savages' of Rousseau's description, and the experience of early voyagers like Captain Cook made the islands appear earthly paradises.

By the early nineteenth century, tales – sometimes true, but often lurid penny-dreadful accounts of the savagery and cannibalism of primitive peoples – had led to a sea change in public attitudes. The noble savage was now widely regarded as a sub-human species of brute creation.

Black Africans and South Sea islanders, especially Fijians, were routinely described as 'cannibals'. Not all were what they seemed. On one occasion a Zulu cannibal was recognized by two women visitors: 'He ain't no Zulu, that's Bill Jackson. He worked over there at Camden, in the dock.'

Of P. T. Barnum's 'Four Fijian cannibals' exhibited in 1872, one was from Virginia and two more had been living in California for some years. None of that prevented Barnum from issuing a press release when one of them died of natural causes, claiming the other three had been interrupted while making a meal of him.

Tales of natives feasting on human flesh in remote and exotic parts of the globe brought a vicarious thrill to Victorian drawing rooms, but both the tattooed skin and the professed flesh-eating culture of the cannibals displayed by the showmen were regarded as clear evidence of the degenerate, primitive and backward nature of societies so alien to the Victorian ideals of decency, morality and duty.

British seamen – white Anglo-Saxons – showing the same stigmata of the tattooing needle, and the same willingness to consume human flesh in extremity, were an uncomfortable reminder that the distance between primitive peoples and English civilization might not be as great as the Victorian upper classes liked to think.

This, even more than the steady encroachment of government regulation over the shipping trade, was the driving force in attempts to outlaw the most abhorrent of all the seafaring practices: the custom of the sea.

The Customs House, Arwenack Street, Falmouth, late nineteenth century.

The Pictorial World
An Illustrated Weekly Newspaper

No. 116, New Series.—(Vol. V.)   *NOVEMBER 13th, 1884.*   Price Sixpence. Post Free, 6½d.

REGISTERED AT THE GENERAL POST OFFICE FOR TRANSMISSION ABROAD.

1. The Castle Gate.   2. Captain Dudley.   3. The Mate.   4. Master Wiese, of the *Montezuma*, who rescued the crew.   5. His Lordship informs the Jury of *his* intentions.   6. Edwin Brooks as witness.   7. Mr. Collins, Q.C., for the Defence.   8. The Trial: The case for the Prosecution.

THE LOSS OF THE YACHT "MIGNONETTE": TRIAL OF THE SURVIVORS AT EXETER.

'The Last of the Barons', Sir John Walter Huddleston.

THE MIGNONETTE TRAGEDY—PORTRAITS AND INCIDENTS
THE LAST RESOURCE
ON BOARD THE MONTEZUMA
CAPTAIN DUDLEY
OF THE YACHT MIGNONETTE
MEETING HIS WIFE
AT SUTTON RY STATION
THE DINGY
TRIED FOR THE
MURDER OF THE BOY PARKER

From *Illustrated Police News*, 15 November 1884.

Lord Chief Justice Coleridge.

Sir William Harcourt.

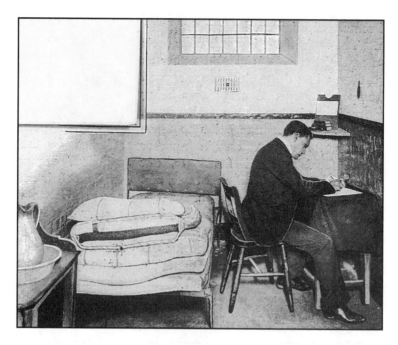

Prison Cell, Holloway Prison, *c*. 1880.

Prisoners at work on the treadwheel and picking oakum, Holloway Prison, 1862.

The exercise yard, Holloway Prison, *c*. 1890.

Meeting discharged prisoners at the gates of Holloway Prison, 1890.

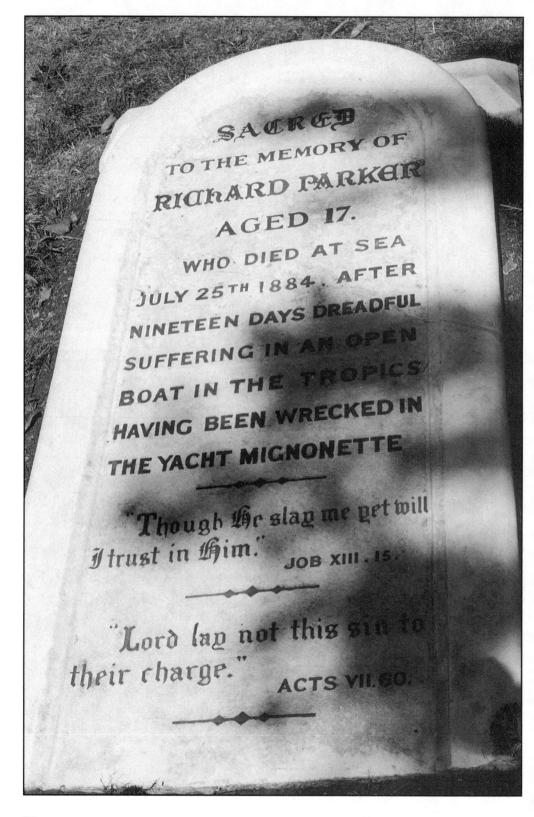

SACRED
TO THE MEMORY OF
RICHARD PARKER
AGED 17.
WHO DIED AT SEA
JULY 25TH 1884. AFTER
NINETEEN DAYS DREADFUL
SUFFERING IN AN OPEN
BOAT IN THE TROPICS
HAVING BEEN WRECKED IN
THE YACHT MIGNONETTE

"Though He slay me yet will
I trust in Him." JOB XIII. 15.

"Lord lay not this sin to
their charge." ACTS VII. 60.

16   The tombstone of Richard Parker, in Pear Tree Churchyard, Itchen Ferry.

CHAPTER 18

The judge chosen to hear the case of Regina versus Dudley and Stephens at the Exeter Assizes was the Baron Huddleston, a haughty and flamboyant character who suited the colour of his gloves to the case before him – white for routine thefts and felonies, lavender for breach-of-promise suits and black for murder cases.

He had acquired a well-deserved reputation for browbeating jurors into verdicts that tallied with his own conclusions and also had some knowledge of the seafaring world from a spell as Judge Advocate of the Fleet and Counsel to the Admiralty. Although, according to his obituary in *The Times*, 'He knew less of the lines of a ship than of the points of the horse, he yet managed to hold his own against the skilled mercantile lawyers of his day.'

As the paper also noted, 'The judge, whose charm of manner and skill in conversation made him afterwards particularly acceptable in distinguished society, began his ascent in not the most fashionable or promising surroundings.'

Born in 1817, the son of a merchant captain, Huddleston grew up in the West Country, but when his father retired from the sea he returned to his native Ireland. The future judge matriculated at, but never graduated from, Trinity College, Dublin.

He began his legal career as an usher but was admitted as a student at Gray's Inn on 18 April 1836, and called to the bar in the summer of 1839, becoming a barrister of the Central Criminal Court and, a diligent attendant at the Old Bailey. A friendly turnkey went up and down the corridors of Newgate touting for dock briefs on behalf of Mr Huddleston. He was admirable in the conduct of a cause, dangerous in cross-examination, and above all things, skilful in presenting his points to the jury.

Huddleston showed an early fondess for good living and the pleasures of society and, as *The Times* acidly noted,

> It will be a surprise to many to learn that in this early period in his career his speciality lay in the argument of Poor Law cases. Society indeed played a large part in his later life and did not leave him that leisure for study which a judge who is satisfactorily to dispose of legal arguments requires. He was fond of exercising the remarkable powers of genial and fascinating address which he undoubtedly possessed, whether or not at heart he was more amiable or less selfish than the majority of successful men.

He was able to make use of the full range of his talents as a counsel in the divorce court, 'repeatedly impressing upon a common jury the precise significance of French words of endearment, pronounced probably on purpose, with the most English of accents'.

Huddleston took silk in 1857, and featured in many great criminal cases at the Old Bailey, conducting a series of memorable defences including that at the murder trial of Edward Pook. Huddleston, 'annihilated the evidence of one important witness on cross-examination, pointed out the weaknesses of the prosecution and then attacked the Police as severely as if his instructions had been similar to the time-honoured: No case; abuse the opposing attorney.'

He also defended Cuffy, one of the Chartists, prosecuted the Countess of Derwentwater, secured the release of Mercy Catherine Newton on her third trial for matricide, was junior to Sir Alexander Cockburn in the prosecution of Dr Palmer for 'wholesale poisoning at Rugeley, and vindicated the character of Mrs Firebrace in the court for matrimonial cases'.

Huddleston also harboured political ambitions, and stood as a Conservative candidate – unsuccessfully at Worcester, Shrewsbury and twice at Kidderminster, before finally winning a seat at Canterbury in 1865. He lost it at the general election of 1868, and made a further unsuccessful attempt on Norwich in 1870.

He succeeded there by forty-seven votes in 1874, greatly helped by his recent marriage to Lady Diana de Vere Beauclerk, sister of the Duke of St Albans. His new wife was well known in Norwich and she and her mother, the Duchess of St Albans, campaigned hard on his behalf.

They had been married at All Saints, Knightsbridge, by Bishop Wilberforce, a notorious snob who characteristically forgot to include in his diary the name of the low-born bridegroom: 'December 18th, to All Saints, Knightsbridge, to marry Lady Di. Back into centre, Bar Committee.'

In February of the following year Huddleston gave up his political ambitions to become a judge in the Court of Common Pleas and was knighted that May. He was transferred to the Court of Exchequer on the death of Mr Baron Pigott, automatically receiving the honorific Baron of the Exchequer, a title that went back to a period before the days of professional judges when the barons of the realm heard cases in the Court of the King. Huddleston was the last to be created before the Court of Exchequer was abolished and delighted in calling himself 'the Last of the Barons'.

He always insisted on having his courtroom, 'heated and protected from currents of air until the atmosphere was oppressive to the verge of endurance, and proved what is called a strong judge, taking a view of his own and almost invariably leading the jury to the same opinion'.

Age and success had not blunted the edge of Huddleston's ambition and, though some of his peers regarded him as insufficiently dedicated to the law to merit consideration as a future Lord Chief Justice, the chance to preside over a great leading case offered him an opportunity to advance his claims.

His first task was to persuade the grand jury in Exeter to arraign Tom and Stephens for trial. Grand jurymen were not the twelve good men and true who heard criminal trials. They were gentlemen 'of the best figure in the county', and their meetings were as much social as judicial occasions, with luncheons and even a ball punctuating their deliberations.

They rarely resisted the recommendations of the judge at the assizes but Huddleston was anxious to remove even that possibility. After all, the grand jury in the US versus Holmes case in Philadelphia had thrown out an indictment of murder and replaced it with one of manslaughter. If the Exeter grand jury had rejected the indictment or substituted the lesser charge of manslaughter, the chance to establish a leading case, and with it Huddleston's hopes of further advancement, would have been lost.

When the grand jury convened on Monday, 3 November, Huddleston first led them through the indictments for the other trials to be heard that week. Following his advice, they rejected an indictment in a case of rape and one of manslaughter, but defied him by also rejecting an indictment against the mother of two murdered children. The father was to be convicted and sentenced to death on the day before Tom and Stephens stood trial.

When he turned to the case of the *Mignonette*, Huddleston did not allow either the prosecution or defence counsel to address the grand jury. Instead he gave a magisterial lecture outlining the 'facts' of the case. These included the assertion that Brooks had not only taken no part in the killing but had 'sternly dissented from it'.

Having established the credentials of the prosecution's chief witness, the baron then gave a formal ruling on the relevant law. He cited such legal authorities as there were and rejected out of hand the precedents in other courts including US versus Holmes, which a barrister, 'Peluca', had cited in a letter to the *Telegraph* as justification for the actions of Dudley and Stephens.

Huddleston also made a brusque dismissal of the possible defences of self-defence and necessity. His closing remarks left the grand jury with no room for doubt about what was required of them. 'It is impossible to say that the act of Dudley and Stephens was an act of self-defence. Parker, at the bottom of the boat, was not endangering their lives by any act of his; the boat would hold them all, and the motive for killing him was not for the purpose of lightening the boat but for the purpose of eating him, which they could do when dead, but not while living. What really imperilled their lives was not the presence of Parker, but the absence of food.'

His reference to 'lightening the boat', was a nod to the US versus Holmes case, no doubt in the hope of swaying the grand jury against a similar substitution of a manslaughter indictment, but it seemed to imply that drowning someone to save yourself from drowning was less of a crime than killing and eating someone to save yourself from starving.

To rule on the facts of a case that had not been tested in evidence was unprecedented. Huddleston's prior ruling effectively made the legal opinion of counsel for the defence irrelevant: whatever arguments he advanced, the judge had already reached his decision. His actions were within the letter of the English law – in which the judge is presumed to know the law, whereas the counsel's job is merely to remind him of it – but they were outside its spirit. At best it was highly irregular, at worst a flagrant abuse of the due process.

The grand jury obliged him by 'finding a true bill' on the indictment, but Huddleston had next to convince the trial jury. He had already laid the groundwork. His exposition of the law had been printed in the local press, and the men who were to form the jury for the criminal trial were therefore made aware of the judge's opinion that the defendants were guilty of murder before the criminal trial had even begun.

Of course, it was by no means certain that they would agree with him. There was a property qualification for jury service, but jury members were rather less socially elevated than grand jurors and often of a much more independent bent. One in five of all murder trials at the time resulted in an acquittal. In another three-fifths the accused was convicted on the lesser charge of manslaughter or found insane. In less than 20 per cent of cases was the sentence of death passed and, through the exercise of the royal prerogative of mercy, in only half of those was it actually carried out. In 1884, for example, a year when a higher proportion than usual were executed, 192 people faced charges of murder, but only fifteen met their end on the rope.

Jury verdicts had to be unanimous. Even if Huddleston's power of argument and force of personality was enough to sway eleven of the twelve jurors, a single member of the jury obstinately refusing to convict would force a retrial.

The widespread popular sympathy for Tom and Stephens and the impending arrival in Exeter of a large number of character witnesses for them also made Huddleston well aware of the risk of a conviction on the minor charge of manslaughter or even an acquittal. Instead of outlawing the custom of the sea, such a verdict would have legitimized it. His imaginative solution was to try to persuade the jury not to reach a verdict at all.

Regina versus Dudley and Stephens opened at the Western Circuit Winter Assize, Exeter – the courts held periodically under a visiting judge to hear cases too serious or complex to be dealt with by the magistrates – at ten thirty on Thursday, 11 November 1884. Tom had caught the mail train, leaving Paddington at four o'clock on a freezing, foggy morning. He stood motionless on the platform at Exeter for a few moments, allowing the crowds of passengers to ebb away around him. Always a solitary, insular character, this morning of all mornings he was anxious to keep his own company.

He glanced up at the monolithic red-brick façade of the building overlooking the platform, and saw the words 'Devon County Prison' carved over the entrance. He looked away, only to see the outline of the castle, where the trial was to be held, rising above the city walls on the next hill.

He ate breakfast in one of the taverns clustered around the foot of Castle Hill, choosing a table in a dark corner and keeping his back to the room as he ate. The snatches of conversation he overheard suggested the only topic on everyone's lips that day was the trial of Dudley and Stephens.

Still not strong enough for the walk up the steep hill to the castle, he hailed a hansom cab. 'You're here for the trial?' the cabbie said. 'You'll be lucky to find a seat. All Exeter wants to see this one.'

'I'm sure they'll find room for me,' Tom said.

It was nine twenty, over an hour before the trial was due to begin, but already the road leading to the Castle Gate was thronged with people. Murder trials were a popular form of entertainment, whether experienced in person or vicariously through the pages of the penny dreadfuls. Frock-coated country squires, sober-suited citizens and their wives, even whole families, hurried up the hill, talking and laughing with such animation that they could have been on their way to the fair.

The old city walls towered fifty feet above them, blocking out much of the light from the narrow street, and the dark cobbles glistened with damp from the night's rain. Next to the Castle Gate was the crumbling, ivy-encrusted masonry of the great tower. Its roof lay open to the sky and it was populated only by crows.

The cab passed under the spiked iron portcullis. It was an uncomfortable reminder to Tom that his freedom might end at this gateway. The courtyard in front of the elegant Georgian building was packed with people. Tom shrank back in his seat as heads turned and people craned to see the occupant of the hansom. The driver inched it towards the triple-arched entrance where a group of policemen were struggling to restrain the crowds.

'Not here,' Tom called. 'The court officials' entrance.'

The cabbie glanced behind him, then shrugged and flicked his whip. He pulled up at a side door guarded by two more policemen. Tom paid the driver and hurried towards them before the crowd could reach him. 'Tom Dudley,' he said. 'I am to be tried here this morning.'

'Indeed you are, Captain Dudley,' one said.

He led Tom through the broad, echoing corridors of the castle and down a steep spiral flight of steps, the treads worn by use, to the holding cell beneath the dock of the court.

As Tom entered, Stephens rose to shake his hand. He seemed to have regained no more weight in the three weeks since Tom had last seen him. His cheeks remained hollow and his eyes were sunken, with deep, purple-black shadows beneath them.

Tom shook his hand then turned to greet the other man in the room. 'Are you in good heart, Mr Collins?'

Arthur Collins was dressed in a dark suit of fine worsted, and the ruddy complexion beneath his greying hair spoke not of fresh air but of rich food and wine. The hand he offered Tom was soft and plump, and his speech was slow and cautious, as if he measured each word before he uttered it. 'I am indeed, Captain Dudley, though I could have wished for the case to be heard by a different judge.'

He shuffled the papers in front of him and cleared his throat. 'Sir William Grove was originally scheduled to preside at the Winter Assizes, but he was replaced by Baron Huddleston after consultations between the Lord Chief Justice, Lord Coleridge, and the home secretary.

'The Baron Huddleston is a man of mature years, but his age has neither blunted his ambition nor improved his temper. He also has a complaint of a delicate nature. They say Judge Jefferies was suffering cruelly from the same complaint when he conducted the Bloody Assizes at Monmouth, executing supporters of the unsuccessful pretender to the throne. It is to be hoped Mr Baron Huddleston is rather less dyspeptic when he takes his seat on the bench this morning.' He gave a brief smile, which Tom did not return.

Just before ten thirty Tom and Stephens were led up the staircase into the dock. Local sympathy for the defendants was as strong in Exeter as it had been in Falmouth. The courtroom was packed and the murmurs of conversation swelled into applause as they came into view. Tom stood at the rail of the dock, where he was to remain throughout the trial, since the lacerations caused by the broken chamber-pot on the Moctezuma still prevented him from sitting for any length of time.

The morning sunlight streamed through the iron latticework covering the windows, forming diamond patterns of light and shade on the floor. Directly in front of and below the dock, in the well of the court, was a large square lawyer's table, smothered in papers and parchment rolls.

Arthur Collins and the other members of the defence team sat on Tom's right. Collins's junior was Henry Clark, the recorder of Tiverton and a member of the Royal Western Yacht Club at Plymouth. The prosecution faced them across the table, led by Arthur Charles, QC, with Charles Matthews as his junior. The stature of the leading counsel for the Crown and the number of other lawyers – no less than fourteen sat around three sides of the table, leaving the other for the clerks of the court – showed the importance the Home Office attached to the case.

The double-banked seats of the jury box stood at the right of the court. The jurors, twelve men dressed in their Sunday-best suits, stared back at Tom, curiosity written on their faces.

Facing the dock was the judge's bench, an ornately carved mahogany chair upholstered in blood-red velvet. The witness box lay to its left and on the other side was a seat, like a box at the theatre, where a lady – of some refinement, judging from her dress – was sitting.

The rest of the well of the court was crowded with country gentlemen, officers in full military uniform and clerics. Most of the seats were allocated by ticket only, doubtless to people of the best figure of the county, but a few, plus the standing areas, were reserved for the general public. Those spaces had been filled as soon as the doors were open, and the benches behind Tom were jammed. Through the open door he could see policemen still battling to repel those who had gathered in the corridors and were determined to force their way in.

After a few minutes the heavy oak doors banged shut. There was a brief silence, then the door behind the judge's bench opened. Flanked by his usher, the Baron Huddleston strode in and sat down, resplendent in the crimson robes of a judge at assize. He glanced to his right and smiled at the woman seated in the wings. She raised her hand in acknowledgement. 'That's his wife,' the turnkey whispered to Tom. 'She always comes to watch his big cases. He passed sentence of death on a poor devil yesterday and she had to put her hand to her mouth to hide a smile.' He smiled himself, showing a mouthful of rotten teeth.

Tom turned his head away. The man's breath stank of tobacco and sour ale, but he also did not want to hear any more of his confidences.

The judge banged his gavel to silence the buzz of conversation. Tom studied him as the clerk of the court began to read the indictment. Huddleston's hair was obscured by his wig, but his long sideburns were grey and he looked to be at least sixty years old. His eyebrows were darker and drawn together in a permanent frown, accentuated by the downturned corners of his mouth.

He was running to fat and his jowls quivered as he leaned forward to speak. His smiles seemed to be reserved for his own wit and for the remarks he addressed to the jury. His manner was impatient, his speech clipped and precise, but every now and again a flat vowel or a mis-pronunciation betrayed his humble origins.

Eleven of the twelve jurors had already sat through seven previous cases during that week's assizes, including the conviction of a thirty-four-year-old man, Edward Bath Edwards, for murder. As the turnkey had said, Huddleston had sentenced him to death the previous day for slitting the throats of his two children.

The clerk laid down the indictment, and faced Tom and Stephens. 'How do you plead?'

'Not guilty,' they said in turn.

Arthur Charles removed the gold *pince-nez* through which he had been studying documents, and got to his feet to open the prosecution, hooking his thumbs into the pockets of his waistcoat. Like Huddleston, he peppered his remarks with Latin quotations, which, from their expressions, were as incomprehensible to the jurors as they were to Tom.

'May it please Your Lordship, gentlemen of the jury, on the part of the prosecution it now becomes my duty to lay the facts of this extraordinary and painful case before you and to submit, I regret to say without doubt or hesitation, that the prisoners at the bar are guilty by the law of this country of the murder of Richard Parker.

'Gentlemen, you must all feel the deepest compassion and sympathy for them in their appalling suffering but that does not free you from the grave responsibility of finding a verdict in this case, according to the law and the evidence which will be laid before you.

'Sympathy and compassion for the shocking and terrible sufferings which these prisoners have undoubtedly undergone may well be urged as a most powerful plea for the remission in this case of the extreme penalty of the law, but it cannot be considered by you in coming to a conclusion as to whether, by the law of England, these men are guilty of the crime of which they stand charged.

'Now comes a question of great importance and of deep interest in this case, and as far as I know, it can only be answered in one way. These men are charged with murder. What is murder? As I understand it, murder is the unlawful killing of anybody by a man of sound mind with malice aforethought.

'Anybody who deliberately or intentionally kills another is undoubtedly guilty of what the law calls malice aforethought. Here we have evidence of the utmost deliberation. You have the statement of Dudley that "Something must be done", the agreement between Dudley and Stephens that unless a sail appeared on the horizon on the morning of the nineteenth day, Parker must be killed. And you have the fact that Dudley killed the boy with his own hand and that Stephens, who had agreed to the act, was within three feet of the boy and therefore in a position to have joined in it, had the boy struggled for his life.

'The facts of the case are practically beyond dispute; I doubt whether the defence will endeavour to dispute them. There can be no doubt that the act was deliberate and was done by persons of sound mind.

'If the prisoners could be held to be of unsound mind, your duty would be a comparatively simple one. Under the Act of Parliament passed last session it would simply be your duty to say they were guilty of the act but at the time they committed it they were of unsound mind.

'You will find that Dudley and Stephens appeared perfectly clear in their mind at the time they did the act. Dudley knew the nature of the act he was doing and he knew it to be wrong, for before he did it, he offered up a prayer for the poor boy and for the rash act he was about to commit.'

It was hardly necessary for Charles to dismiss this line of possible defence. Given the deservedly terrible reputation of the Victorian asylums, even a man facing the gallows would have thought hard before pleading insanity, though Collins could certainly have entered a plea of temporary insanity and might well have found the jurors sympathetic to the idea.

Charles went on to reject the tiny handful of precedents in other courts, including US versus Holmes. 'Another topic of defence which has already been publicly urged in the case, and which I presume will be raised again, was that it was an act of justifiable or excusable homicide. There can be no doubt that there are cases known to the English law when homicide is justifiable or excusable, but I am obliged to submit that I can find no trace that this was one of those cases.

'I cannot help thinking that it is a total misconception of the meaning of the doctrine to apply it to this case. They might kill a man in order to prevent his killing them – that is self-defence – but in this case the prisoners were in no danger at Parker's hand. He was not assailing them, he was lying in the bottom of the boat where he had been for many hours.

'What they were really in danger from was the violent and fierce assault of hunger and thirst, and it was in order to prevent their being killed by that, that they chose to sacrifice an innocent victim. Homicide is only justifiable by the law of England when committed in defence of one's life, but they did not do it in defence of themselves from Parker, they did it having come to the conclusion that he was weaker than them, not likely to live as long as them and had a life not so valuable as their own, in as much as he had no wife and children dependent on him.

'They put an end to his existence. Gentlemen, it seems to me that having done that, and having been, as I pointed out to you, sound in their own minds, the prisoners are guilty by the law of this country of the crime of wilful murder.'

CHAPTER 19

Before Collins could begin his opening statement for the defence, Baron Huddleston stirred himself. 'Mr Collins, I presume you traverse the law?' It was an archaic and recondite way of asking him if he opposed the prosecution's contention, as if the matter was being discussed in the Wig and Pen Club, not an open courtroom.

'Yes, My Lord,' Collins said.

'And you rely on those cases mentioned by learned counsel for the prosecution, I suppose?'

'I rely on those cases, and I say that if necessity compelled these men in taking the life they were justified in so doing.'

'I may say at once that it is a doctrine that I cannot assent to,' Huddleston said. 'I have already expressed my opinion as to what is the law and I shall tell the jury to act upon that.'

'If Your Lordship pleases.'

'I shall lay down as a matter of law there was no justification,' Huddleston said. 'I shall lay that down distinctly and absolutely.'

'I must address the jury on that point.'

'Yes. I shall rule it distinctly. I am firm on that point. That is my own opinion of the law and I must rule firmly on that point.'

'Yes. I will address the jury upon my view of the case. Your Lordship will, of course, adopt what course Your Lordship pleases after that.'

Huddleston noticed a couple of the jurors exchanging muttered words and sweetened his tone. 'But I shall take every opportunity to lay this case before a superior tribunal that they may decide upon it, and it has occurred to me that there are two modes in which that may be done. One is that the jury, obeying my directions, find the prisoners guilty and the case will be referred to the Court of Crown Cases Reserved.'

Judges had always successfully resisted attempts by Parliament to impose a system to review their verdicts, but though there was no Court of Appeal, a mechanism did exist for ruling on purely legal points in cases where the law was believed to be uncertain. The Court of Crown Cases Reserved, a panel of five judges sitting under the Lord Chief Justice in London, could establish an unshakeable legal precedent, but only once a defendant had been convicted. No referral was possible after an acquittal.

Huddleston swept his hand across the bench in front of him, brushing away that possibility. 'The other course is a Special Verdict, whereby the jury find all the facts of the case and refer to the court to say what offence in law was committed. It is not very familiar in modern days but is one which I find repeatedly in the old books, and it is the course that I feel inclined to adopt.'

Collins rose to his feet at once. 'My Lord, I am powerless to consent to this.'

'I do not ask you to,' Huddleston said. 'I shall take it upon myself to do it.' He turned to the jurors and bared his teeth in a smile. 'Members of the jury, the facts of this case are not in dispute, but as you have seen, there is a difference of opinion on the points of law arising from it. I would like to offer you a way to spare yourselves the pain of hearing again the awful sentence of death pronounced.'

He paused, giving them time to recollect the previous day's events. 'It is within your rights to return a Special Verdict instead, in which you, the jury, establish the facts of the case and then leave it to a judge or judges to rule on the points of law and thereby determine the guilt or innocence of the defendants. These men's best chance of having the legal opinion of their eminent counsel considered is to follow the course I have just outlined.'

Neither he nor, surprisingly, Collins told them that they were quite at liberty to reject the idea. Having effectively dismissed the defence case from consideration, Huddleston then allowed the prosecution to begin presenting its evidence. Brooks was the first to take the stand. His answer to Charles's first question to him provoked Huddleston to a deep, theatrical sigh.

'Are you thirty-nine years old?'

'No, thirty-eight last May. That was a mistake of mine.'

Charles began to lead Brooks through his testimony but Huddleston repeatedly intervened. As Brooks was recounting the events following the sinking of the *Mignonette*, Huddleston interjected, 'How far do you suppose you were from shore at the time of the sinking?'

Brooks looked blank. 'I could not say, I am no navigator.'

'But you knew where you were?'

'The Captain and mate did, I did not.'

The judge lapsed into silence, shaking his head.

The courtroom was still as Brooks told the rest of his by-now well-polished tale, culminating in the death and dismemberment of the boy.

Collins rose to cross-examine. Brooks watched him approach the witness box with the same enthusiasm he had shown when the shark was circling the dinghy.

'Now, by the eighteenth or nineteenth day,' Collins said, 'you have told us you were ravenous for food, or rather for liquid. The thirst was worse than the hunger, was it not?'

'Much worse. A great many days we were compelled to drink our own water. The effect was very bad. Our lips blackened and our tongues were parched up like stones.'

'You were all very bad, I suppose. You must have been in a fearful state at that time, all of you?'

'Yes, we were all very bad.'

'I do not know whether you were quite as bad as those two men.'

As Brooks hesitated, Huddleston intervened, 'He has already said during his testimony he was better than them.'

'I'm grateful to Your Lordship.' Collins turned back to Brooks. 'And for some days they could not lie down or stand up?'

'No, they could not rest, they had such aches and pains. We had sores all over our bodies and Dudley and Stephens's legs were swollen dreadfully as far as the knees. I had boots but they had none, and they suffered more than I did.'

Collins nodded. 'Now you said, what I have no doubt is true, "Except for the death of the boy I think we should have died of hunger and thirst."'

'Yes.'

Huddleston again interrupted, the edge in his voice betraying his testiness. 'No, you said except for the sustenance you had from the boy, "Except for the body of the boy, we would not have survived to be picked up."'

Collins once more bowed to his lordship. 'I see you have also said when sworn before the magistrates that Captain Dudley was a good skipper and you found him a kind and good captain.'

'Yes.'

Huddleston was now drumming his fingers on the bench.

'You told us that you yourself dissented from the casting of lots,' Collins said.

'Yes, I could not agree to it. My heart would not let me. I said, "Let us all die together. I should not like anyone to kill me, and I should not like to kill anyone else".' The numerous repetitions of his story for freak-show customers had greatly improved Brooks's delivery, which was now much more fluent than it had been in the Falmouth courtroom.

'Did the boy consent to it, or was he asked?'

'I am sure I could not say now.'

'But there were no lots drawn?'

'No.'

'The boy had been at the bottom of the boat some hours, I believe. Did he appear to be dying?'

'He was very bad. He was very quiet in the boat, he did not say anything at all scarcely.'

'You said before the magistrates – and I suppose it is true – that to the best of your judgement he appeared to be dying. He was lying with his face on his arm, I believe, not speaking or taking any notice of anything for a great many hours. Did it appear to you that the boy was likely to die sooner than any of you other three?'

'He seemed weakest. I could not say.'

'When you saw the captain putting the knife into the boy, I take it for granted there was no sail in sight?'

'No, there was not.'

Collins paused and raised an eyebrow. Brooks had not argued with his assertion that he had seen Tom put the knife into the boy, but the lawyer did not pursue the point. It was a strange omission; if he could have shown that Brooks was as complicit as Stephens in the act, one of the pillars of the prosecution case would have fallen.

'You could not resist the sight of the blood,' Collins said. 'I believe you asked for some, you were in such a state?'

'I could not, I was obliged to ask for some.'

'Horrible as it was, you were obliged to have some?'

'Yes.'

'And you were reduced to feeding upon the heart and the liver of the boy. And for those four days was life kept in you by this unfortunate boy's body?'

'Yes, no doubt it was, sir. I believe so.'

Huddleston had been growing increasingly restive at Collins's tone and line of questioning, and his patience was now exhausted. He interrupted again: 'Mr Collins, we have covered this ground already in ample detail. Can we now move on?'

Collins's lips tightened, but he kept his voice even. 'As Your Lordship pleases.' He bowed and resumed his seat.

After Brooks had left the witness box, one of the sailors from the *Moctezuma* was called to give his evidence. Their ship had received orders and sailed for Hamburg two weeks previously but Julius Wiese and Christopher Drewe, the two crewmen who had examined the dinghy after it was brought on board, were required as Crown witnesses and had been left behind.

'I saw in the dinghy some small pieces of flesh and one little piece of a rib,' Wiese said. 'I could not tell what sort of flesh or bone it was. We were ordered by Captain Simonsen to throw everything overboard.'

Huddleston curtailed Wiese's evidence and Christopher Drewe was not called at all. The Falmouth pilot, Gustavus Lowry, then began to testify to what Dudley had told him on board the *Moctezuma*. 'I asked him who had killed the boy, Dudley said, "I did", and before he did it he offered up a prayer to the Lord to forgive him if he did any rash act. I asked how he killed him. He said by putting the knife under the ear. They had about a quart of blood. He and a mate had the first drink then he looked around and saw the other man coming for his share. They cut the boy's clothes off and opened him, took out and ate his heart and liver, and lived on him until they were picked up.'

Huddleston leaned forward. 'I think it is superfluous to go into all these unnecessary repetitions unless there are variations from the captain's statements.'

Lowry was followed into the witness box by the collector of customs, Robert Cheesman, who lasted only slightly longer. He described the conversation he had with Dudley in the Long Room of the Customs House. '. . . "the blood spurted from the wound and we caught it with the baler," Dudley said, "and I and Stephens drank some of it immediately. We then stripped the body and cut it open—"'

'You need not go any further,' Huddleston said.

The clerk of the court then read the depositions of Dudley and Stephens into the record.

Richard Hodge, the waterman who had brought the items from the dinghy ashore in Falmouth, was called to testify that they included Dudley's papers, but before he could even open his mouth, Huddleston once more intervened: 'Mr Charles, is there any necessity for this man to give evidence when the facts are already so well established?'

Hodge retreated, showing the same mixture of relief and resentment as his predecessors in the witness box.

Sergeant Laverty was the final prosecution witness. He rushed through his statement, running his words into each other, as if fearing that Huddleston would seize on any gap to dismiss him. 'I received the clothes from Hodge and in the borough lock-up in front of Superintendent Bourne, Dudley admitted the documents they contained were in his handwriting and contained further versions of the sinking of the *Mignonette* and the subsequent events. He told me they were his private papers. I heard Captain Dudley say that the knife produced in court was the knife with which he did the killing.'

'The papers may be put into the record,' Huddleston said, 'but there is no necessity to read them. It is only right to say that Captain Dudley has never varied in his story and has never attempted to conceal anything.' He paused. 'Mr Charles, has the prosecution any further witnesses to call?'

Charles rose to his feet. 'No, My Lord. That is the case for the prosecution.'

Huddleston pulled his pocket watch from his waistcoat pocket and glanced at it. His face registered disappointment and he exchanged a look with his wife at the side of the court. 'We will hear from you now, Mr Collins.'

Collins called no witnesses and raised only two obscure legal points. The first was the question of jurisdiction, the right of the court to hear the case at all. His argument depended on the *Mignonette*'s dinghy not being regarded as a British ship. Huddleston graciously conceded that the Special Verdict he was proposing could be widened to include discussion of this point.

Collins then sought the final right of reply after the prosecution's summing-up. Having called no witnesses, it was normally the defence's right to do so, but Charles claimed that the precedent in cases where the prosecution appeared on the instructions of the Treasury solicitor, gave him the right to the last word. At the time it was a contentious issue in the courts.

'I will hear both of you before I decide,' Huddleston said, 'but I have an opinion of my own upon it.'

Collins's expression suggested that he already knew what that opinion would be. After making his case, he showed no surprise when Huddleston ruled against him.

Collins turned to address the jury. 'May it please Your Lordship, gentlemen of the jury, I am not going to make a grievance about the decision which My Lord has just given. I know my friend Mr Charles too well to believe that he would take any unfairness from the decision, and if there was any unfairness taken, I know perfectly well that My Lord who presides in this court would soon put it right with you.'

Collins's tone was even and his face impassive, but the stare that Huddleston directed at him showed his displeasure.

'As I said, and I will not say another word about it, it may become a dangerous practice. It might, and doubtless will, give a very considerable support to Crown cases which perhaps sometimes they do not deserve.'

Irritated beyond his normal caution, Collins had come as close to open insubordination as was possible. Huddleston's face was a mask, but he leaned further forward on the bench, advancing his chin as if awaiting the opportunity to pounce.

'Gentlemen,' Collins said, 'I have to address you on as painful a case as ever any twelve gentlemen adjudicated upon. You are to try these two men in the dock for one of the highest offences known to our law: the crime of murder. As you know, the punishment for that crime is laid down by the law as death. The question for you is: are these men guilty of murder? Putting it, as My Lord says, another way, you will have to answer certain questions and upon your answers My Lord will submit the case to a higher court. But standing as you do, as a jury between the Crown on the one hand and the prisoners on the other, you gentlemen are paramount as regards the facts.

'You have, as twelve men, to say whether or not upon the facts stated by My Lord these men are guilty or not guilty of the crime of wilful murder.

'Are they murderers? What do you think? Gentlemen, I have put it to My Lord and My Lord is against me on this point, but I submit that I am entitled to have your opinion upon it: that the circumstances of this case excuse the act which these men did. They did not commit the crime charged on the indictment, that of wilful murder.'

Huddleston reddened and opened his mouth as if to interrupt again, then closed it and sat back, once more drumming his fingers on the bench.

'We know perfectly well that in many instances unfortunate men have been driven through stress of hunger and thirst to eat their fellow creatures,' Collins said. 'I believe I am right in saying that in no civilized country has the government of the day ever prosecuted a single person for the offence. It is evident that these men, on their return to this country, did not dream that they had committed any criminal offence.

'It is pointless in this courtroom to talk of remission or mercy once the law has run its course. It may be that the Crown will not say that the two men have suffered enough. It may be that the attorney general and those in office take a different view from My Lord's.

'I cannot and will not speculate upon these matters, but what I have to press upon you is this, that this is the first prosecution known to the English law under the awful circumstances which have been detailed to you by the witnesses.

'These men for eight days – do, gentlemen, consider the time – were without food, and without water for five. Now I ask you, gentlemen, to put yourselves, if you can, in these wretched men's places.

Think of what they were suffering, their throats and their lips dry and black, their tongues as hard as stone. They were in about as awful and miserable a condition as human beings with life in them could be.

'Famine, despair, cold, thirst and heat had done their work on them. They were in a condition which every man, woman and child in this world must view with pity. They were respectable men, God-fearing men of some reputation. They were so ill that, Brooks says, Stephens especially could not stand upright but had to crawl along the bottom of the boat.

'Brooks, of course, is a witness for the prosecution. He has been taken on the advice of those who instruct my learned friends to give evidence against the others and he has done so, as you heard, apparently very fairly without pressing upon one or the other, but giving what I suppose you believe is the truth.

'The captain, who saw the desperate state things were in, suggested the drawing of lots. The other men refused and no lots were drawn. On the morning of the nineteenth day, these men knew and felt what state they were in and saw the unfortunate boy lying, as Brooks said, apparently dying at the bottom of the boat. These men, fathers of families, husbands of wives, came to the resolution that "without something was done", to use Captain Dudley's own expression, they must all die.

'Gentlemen, as I said and say again, if there was ever a case in which necessity can be a plea for an act of this nature, surely each and every one of you will agree with me that there could not be a more awful and more dreadful case than this.

'They did it to save their lives and I do not think that you can have any doubt that if that unfortunate boy had not been killed in the manner described by Dudley, he could not have lived through the day or the next night. You can have no doubt that the awful food did save their lives. If these men had not done what they did there would not have been a single soul alive on the morning when they were picked up by the barque.

'They knew perfectly well the perils and the dangers they had gone through. They knew perfectly well the awful straits they were reduced to. They knew perfectly well the awful act of the taking of life – even if justified by necessity – and they make no thought or description of concealment of it but give the information to the Customs House. They tell their sufferings and what they were compelled to do.

'Gentlemen, you have the whole facts before you and will have under the direction of My Lord to answer as to certain facts in this case, but you will recollect on this indictment we are enquiring as to whether these men committed wilful murder or not, and you twelve gentlemen must be unanimous before you can find them guilty of anything.

'Gentlemen, I put it to you again, that taking the undisputed facts of this case, taking into consideration the dreadful state those men were in, that the necessity which compelled them to sacrifice the boy who was apparently dying at the time, is not a crime which you would call murder.'

Neither the prosecution nor the defence had referred to the possibility of the case being one of manslaughter. The doctrine of inevitable necessity that Collins was advancing as grounds for acquitting his clients of the crime of murder could have been argued with equal or even greater force as a justification for reducing the charge to one of manslaughter.

While Huddleston and Charles had their own reasons for not wishing to alert the jury to that, it was a curious omission on the part of Collins. It may be that he had already despaired of a fair trial under Mr Baron Huddleston's less than benevolent despotism, and was hoping to raise the defence before a higher court, but in the event he was never to do so.

Charles rose to make the concluding speech for the prosecution. Its brevity reflected his confidence in the outcome. 'Gentlemen, I think it would be a very long time before you said that, however hardly the poor men might be pressed, it is the law of England and the opinion of the jury that the weakest must go to the wall. That is the only observation I make in reply to my friend on the facts of the case. Gentlemen, I leave the case to My Lord.'

Huddleston gave a bleak smile but before he could speak, the junior for the defence, Henry Clark, rose to his feet. 'I may mention, My Lord, that we have a number of witnesses to character, including every captain under whom Captain Dudley has ever served. I think it right to mention that, as they have come an enormous distance at their own expense, many of them from the north of England and Scotland. If they are not to be heard, are they at liberty to go?'

'Yes, certainly.' Huddleston again consulted his pocket watch, ignoring the clock set in the wall facing him, then turned to face the jurors. 'Gentlemen of the jury, I am very glad I have the advantage of receiving in this case the assistance of gentlemen who have in other arduous cases manfully discharged their duty, and I am quite satisfied that, notwithstanding every feeling of sympathy for these two men in the dock, they will again discharge their duty in a way which they owe it to themselves to discharge.'

He favoured the jurors with a smile. 'Whatever may be the result of this case hereafter, I am quite satisfied of this, that outside the facts of this unhappy case there is no reflection on either the prisoners' character or their humanity.

'Though, gentlemen, you and I have to discharge a painful duty, I have to tell you what I believe to be the law of the land and I take upon myself the whole responsibility of that. You, gentlemen, have to deal with the facts but you are bound to obey to the letter the law of the land as I lay it down. If you were, as you were invited covertly to do–' he broke off to stare at Collins '– if you were to disregard my ruling as to the law, I should be obliged to require you to adopt the law as I lay it down to you.'

He softened his tone and gave them another smile. 'But it has occurred to me that you will be anxious and desirous of having the very best and ultimate decision of the law, and as I have already intimated, you would probably like to state what in your judgement were the facts of the case. Then, instead of delivering the verdict with which these men are charged, you would adopt a course at one time very commonly adopted by juries and say, "The facts might be true but whether upon the whole matter the prisoners are guilty the jury are ignorant and therefore refer to the court."

'I will carefully go through the whole of the facts with you, taking the mildest view that can be taken of them in favour of the prisoners.' Once more the smile was in evidence. 'And having given your finding upon those facts, you will refer to the court the question as to whether or not the men were guilty of the crime of murder.

'You will refer it not to myself individually but to a court to be appointed in London consisting of the whole of the judges of the land who would satisfactorily lay down the law as the opinion of all the judges forming that court.

'Gentlemen, the learned counsellor has urged, and urged with a force and ability which we should expect from one of the leaders of this great circuit,' his voice dripped sarcasm as he spoke, 'that there may be a law which is beyond the law of the land – the law of necessity – which would justify the stronger man taking the life of the weaker. If several men were in a position of peril the weakest man should be sent to the wall.

'That is a proposition from which I entirely dissent. I think it would not be fair to Dudley as a brave man not to say that he suggested from the beginning, "Let us draw lots and let us see who is to go." I merely mention that because I must deal with this point. They are points which were well urged and likely to captivate the mind and lead the judgement astray.

'But now, gentlemen, let us consider the suggestion that a man may in a certain state of things arrive at a position when he will be justified in taking the innocent life of another for the purpose of saving his own.

'I know, gentlemen – I say it here with the responsibility there is upon me – I know of no such law in the laws of England. The founders of our constitution thought it better to vest in the Crown the power of pardoning particular objects of compassion. If in laying down the law there seems to be great hardship, the law must be followed and the law must be adopted, but there is a throne of mercy . . .' he paused and raised his eyes to the bas-relief of the royal coat-of-arms on the wall '. . . from which any supplicant is never spurned.

'Captain Dudley shows the deliberation with which he took the step. I daresay he thought he was justified, perhaps from reading some wild books upon the subject, but I am now dealing with the question of deliberation. He addressed a prayer to the Almighty to excuse him, as he says, from his own rash act.

'Gentlemen, there was deliberation and there was deliberate homicide, and if I was to direct you to give your verdict I should have to tell you,' his voice rose to emphasize the point, 'and you would be bound to obey me, that you must return a verdict of guilty of wilful murder.'

He paused, studying their faces. 'Now, I hope I may deserve from you some consideration for putting you in a position of merely finding the facts and not finding the verdict of guilty of wilful murder. If you will be kind enough now to follow me in the facts that I have prepared and give your consent to each paragraph as I read them to you, when the whole of these paragraphs or facts are found by you, the matter will be referred to the court for the purpose of the court saying what is the law upon the subject, and that must be some satisfaction, I hope, to you.'

Without pausing for breath or allowing the jurors to assent to his proposal, Huddleston began to read from the draft Special Verdict he had already prepared. 'I propose to say that if the men had not fed upon the body of the boy they would probably not have survived to be picked up and rescued, and would within the four days have died of famine.'

As he prepared to continue, the foreman of the jurors, Samuel Widgery, raised his hand. 'To the last, Your Lordship, they would have died if they had not had this body to feed on.' He put particular emphasis on the words 'would have died'.

'That is as I put it,' Huddleston said. 'I will read the paragraph again. "That if the men had not fed upon the body of the boy they would probably not have survived to be picked up and rescued, and that within the four days would have died of famine."'

Huddleston's apparently trivial addition of the word 'probably', made a defence of necessity almost impossible to sustain; what is merely probable cannot be a necessity. There was no objection from Collins.

'You will consider whether the boy was in such a condition as he was likely to die before them or not.' Huddleston looked across at Widgery. 'It is for you to say.'

'We all think so,' Widgery said.

'Then I will take that. There appeared to the prisoners every probability that unless they then or very soon fed upon the boy or one of themselves,' he paused, 'you must draw that distinction – one of themselves – they would die of starvation. What do you say to that?'

The jurors conferred briefly and then Widgery nodded.

Huddleston had produced three different drafts of the statement on the necessity of killing Richard Parker. His first read, 'Was there any absolute necessity for killing Parker rather than any one of the other three men?'

Fearing that the jury might reply, 'Yes,' he deleted it and replaced it with a statement of fact. 'It was no more absolutely essential to kill Parker than any of the other three men.'

This still left open the possibility of the jury disagreeing with him and he finally produced a third version. His explanation of it to the jury was a masterpiece of obfuscation. 'There was no more necessity that they should kill the boy than that they should kill one of themselves. All they required was something to eat, but the necessity of something to eat does not create the necessity of taking or at least excuse the taking of the boy.

'That is the question: was there any necessity for taking that boy rather than drawing lots? I should think you would consider no, therefore I propose to add this: that, assuming any necessity to kill anyone, there was no greater necessity for killing the boy than any of the other three men. You adopt that, gentlemen?'

He moved on without waiting for their reply. The jurors' faces showed their puzzlement as they struggled to keep up with him. They might even have imagined that they were reaffirming the drawing of lots as part of the custom of the sea, but what Huddleston's carefully chosen phrasing had actually done was to deny the necessity of killing anyone. Had they found that the reverse was true, it would have been impossible for a court to rule that the act was illegal: if it was essential, how could it be unlawful?

The custom of the sea remained untested by the courts. Since Tom had not cast lots, the defence could not advance the argument that the practice, which gave all an equal chance of life or death, justified homicide in extreme circumstances. Huddleston had dismissed the notion, describing it as 'blasphemous', but it was never rejected by a jury, except in the deliberately obscure terms of the Special Verdict he persuaded them to adopt.

'Your verdict when returned will conclude that you return these facts and whether upon the whole matter the prisoners were and are guilty of murder, the jury are ignorant and refer to the court. That is to say, you will ask on the point of law, looking at all these circumstances, is this murder or is it not? Gentlemen, that will be the Special Verdict which will be taken in this case.'

It was the first use of a Special Verdict for a century.

Huddleston laid his papers on the bench and beamed at the jurors. Widgery conferred with the others and then cleared his throat and stood up. 'We would like to add a recommendation for—'

Huddleston interrupted him. 'I see what you are going to suggest to me. You wish to accompany your finding with some expression—'

'It is just my idea,' Widgery said.

'And mine,' another juror added.

'I take it you are very desirous that I should convey to the proper quarters your strong feeling of compassion for the position these men are placed in,' Huddleston said, again choosing his words with the utmost care. There could be no recommendation to mercy in a case where the accused had not even been found guilty.

'Yes, My Lord,' Widgery said.

'It shall be done.' He glanced at Collins. 'Pending the decision of the case by the superior court, the accused will be liberated on bail.'

'The same bail as before, My Lord?' Collins said.

'The same as before.'

Thomas Houston Kirk, a Glasgow lawyer and one of the men whose yachts Tom had once captained, stood surety for his £200 bail.

Huddleston rapped the bench with his gavel. 'The court stands adjourned.' He could not hide a smile of triumph as he turned to look at his wife before sweeping out of the court.

The *Exeter & Plymouth Gazette* shared his opinion, describing his summing up as, 'A charge of singular ability, reminding one of the luminous and comprehensive judicial addresses of Lord Chief Justice Cockburn.'

The Times also applauded Huddleston's handling of the trial:

Thus was raised sharply and clearly and in a striking manner a question that has often been referred to as a legal curiosity, a point for casuists to split hairs about, but which has never before apparently required to be practically settled.

Baron Huddleston could refer the jury to no case in which

the question has been decided in an English court of law and he had to do what English judges are frequently to do under the guise of interpreting the law, he had to make it.

Though there is no case exactly in point, the genius of the English criminal law as opposed to the multiplication of excuses for acts of violence and especially those that end fatally, is that the English law has always been very chary of admitting the excuse and necessity for homicide. The fatal blow was not struck in self-defence.

The English law as laid down by Baron Huddleston is averse from entertaining the notion that peril from starvation is an excuse for homicide and it seems best to adhere to this rule. It would be dangerous to affirm the contrary and to tell seafaring men that they may freely eat others in extreme circumstances and that the cabin boy may always be consumed if provisions run short.

Would the three men have waited so many days and endured the agony which they bore so long if they had not been well aware that killing by hungry men was not murder, and if they had not grown up with the belief that killing a human being was all but universally criminal?

Where is the doctrine of necessity in this loose sense to lead, if once it is enshrined as law? It must be, for reasons still stronger, a good excuse for crimes of a less serious nature than murder. A man would only have to plead extreme poverty to be free to steal. As soon as one such exception is admitted we quit solid ground, but it would be a mistake to seek to wrest and pervert that simple distinction through any desire, natural though it may be, to shield unfortunate men from all punishment.

It would be unfortunate if, in any form, the notion got abroad that at sea in times of peril all legal restraints are withdrawn. From time to time duty comes in a sterner form with as pitiless a face as it could have presented to them, famished though they were. It is the honour of our nature that men are found equal to this hard obligation and that they meet death side by side.

We are not all to be sure, of the stuff which goes to the

making of heroes and martyrs, and there must be allowance for the frailties of those who act as Dudley and Stephens did in their terrible situation, but society cannot be too jealous as to the maintenance of the safeguards which experience has reared for the protection of life.

Hard cases, it is notorious, do make bad law. The lot of men who have been for days in an open boat without food was cruelly hard, but justice will be done in this instance and no embarrassment will be created in the future, if the matter be determined with as little reference to sympathy as possible.

While also backing Huddleston, the *Spectator* expressed regret at the necessity of his legal sleight-of-hand.

So strong is the prejudice in seaport towns that the jury might in defiance of the judge have acquitted the prisoners but it is melancholy that there still should be need for such a reference.

The convention that some murders are justified by the law of self-defence and are not therefore illegal is so general amongst seafaring men and has so infected naval literature that the solemn judgement to the contrary announced by more than one judge has become indispensable.

How an idea so directly contrary not only to morality and law but to the comradeship of seafaring men can ever have grown up is inexplicable but of its existence there is unhappily no doubt. Even now, probably one person in three of all inhabitants of seaport towns would declare the sailors of the *Mignonette* guilty only in not casting lots for the victim to be selected.

CHAPTER 20

The last act in the case of Regina versus Dudley and Stephens was set to be heard in London on Thursday, 4 December 1884, before the five most senior judges in the land, but before the hearing itself two meetings were convened to wrestle with the knotty procedural problems created by Huddleston's imaginative use of a Special Verdict.

On 25 November Huddleston met in his chambers with the attorney general, Sir Henry James, and Arthur Collins. Much of the meeting was taken up with a discussion about what title would be given to the court that was to hear the case. The Court of Crown Cases Reserved could only adjudicate on a case after a prisoner had been convicted, and the Court of Queen's Bench, to which Special Verdicts had formerly been referred, had been abolished in 1873, when the archaic system of separate and quasi-independent courts was unified into a single High Court of Justice.

Almost the last case heard by the Court of Queen's Bench before its abolition had been the libel action against Samuel Plimsoll. The court now survived only as a purely administrative division within the High Court of Justice.

The attorney general initially proposed that the court should simply be regarded as an extension of the Assizes of the Western Circuit, convening in London instead of Exeter. The proposal created as many procedural problems as it solved, but it was accepted for the moment as the only workable solution.

Before they adjourned, Mr Collins, who had been studying the final version of the Special Verdict produced for the court, made a request that appeared to disconcert Baron Huddleston.

'My Lord,' Collins said. 'We have made an application to the Treasury and I believe there is some difficulty about it, but I have no doubt the attorney general will be good enough to comply with my request to be furnished with a copy of the shorthand notes.'

'The shorthand notes of what?' Huddleston said.

'Of the trial.'

Sir Henry intervened: 'My friend need not trouble Your Lordship. He shall have anything he asks for. Whatever we can give my friend, he shall have.'

'You can have a copy of my notes if you like,' Huddleston said. 'But what do you want the shorthand note of the trial for?'

'I wish to read it, My Lord.'

It was close to an open challenge from Collins: a suggestion that the final version of the Special Verdict did not accord with that found by the jury. Huddleston's lips whitened, but he suppressed his anger before he spoke. 'Very well, Mr Collins. It shall be done.'

A week later, on 2 December, only two days before the hearing, Huddleston, Collins and the attorney general reassembled before the Lord Chief Justice, Lord Coleridge, who had decided that there were legal difficulties in maintaining the fiction that the judges were to sit as an extension of the Assizes of the Western Circuit.

He had asked Sir Henry to propose a suitable alternative. He now suggested that, 'The court, certainly as far as it can be constituted, should sit not as the old Court of the Queen's Bench, but as the Queen's Bench Division. There was a transfer to this court and it is to this court that I shall have to bring this record of the trial at Assizes.'

The diffidence with which Sir Henry spoke reflected his uncertainty. As components of a single High Court of Justice, the Queen's Bench Division had no more authority than the Assizes of the Western Circuit. There was also a further problem. To give the court that they had re-awoken from oblivion the legal weight required to establish a leading case, it was to be packed with five senior justices. However, the 1873 Judicature Act, which had abolished the Court of Queen's Bench, had specifically limited the number of judges sitting together to consider 'such cases and matters as are not proper to be heard by a single judge' to a maximum of three.

Even if the transfer of the case from Exeter to London was lawful – itself by no means certain – the court that was to assemble in two days' time was improperly convened and therefore illegal by the letter of the law. If challenged, its rulings could not fail to be overturned.

Any half-competent defence counsel, let alone one of Arthur Collins's standing, would have been expected to have noted and raised this in the interests of his clients. He never did.

When Tom travelled up to London on the morning of 4 December 1884, his mood was black. His thoughts were focused not on the hearing that morning but on his youngest daughter, Winifred. She had been seriously ill for several days with congestion of the lungs and it was thought unlikely that she would live. He had been nursing her night and day and could think of nothing but her pale, feverish face as the train rattled in towards Victoria. The thought gnawed at him that, even if he was released that night, she might already have died.

As he walked along the Strand, he saw a large crowd of people thronging the entrance to the Royal Courts of Justice. A street vendor had set up a brazier near the crowd and the sweet, smoky smell of roasting chestnuts filled Tom's nostrils. He paused, the scent transporting him in an instant to a long-distant Christmas in Tollesbury.

They had eaten a wild duck, shot by his father on the marshes, then sat around the iron range roasting chestnuts while his father told them tales of the sea. He could still recall nestling on his mother's knee, drowsy from food and warmth, hearing the soft crack of chestnut shells as they split in the heat of the fire. It was the last Christmas before his mother had died.

The memory seemed an ill omen and, lost in his own dark thoughts, he hurried past the vendor and pushed his way through the crowd to reach the entrance to the court.

The hearing opened at eleven, before the five most senior judges in England: Lord Chief Justice Coleridge, Mr Justice Grove, Mr Justice Denman, Mr Baron Pollock and Mr Baron Huddleston. The attorney general himself led for the Crown, assisted by Arthur Charles, Charles Matthews and William Danckwerts. Arthur Collins again appeared for

259

the defence, with Henry Clark and Lionel Pyke, who practised at the Admiralty Bar and was, like Danckwerts, a specialist in wreck inquiries.

The attorney general first sought a ruling on whether the prisoners should be present. 'They have had notice to appear and, I believe, are in the precincts of the court.'

'We think it better they should be here,' Coleridge said.

Knowing of Tom's anguish over his daughter, Collins made some attempt to have the two men excused from attending. 'Your Lordships order that they should be present? They were bailed to appear in Exeter, not London.'

Coleridge waved the question away. 'Yes, we think it will be proper.'

Tom and Stephens were summoned and took their seats alongside their counsel. The Master of the Crown Office then began the interminable reading of the formal record of the proceedings of the trial in Exeter. 'The jurors for our said Lady the Queen upon their oath do present that Thomas Dudley and Edwin Stephens on the twenty-fifth day of July eighteen eighty-four with force and arms on High Seas within the jurisdiction of the Admiralty of England, feloniously, wilfully and of the malice aforethought of them, the said Thomas Dudley and Edwin Stephens, did kill and murder one Richard Parker against the Peace of our said Lady the Queen, her Crown and Dignity.'

The recital included the commission of the Assizes of the Western Circuit, the name of every judge qualified to sit there, the findings of the grand jury, the record of the trial and finally the Special Verdict.

When it was at last at an end, Collins got to his feet. 'I have to raise before Your Lordships an objection to that record. It does not set forth the real Special Verdict given by the jury.'

'What are the words that you object to?' Huddleston said, his voice like ice.

'"A registered British vessel," and "belonging to said yacht". Those words were never in the Special Verdict and are not in the copy of it, nor the shorthand note supplied by the Treasury. The jury did not return that verdict.'

When the Special Verdict was being transcribed, Huddleston had realized that he had made a potentially critical error by not stating that the *Mignonette* was registered in England and that the dinghy belonged to the *Mignonette*. Knowing that Collins would use the omissions to query the court's right to try the case at all, Huddleston had amended the verdict to block the loopholes.

He held his expression neutral. 'It is true those words were not in the actual findings of the jury, but they were upon my notes and there are precedents for a Special Verdict being amended from the judge's notes.' He paused, aware of the eyes of the other justices upon him. 'However, these statements are not material.'

'Then they may be struck out by consent,' Coleridge said. 'We will strike those words out.'

Collins next turned to Huddleston's second falsification. The Special Verdict had originally ended: 'And whether upon the whole matter the prisoners were and are guilty of murder, the jury are ignorant and refer to the court.'

Worried about the implication that the judges, not the jury, were thereby pronouncing the verdict, Huddleston had added, 'And find accordingly.'

Once more, Collins had detected the alteration. 'That was never found by the jury.' He paused. 'If I make the objection, it is only for my clients.'

Tom looked up in surprise. It was a curiously apologetic way for Collins to voice such a crucial objection. If it could be demonstrated that the jury had not found a verdict at all, it would be impossible for the judges to convict.

'You say that the jury in fact find him guilty or not guilty?' Justice Grove said.

'I say it was an abortive trial altogether.'

'The only result of that would be a trial *de novo*' – a retrial.

'I will meet that difficulty when I have to deal with it, My Lord.'

'But the jury are upon the record made to find guilty or not guilty, according to certain conditions,' Grove said. 'Then it does not matter whether that is omitted. You may strike it out and leave what was actually found by the jury.'

The attorney general at once rose to his feet. 'The jury must go further. If they find certain facts, they must point out some result from the facts. If you strike that out, we should have no result. We shall have a path without an end.'

A long argument ensued in which all the justices participated. Collins continued to argue, albeit in a curiously diffident manner, that the un-amended version of the verdict showed that the jury had made no finding at all, making the five justices in effect the jury.

Sir Henry argued that, whether or not the jury actually made the finding, it was implicit in their verdict: 'the natural intentment from their submission'.

Grove gave a weary shake of his head. 'I must say, my difficulty is not removed. I do not wish at all to dissent in a case where it is pure form, almost a clerical matter.'

Pollock then intervened: 'I think we must take it that it is the intention of the jury.'

'We do not know what they intended to do,' Collins said.

Coleridge had grown increasingly restive during the protracted discussion. 'In my view, it is wholly immaterial,' he said. 'They have found the facts and the court is to give judgement upon the facts they have so found. It is not a question of verdict at all.'

His ruling ended the discussion and Huddleston's three-word addition to the Special Verdict was allowed to stand, but the argument had discomfited the justices. Collins's objection had forced them to con-front the unsavoury reality: five judges sitting in London, not twelve good men and true in Exeter, would pronounce the verdict of guilty or not guilty on Tom Dudley and Edwin Stephens. Lord Coleridge and his fellow justices were to be both judge and jury.

The attorney general then stated the case for the Crown. 'I have to submit, Your Lordships, that it should be your opinion that the killing of Richard Parker amounted to the crime of felony and murder. I agree that the case should be taken in the way most favourable to the defendants, and therefore I take it that at the time of the killing of the boy they believed that they would otherwise have died, and that it was probable that they would have died if they had not killed and eaten him. But there was a chance of their being saved within the four days, so they took away not only the boy's life but the chance of its continuance.

'It is clear that they deliberately took his life and I submit that except in cases of legal process or actual warfare it can only be justified on the grounds of self-defence.'

As Sir Henry began to marshal his arguments to counter the defence's plea of necessity, Coleridge called a halt to confer with the other judges. 'I have consulted my learned brethren and this proposition of necessity is so entirely novel and startling to every one of us, and the present impression of our minds is so clear that it clearly is murder by the law of England, that we think we should like to hear what Mr Collins has to say to remove that very strong impression from our minds.'

Collins got to his feet. 'By the findings of the jury in the Special Verdict, these men are guilty of neither murder nor manslaughter.'

Coleridge at once interrupted him. 'It is murder or nothing, we all think. You need not trouble us about the manslaughter.'

'If Your Lordship pleases,' Collins said. 'It is murder or no crime at all.'

The defence juniors, Henry Clark and Lionel Pyke, exchanged a look of astonishment. While arguing that necessity provided a defence against a charge of murder, Collins was once more tossing away without a fight any claim that the same doctrine could reduce the charge to manslaughter.

'The verdict states that there was no appreciable chance of saving life,' Collins said, 'except by killing someone for the others to eat. If that was so, it reduces that act from the crime of murder by the doctrine of necessity.

'Mr Justice Stephens says a man is under compulsion when he is reduced to a choice of evils: when he is so situated that, in order to escape what he dislikes most, he must do something which he dislikes less, although he may dislike extremely what he determines to do.

'The same illustration shows the true meaning of freedom. These were men in a place where no assistance could be given them. Their extreme necessity drove them to an act that would otherwise be a crime. Your Lordships will recollect that I put it that the real question for the jury was: "Did they act from necessity?"'

Huddleston interrupted at once. 'I should not have left that question to the jury.'

'Your Lordship did not leave that question to the jury, but I submit that it was a proper question to leave to them. Lord Mansfield has found that if a man is forced to commit an act of high treason and the jury are of the opinion that the force is such as human nature could not be expected to resist, the man is not then guilty of high treason. My Lords, force I apprehend does not only mean physical force.'

'But you must then go the length of saying that no act, however base or wicked, can be punished if a man can save his life by doing it,' Coleridge said.

'That is for the jury,' Collins said. 'But if he is forced into it by the great law of Nature and self-preservation, he is justified in saving his own life.'

'However base and cruel the act? You must take that.'

'I put it in this way,' Collins said. 'When a man is under the absolute necessity of force, his will does not go along with the act and therefore wherever a case turns upon natural necessity it is to be determined by a jury and by a jury only. I put it in this case that you cannot have a greater natural necessity than that which these men were under.'

'Surely this is a case in which you cannot say that these men had not the will and intention of the mind.'

'Very well,' Collins said. 'The intention was to save their own lives.'

Coleridge shook his head. 'But the jury meant to leave to the court whether there was any evidence of necessity.'

'They said that there was no chance of saving life except by killing someone for the others to eat.'

Huddleston took up the cudgels. 'The Special Verdict goes on to say that there was no greater necessity for their killing Parker than killing any one of the others. Why was it more necessary for Dudley and Stephens to kill Parker than the other man who shrank from it and would not do it?'

'Because someone had to do it. If one committed the act, the others need not.'

'No,' Huddleston said. 'Brooks said, "I would rather die myself, I will have nothing to do with it," and they knew it because they ordered Brooks to go to sleep while they proceeded to kill the boy.'

Collins shook his head. 'That is what he said but, with great respect, it does not meet what I was saying about unavoidable necessity. Someone must be killed, and although he says he went to the other end of the boat, the moment the boy was killed, Brooks took a share of the flesh and blood.'

He paused and glanced along the row of judges facing him. 'Those are the only points I have to urge why these men are not guilty of the crime charged against them.'

'Mr Attorney General,' Coleridge said, 'if we wish to hear further from you, we will let you know when we come back.' The five judges retired to consider their verdict.

Sir James Fitzjames Stephen's *History of the Criminal Law of England*, written the previous year, had made the prophetic remark that the law on the subject of necessity was 'so vague that, if cases raising the question should ever occur, the judges would practically be able to lay down any rule which they considered expedient'.

There was never any doubt what the five judges in this case would find expedient. They were out of the courtroom for less than ten minutes. When they returned, Coleridge announced, 'I have had an opportunity of conferring with my learned brothers and we were all of the opinion that the conviction should be affirmed.'

There had been no conviction and yet the Lord Chief Justice and his fellows had confirmed it. Their Lordships then tied themselves in further linguistic knots in trying to avoid the appearance – the reality was not in doubt – of usurping a jury's function by pronouncing a verdict.

Coleridge looked at the attorney general. 'Can you tell me what course you propose to invite us to take?'

'By law, in order that the proceedings should be regular, the only course that I am aware of will be to ask Your Lordships in this court to pronounce judgement.'

'To pronounce judgement on the question of guilty or not guilty?'

'Yes, and continue the judgement by passing sentence. Judgement must be passed after sentence,' Coleridge said.

Sir Henry nodded. 'But would not a convenient course be for Your Lordships to say, "We do not formally convict until four days have elapsed"?'

Coleridge sighed. 'It is very difficult when we get into these technical things. If we do that, what is there for the prisoners to appeal against? They cannot appeal against a mere conviction.'

Tom sat with his head in his hands. 'They have set themselves up to be judge and jury of us,' he muttered to Stephens. 'Now they wish to pretend that it isn't so.'

Once the justices had settled that procedural point, the defendants were then forced to sit through a further lengthy argument about when and where the sentence of death – there was no other penalty for men convicted of murder – should be pronounced and carried out.

Huddleston argued that the case should be returned to the Assizes for sentencing, but Coleridge overruled him. 'We will give our formal judgement now,' he said, 'and we will give our reasons accompanied by the sentence on Tuesday next. In the meanwhile, Mr Collins, you will understand that the judgement is formally given against you?'

'If Your Lordship pleases,' Collins said.

The four-day adjournment was to give Collins the chance to prepare 'a motion in arrest of judgement', the standard process by which a condemned man was asked if he could put forward any reason why sentence of death should not be pronounced.

The attorney general again got to his feet. 'I have to ask what direction you think right for the disposition of the prisoners?'

'We have considered that and I think they must remain in the custody of the court now.'

'We have bail for them,' Collins said.

'But it was a very different thing before today.' Coleridge gestured to Huddleston. 'My learned brother had not decided the point. We have done so now.'

'I will not argue with the court,' Collins said, 'but they surrendered to the court today merely on a notice. They were not bound to.'

Coleridge shook his head. 'We are all of the opinion that it would not be right to free them from custody. They will be sent to Holloway Prison, which I understand, as far as there is a difference between prisons, is the most comfortable for them.'

Both men were too shocked and distraught to be much consoled by Coleridge's generosity. Still frantic with worry about his daughter, Tom was taken down from the court and manacled to Stephens. Collins followed them down from the courtroom. 'I would wish a private word with the prisoners before they are taken away.'

The police sergeant in charge gave a grudging nod and led the two constables a few paces away.

Collins removed his wig and dabbed at his perspiring forehead with a linen handkerchief. 'Captain Dudley, Mr Stephens, I have tried to prepare you for this moment, but I am afraid you have not been of a mind to heed the warnings I have given.'

He hesitated. Stephens kept his head bowed, not even seeming to hear him, but Tom's steady gaze was fixed on Collins's face.

'The merits or demerits of your particular case are not and never have been the central issue in these proceedings.' Collins paused again, his expression showing his discomfort. 'For some years, the Home Office has been seeking to establish an unshakeable legal precedent outlawing the custom of the sea. They have tried before and failed.'

Tom nodded. 'I know of the case.'

'You provided them with another opportunity and the home secretary took all necessary steps to ensure that you were prosecuted without any risk of an acquittal. Baron Huddleston was hand-picked to hear the case. As you have seen, he is a clever man,' Collins's lip curled, 'and still a very ambitious one. Even at his age, he yet harbours hopes of further advancement.

'Huddleston had been left in no doubt that the home secretary required a precedent to be established. A case before a single judge, delivered on assizes, was not regarded as binding on other courts, and Huddleston had to ensure that the case came before a bench of judges in a higher court.

'The Crown's first step in that process was to offer Brooks immunity from prosecution and enlist him as a hostile witness. The fact that his deposition to the collector of customs in Falmouth had allegedly been lost was not without significance. The Crown undoubtedly had no wish to have self-incriminating or contradictory testimony from their chief witness available to the defence. Without even allowing me to address them, Huddleston then delivered his lecture to the grand jury, rejecting out of hand the possible defences of necessity and self-defence.'

Collins paused, avoiding Tom's eyes. 'To rule on a case before hearing the evidence is in my experience without precedent.' He checked, as if surprised by the force of his own anger. 'The grand jury found a true bill, but the baron now had to convince the trial jury. He was well aware of the risk of an acquittal.

'He allowed the prosecuting counsel to outline its case but prevented me from putting to the jury a defence based on the necessity of the act until he had planted in their minds the idea of finding a Special Verdict. When I insisted on stating my case to the jury, he immediately directed them to ignore my remarks.'

Collins's voice grated in Tom's ears. It had taken on a plaintive, almost whining quality, as if the greater offence had been to prevent Collins from speaking, rather than the injustice perpetrated on his clients.

'Where is this leading, Mr Collins?'

The lawyer again mopped his brow and darted a glance at him, but looked away at once. 'The improperly constituted court, and Baron Huddleston's disregard for due and correct legal procedures, do give me some technical grounds for an appeal. However, even if successful, the result will not be an acquittal but a retrial, and . . .' He fell silent, his jaw working as he steeled himself for what he had to say next.

Tom watched him for a moment. 'Mr Collins, what you have told me shows that you knew that the trial was a charade from beginning to end. Yet you chose to leave Stephens and me – the men you were defending – in complete ignorance of this. You allowed us to nurture the hope of acquittal, when you already knew—'

'I swear I did not know this myself until the trial had begun,' Collins said. For the first time, he raised his eyes and met Tom's gaze. 'Captain Dudley, you are a truthful man, even when it is to your detriment. I owe you at least as much honesty and I apologize for concealing this from you, but I felt it better for you to live in hope than to go through the ordeal of the trial knowing that your fate was already sealed.' He hurried on before Tom could speak. 'Huddleston summoned me to his chambers to remonstrate with me over the line of defence I was pursuing. He let it be known that the home secretary was taking a personal interest in the case and that the future prospects of us both depended on the correct verdict being reached.'

He glanced towards the waiting policemen and lowered his voice. 'As I was dining at my club some nights later, I received a visit from an emissary of the home secretary. It was made clear to me that, providing there were "no mishaps or unforeseen errors" on my part, I was to be recommended to Her Majesty for a knighthood and elevated to the bench within the year.'

'And that is your reward for your part in this,' Tom said. 'I congratulate you on your good fortune.'

Collins flinched at the contempt in his voice. 'I understand your anger, but I hope, sir, that when you have time to reflect on this, you will feel that I have continued to defend you to the best of my abilities despite those blandishments. As I said, there were a number of legal failings in the proceedings, which I could use as grounds for an appeal, but I must advise you that there is nothing to be gained by further prolonging the case.

'The full weight of the establishment, from Her Majesty the Queen and the home secretary to the justices sitting in judgement upon you, is united against you. They are determined that this case will end in your conviction and a sentence that will deter others from doing as you have done.

'You have my sympathy, but you must prepare yourself for the awful sentence which must be passed to uphold the laws of England. And rest assured, as soon as things can go through their form, you will be granted a free pardon, we are all sure.'

'Let them do their worst,' Tom said, 'and be damned with you and all of them. You and your peers have conspired to heap further trials on ourselves and our families, who had already suffered as much as human souls can endure.'

'But the laws of England must be upheld,' Collins said.

'Even if upholding the laws of England requires the denial of justice to Englishmen?'

'It has been done to outlaw the custom of the sea.'

Tom gave a bitter laugh. 'It has done no such thing. What it has done is to outlaw the truth. Ships will still wreck and men will still be cast away. Men will thirst and men will starve, and men will do what they always have done in order to survive, for no instinct is stronger than that. But never again will men return to these shores and freely confess what they have done. The evidence will be hidden, consigned to the deep; and the survivors will say that they lived on tallow candles, shoe leather, plankton or God's fresh air. They will know the truth of it, and their interrogators will know, but that truth will never again be expressed. The custom of the sea will continue but, like the whores in the crimps and rookeries, polite society – your society, Mr Collins – will be able to pretend that it does not exist. Common folk like me will know better.'

He stared at him. 'I hope your career brings you satisfaction, Mr Collins. I bid you good-day.' He turned his back until he heard the door clang shut behind him.

Stephens's head was still bowed, but Tom could see tears falling in the dust around his feet.

They were led out to the waiting Black Maria – a dark, stinking, horse-drawn wagon, with a central corridor dividing cells so cramped there was barely room to stand. They were driven slowly north towards Holloway, the horses straining to pull the ironclad wagon up the steep hill from Islington.

When the great doors of the prison at last closed behind them, Tom and Stephens were taken from the Black Maria and made to stand before the reception counter while a clerk recorded their age, religion, offence and sentence. All their possessions were noted in the ledger, which the two men had to countersign. They were stripped of their clothes, which were taken away to be cleaned and stored against their release. The garments of particularly filthy or verminous prisoners were simply burned.

Naked and shivering with cold, Tom and Stephens were weighed and medically examined, then forced to wash with lye soap and hosed clean. They were issued with prison clothes, given a lecture on the prison regime by the head jailer and then taken to their cell-block.

As the door clanged shut and Tom was left alone in silence and semi-darkness, the displays of waxworks in the Chamber of Horrors at Madame Tussaud's were already being rearranged to include a crude likeness of 'The Cannibal Captain, Tom Dudley'.

CHAPTER 21

Holloway was a prison for men, women and boys of eight years and over. As Lord Coleridge had suggested, it was newer and better equipped than the notorious jails like Newgate or the rotting prison hulks moored on the Thames at Woolwich, but the system it operated was as cruel and degrading as any in the civilized world.

Always brutal and dehumanizing, the prison system in the early nineteenth century had also been irredeemably corrupt. In the 1830s turnkeys were doubling or trebling their wages through the sale of food, liquor and tobacco to inmates with the means to pay for them and bribes to allow male prisoners access to female inmates willing to act as whores. The infirmary was also full of healthy prisoners paying bribes to sleep in a bed.

Captain George Chesterton, the governor of Coldbath Fields prison, introduced a new regime, 'the silent system', in 1834. It removed much of the corruption, but it also replaced the random cruelties of earlier eras with a system requiring the isolation and degradation of every single prisoner. The regime was enforced by whippings and floggings which Chesterton described as 'beneficial, nay indispensable'.

There was no heating or lighting, and no instruction or productive employment of prisoners. Every inmate was totally anonymous, addressed only by the number of his cell incised on the brass badge on his cap. The work of hard labour was mostly carried out in the cells, prisoners ate alone and never communicated with or even saw the other inmates. They were hooded whenever they left their cells for exercise or any other reason.

The punishment for talking was normally confinement in one of the refractory cells in the basement on bread and water. Those cells had only a wooden bench for a bed and a chamber-pot, and when the door was shut, according to Henry Mayhew and John Binny, who wrote a contemporary book on London prisons, 'They not only exclude a single beam of light but they do not admit the slightest sound.'

One warder said, 'It is impossible to describe the darkness. It is pitch black, no dungeon was ever so dark.'

In a single year, 1836, there were 5,138 punishments for talking and swearing in that one prison alone. Even for prisoners confined in the normal cells, the psychological damage inflicted by months of sensory deprivation through darkness and silence was so severe that prisoners being released showed no excitement, 'staring stupidly around them'. They were also often suffering from tuberculosis and other diseases that made them unemployable and, if they survived long enough, were prone to commit further crimes.

Dickens saw similar results during a visit to a US penitentiary, Cherry Hill, which also used the silent system.

> Every prisoner who comes into the jail comes at night, is put into a bath and dressed in the prison garb, and then a black hood is drawn over his face and head, and he is led to the cell from which he never stirs again until his whole period of confinement has expired. I looked at some of them with the same awe as I should have looked at men who have been buried alive and dug up again.

Chesterton's silent system did not become universal until 1863, when a wave of crime in London, particularly robbery with violence, led to the setting up of a Select Committee under Lord Carnarvon.

The committee's conclusion was that, 'A separate system must now be accepted as the foundation of prison discipline. Its rigid maintenance is a vital principal to the efficiency of county and borough jails. Other means employed for the reformation of offenders should always be accompanied by due and effective punishment.'

The committee made a statutory definition of hard labour. It was to be an endless, painful cycle of meaningless repetitions of a gruelling task. The aim was exhaustion and humiliation, not rehabilitation.

First-class hard labour was the treadwheel, the crank, the shot-drill, the capstan and stone-breaking. Of these, 'The treadwheel and the crank performed the principal elements of prison discipline.'

The treadmill at Holloway at least had a function: driving the pumps that supplied the prison's water. It was fifty-four feet long and twenty-four feet in diameter and had places for twenty-four prisoners – sixteen men and eight boys. They stood in numbered compartments, gripped a horizontal bar for support and pushed the treads down with their feet.

Although relatively safe compared to the ancient treadmills in use at other prisons – three separate incidents of prisoners being crushed to death inside the treadmill were recorded at Aylesbury prison in a single year – careless or exhausted prisoners at Holloway could become caught by the foot or leg and it was impossible to stop the wheel in time to prevent the mutilation or even death of a trapped person.

The crank was,

> A narrow drum placed on legs with a long handle on one side which, on being turned, causes a series of cups or scoops in the interior to revolve. At the lower part of the interior of the machine is a thick layer of sand which the cups as they come round scoop up and carry to the top of the wheel, where they throw it out and empty themselves after the principal of a dredging machine. A dial plate fixed in front of the iron drum shows how many revolutions the machine has made.

Cranks were set up in each prisoner's cell and they were forced to work them in silence and isolation. Failure to do the prescribed number of turns led to confinement in a dark cell or a flogging.

The shot-drill drew from Mayhew and Binny the comment that, 'It is impossible to imagine anything more ingeniously useless than this form of hard labour.'

Prisoners were lined up in a row in the exercise yard next to a pyramid of shot – iron cannon balls. The first prisoner in the row would pick up a cannon ball, place it at his feet, then pick it up again and pass it to the next man. This was repeated all the way down the line to the last man who built the cannon balls into another pyramid. Then they were passed back down the line again.

Second-class hard labour, such as oakum-picking, was less onerous, but prisoners only graduated to that after at least three months of first-class hard labour. It required old ship's rope to be unpicked by hand, first into its individual strands, and then into their constituent threads. Each day three pounds of it had to be reduced to 'a fine soft tow by the bare fingers of each man, before he lays down to rest'. If not enough had been produced a punishment would result.

The Holloway regime alternated twenty minutes on the treadmill with twenty picking oakum. The oakum was made into mats by prisoners on secondary hard labour and the prison even made a profit on their sale to railways and other institutions. The clothing workshops also sold prison uniforms to other gaols and to the convict colony in Gibraltar.

The penalty for offences committed in prison was 'degradation from a higher to a lower and more penal class, combined with harder labour and a more sparing diet, but where the offender is hardened and the offence deliberately repeated, corporal punishment is the most effective, and sometimes the only remedy'.

The committee's proposals were embodied in the Prison Act of 1865. Under its provisions, the distinction between 'Houses of Correction' like Holloway and Pentonville, which had housed male and female convicts serving sentences from seven days up to two years, and the ancient and decrepit jails and prison hulks where long-term prisoners were held, was abolished.

All prisoners were now to be

> prevented from holding any communication with each other, either by every prisoner being kept in a separate cell by day and night, except when he is in chapel or taking exercise, or by every prisoner being confined by night in his cell and being subjected to such superintendence during the day as will prevent his communicating with any other prisoner.

Prison food was kept deliberately meagre and plain – gruel and half a pound of bread twice a day – thin rations for men condemned to back-breaking hard labour.

Hammocks were replaced by bare wooden beds, and chains and irons were reintroduced for troublesome prisoners. The governor's office included an arsenal of muskets, pistols, bayonets and cutlasses in case of a riot.

Governors were also given powers to punish other breaches of the rules with up to three days and three nights of solitary confinement in a dark cell on bread and water, and visiting justices could extend that to as much as a month or order a flogging at the jail whipping-post.

As the *Illustrated London News* reported,

> The flogging box is a combination of the principal of the pillory with that of the stocks. The hands are held fast in an erect frame before the patient's face and his legs are secured in two holes in the wooden box where he stands during the process of manual expostulation applied by means of a nine-lashed scourge, or a birchen rod for boys.

An additional punishment was deprivation of work, for even hard labour was preferable to the monotony of being forced to stay silent and motionless in a dark cell all day and all night.

Mayhew and Binny described the system as 'penal purgatory, where men are submitted to the chastisement of separate confinement so as to fit them for the after state' – hard labour or transportation.

Transportation to the colonies was one of the leftovers from an earlier age, abolished soon after the Prison Act became law. The last women convicts had been transported in 1852 and the last convict ship with male prisoners aboard sailed in 1867.

Public executions were also abolished. Hangings outside Newgate had been a popular attraction for centuries, but a body of influential opinion, which included that of Charles Dickens, who had witnessed a double hanging with his wife, led to their abolition in 1868.

From then on hangings were carried out in a gallows-shed built near the chapel. Under Home Office rules, executions took place 'at 8 a.m.

on the first day after the intervention of three Sundays from the day on which sentence is passed'. The prison bell tolled for fifteen minutes before and fifteen minutes after executions, and a black flag flew over the prison for one hour.

The typical prison routine at Holloway followed the harsh prescription of the Prison Acts: six months' separate confinement, followed by six months' 'silent association'. Holloway did not quite extend the full brutality of the silent regime, but though prisoners were not masked, they were forbidden to speak and made to work in high-sided booths, invisible to each other. Hard labour was interrupted only by sleep, meals and chapel services.

Despite improved facilities, the complete separation of prisoners under the silent system led to ten times the rates of insanity at the more modern prisons like Holloway and Pentonville, than in jails that were far worse in every other way.

Even the prison authorities in Tsarist Russia were moved to condemn the savagery and inhumanity of the English penal system, but the terrible ordeal of enforced silence and hard labour remained in force until the Prison Act of 1898. It came far too late for prisoners 5331 and 5332, Dudley and Stephens.

On Tuesday, 9 December, Tom and Stephens were taken from their cells and transported back to the High Court in the Black Maria to face sentence. A huge crowd was once more thronging the Strand outside the courts.

The two men entered the courtroom half an hour before the judges but instead of being placed in the dock, they were seated in the well reserved for solicitors, between two prison warders. The body of the court was jammed with members of the bar and the public gallery was overflowing, but Philippa was not among the crowd. Tom had told her not to come to the court. His daughter Winifred remained seriously ill, but he also could not bear the thought of seeing Philippa's face if the sentence went against them, as he knew it surely must.

The five judges entered at a quarter to eleven and the clerk first read out the Special Verdict. The formal judgement was then read by the Lord Chief Justice. Tom and Stephens were allowed to remain seated as he spoke.

'From these facts,' Coleridge said, 'stated with the cold precision of the Special Verdict, it appears sufficiently that the prisoners were subject to terrible temptation, to sufferings which may break down the bodily power of the strongest man and try the conscience of the best.

'Other details yet more harrowing, facts still more loathsome and appalling were presented to the jury and are to be found recorded in my learned brother's notes. Nevertheless this is clear: that the prisoners put to death a weak and unoffending boy upon the chance of preserving their own lives by feeding upon his flesh and blood after he was killed.

'The verdict finds that if the men had not fed upon the body of the boy they would probably not have survived and that the boy, being in a much weaker condition, was likely to have died before them. They might possibly have been picked up by a passing ship the next day, they may possibly not have been picked up at all. In either case it is obvious that the killing of the boy would have been an unnecessary and profitless act.

'Mr Collins contended that the conclusion of the Special Verdict, that the jury found their verdict in accordance with the judgement of the court, was not put to them by my learned brother. The answer is twofold. First that it is really what the jury meant and is the clothing in legal phraseology of that which is already contained by necessary implication in their unquestioned finding, and two that it is a matter of the merest form – it has been the form of Special Verdicts in criminal cases for upwards of a century at least.'

As Lord Coleridge was well aware, there had been no Special Verdicts at all for ninety-nine years.

'There remains to be considered the real question in the case, whether the killing under the circumstances set forth in the verdict be or be not murder. The contention that it could be anything else was to the minds of all of us both new and strange but at once dangerous, immoral and opposed to all legal principle and analogy.

'We are not in conflict with any opinion expressed on this subject by the learned persons who formed the commissions for preparing the criminal code. They say on this subject: "We are not prepared to suggest that necessity should in every case be a justification. We are equally unprepared to suggest that necessity should in no case be a defence. We judge it better to leave such questions to be dealt with when, if ever, they arise in practice by applying the principles that the law took in the circumstances of the particular case."

'Now, except for the purposes of testing how far the conservation of a man's own life is in all cases and under all circumstances an absolute, unqualified and paramount duty, we exclude from our consideration all the incidents of war. We are dealing with a case of private homicide, not one imposed upon men in the service of their sovereign and in the defence of their country.

'The law and morality are not the same and many things may be moral which are not necessarily legal, yet the absolute divorce of law from morality would be a fatal consequence and such divorce would follow if the temptation, the murder in this case, were to be held by law to be an absolute defence of it. It is not so.

'To preserve one's life is, generally speaking, a duty, but it may be the plainest and the highest duty to sacrifice it. War is full of instances in which it is a man's duty not to live, but to die. The duty, in case of ship-wreck, of a captain to his crew, of the crew to the passengers, of soldiers to women and children, as in the noble case of the *Birkenhead*; these duties impose on men the moral necessity, not of preservation, but of the sacrifice of their lives for others, from which in no country, least of all it is to be hoped England, will men ever shrink, as indeed they have not shrunk.

'It is not correct, therefore, to say that there is any absolute and unqualified necessity to preserve one's life. It would be very easy and a cheap display of commonplace learning to quote from Greek and Latin authors, passage after passage in which the duty of dying for others has been laid down in glowing and sympathetic language as resulting from the principles of heathen ethics. It is enough in Christian countries to remind ourselves of the Example which we profess to follow.

'It is not needful to point out the awful danger of admitting the principle which leaves to him who is to profit by it to determine the necessity which will justify him in deliberately taking another's life to save his own. "So spake the fiend and by the tyrant's power, Necessity excused his devilish deed."

'In this case the weakest, the youngest, the most unresisting, was chosen. Was it more necessary to kill him than one of the grown men?

The answer must be, "No". It is quite plain that such a principle once admitted might be made a legal cloak for unbridled passion and atrocious crime.'

Tom turned to Stephens. 'He has not even addressed the question that faced us – rather than for all to perish, was it better for one to die that the others might live?'

A warder shoved him in the back. 'Be quiet or it will be the worse for you.'

Coleridge paused for a moment. 'There is no path safe for judges to tread but to ascertain the law to the best of their ability and to declare it according to their judgement, and if the law appears to be too severe on individuals to leave it to the Sovereign to exercise that prerogative of mercy which the constitution has entrusted to the hands fitted to exercise it.

'It must not be supposed that, in refusing to admit temptation to be excuse for the crime, it is forgotten how terrible the temptation was, how awful the suffering, how hard in such trials to keep the judgement straight and the conduct pure. We are often compelled to set up standards we cannot reach ourselves, to lay down rules which we could not ourselves satisfy, but a man has no right to declare temptation to be an excuse though he might himself have yielded to it, nor allow compassion for a criminal to change or weaken in any manner the legal definition of the crime.

'It is therefore our duty to declare that the prisoners' act in this case was wilful murder; that the facts as stated in the verdict are no legal justification of the homicide, and to say that in our unanimous opinion they are upon this Special Verdict guilty of murder.'

There was absolute silence in the courtroom as the attorney general rose to speak. 'My Lord, it is my duty now to pray the judgement of the court.'

The master of the Crown Office got to his feet. 'Prisoners at the bar, you have been convicted of murder. What have you to say why the court should not give you judgement to die?'

Tom stood up. There were a thousand things he could have said, a score of ways to vent his fury at the sham show-trial they had been forced to endure, but as he glanced along the row of unblinking faces ranged in front of him, he shook his head. To anger them would serve no useful purpose and could only make his fate worse.

He drew a deep breath. 'What I have to say, my lord, is this. I hope you will take into consideration the extreme difficulties I was in when the deed was committed and I trust I shall have the mercy of the court.'

'I also say the same, My Lord,' Stephens said, his voice barely a whisper.

The two men stood at the rail of the dock to receive sentence. Tom was impassive, but Stephens's face still betrayed his bewilderment.

Coleridge's usher approached him with the black cap but he waved the man away with an irritable gesture. It gave Tom a faint hope that even at this late stage, the judges might be moved to show mercy to them.

Lord Coleridge's opening words seemed to offer confirmation of that hope. 'You have been, each of you, convicted of the crime of wilful murder,' Coleridge said, 'but you have been recommended most earnestly to the mercy of the Crown, a recommendation in which I understand my learned brother who tried you, and we who have heard this argument, unanimously concur. But it is my duty as the organ of the court to pronounce upon you the sentence of the law.

'For the crime of wilful murder, of which each of you is now convicted, the sentence of the court is that you be taken to the prison whence you came, and from thence, on a day appointed, that you be taken to a place of execution; that you be there hanged by the neck until your bodies be dead; and that your bodies when dead be buried within the precincts of the prison in which you shall be confined after this your conviction.'

It was the first time the death sentence had been pronounced in the Court of Queen's Bench since the Jacobite rebellion of 1745.

As Tom and Stephens were led away, the only sound in the courtroom was their footsteps on the stairs leading down to the cells. They were taken straight to the Black Maria and returned to Holloway to await their fate.

The crowd, noisy and exuberant as Tom and Stephens had entered, watched their departure in almost complete silence, some even doffing their hats as if a hearse, not a Black Maria, was rumbling down the street.

Home Office officials were at pains to inform the reporters gathered at the court that the sentence of death was purely 'formal', and the newspaper reports the following morning, 10 December, were unanimous in supporting the decision of the court.

The Times led the applause.

> The judgement delivered by Lord Coleridge yesterday brushed aside the few unsubstantial excuses set up in defence... It is singular that it should have been reserved to these latter days to condemn in set terms a view which would lead to revolting consequences. But that is now done. It is found that the doctrine of necessary homicide has as little foundation as the view that butchers may not sit on juries, or that Englishmen may lawfully sell their wives in market overt...
>
> The situation was terribly trying and the temptation only too likely to deaden conscience, but we protest against the notion that in the extremity of hunger or thirst, men are to be considered as released from all duties towards each other. It is an abuse of words to speak of the crime as due to necessity. It was a necessity which one of the men on board was, it would seem, perfectly able to resist, and which people placed in circumstances equally trying have been known to master. Our columns in 1836 contained an account of the perils of a shipwrecked crew who suffered hardships as cruel as befell the survivors of the *Mignonette*, but no one among them suggested the idea of killing any of their number, and the dead, we are told, were cast overboard lest the living be tempted to forget their misery in a horrible repast.
>
> Miners who are walled up in a subterranean gallery with no food or water, devour in the agony of hunger, candle ends and even the soles of their boots, and then die heroically, and the records of war are rarely tarnished with horrors such as those of which the crew of the *Mignonette* were guilty...
>
> There will be no ground for complaining if a crime of the same nature be henceforth treated as murder with the con-

sequences which usually follow it. There is no wish to deal hardly with Dudley and Stephens, though they have been the subjects of somewhat mawkish, ill-directed sympathy . . . But it would be a great scandal if anyone who hereafter yields to similar temptation to that which Dudley and Stephens yielded should be looked upon as entitled to the same mercy.

CHAPTER 22

Collins had assured Tom and Stephens that they would be granted a Royal Pardon and released at once, but their doubts began to grow as the days passed without any word from the Home Office.

The home secretary, Sir William Harcourt, had at least taken immediate steps to remove the threat of death hanging over them, expediency and principle for once pushing him towards the same conclusion. Harcourt had advocated the abolition of capital punishment in a speech in 1878 but he was aware that neither public nor parliamentary opinion supported him, and by the time he became home secretary he was able to declare that he 'firmly believed in capital punishment'.

He did introduce a Bill in 1882 aiming to retain the death penalty only for first-degree murder – killing with deliberate intent – but opposition from Parliament and the judiciary forced him to drop the proposal.

On the day that Tom and Stephens were sentenced to death, Harcourt instructed his under-secretary of state,

> I am respiting the sentence, during the Queen's pleasure, but reserving the question of the actual term of imprisonment. Inform the Prison Governor that the prisoners are to be kept where they are for the present and not to be removed or placed

in the condemned cell or anything of the kind. In short that they are to remain for the present absolutely *in status quo*.

While content that the custom of the sea had been formally outlawed, Harcourt was still determined to commute the sentence only to life imprisonment with penal servitude. He argued that, like an acquittal, commuting the sentence further would send the wrong signals to ships' crews.

> I should pronounce it an innocent act and deserving of no punishment. If I were to do that I should condemn the law and say I believe that it has arrived at an unjust conclusion. If to kill an innocent person to save your own life is an act deserving of pardon, by what right can a Fenian assassin be punished who kills because the lot has fallen upon him to do the murder and if he does not execute it, he knows his own life will be forfeited?

It was at least a more concise and articulate defence of the judgement than the five judges had been able to produce.

Harcourt was at once warned by the attorney general that a sentence of life imprisonment would be unenforceable and might even lead to riots. 'You will never be able to maintain such a decision and you will have to give way.'

Sir Henry also confirmed Collins's negligence or connivance in ignoring the possible plea of manslaughter. 'The men had been in a state of phrensy quite upsetting the ordinary balance of the mind. If Collins had sought to obtain a verdict of manslaughter, the jury would certainly have found the verdict and no judge would have inflicted more than three months' imprisonment.'

Harcourt at first rejected the advice. 'Everyone knows that the vulgar view of this subject at first was that the men had committed no crime. The judgement of the court in this case pronounces that to slay an innocent and unoffending person to save a man's own life is not a justification or excuse. It is, therefore, on moral and ethical grounds, not upon technical grounds, that the law repels the loose and dangerous ideas floating about in the vulgar mind that such acts are anything short of the highest crime known to the law.'

Harcourt's son, Lewis, a friend of Sir Henry, was working as his father's private secretary at the time and also argued for leniency. 'It would be very mischievous to excite sympathy with them by the infliction of a long term of imprisonment. I suggest no more than six months.'

Harcourt was mindful of Queen Victoria's intransigent views on crime and punishment, however. He had already had a number of bruising encounters with her when arguing for leniency in other cases, and had been forced to threaten to resign over her refusal to commute a death sentence on a nineteen-year-old labourer convicted of murdering his wife.

Only six months before the *Mignonette* case came up for review, the Queen and Harcourt had again been at odds over the fate of Emily Wilcox, who had killed her own two-year-old child. At first the Queen had refused even to consider clemency, and all Harcourt's efforts to persuade her had only resulted in the sentence being commuted to life imprisonment.

He braced himself for another acrimonious dispute over the *Mignonette* case, but fortunately for Dudley and Stephens, the Queen was so preoccupied with the fate of Sir Garnet Wolseley's expedition to rescue General Gordon at Khartoum that she displayed little of her customary interest in securing the maximum rigour of the law for convicted murderers.

Harcourt reached his decision on 11 December and the document commuting the sentence was drawn up that afternoon, but that decision was not communicated to Tom and Stephens for another two days. On the morning of Saturday, 13 December, they were summoned to appear before the prison governor, Lieutenant Colonel Everard Milman. They stood to attention before his desk, waiting with mounting impatience as the clerk read the lengthy preamble to the decision.

> To our trusty and well-beloved the Justices of our High Court, the Sheriffs of London and Middlesex, our Justices of Assize for the Western Circuit, the High Sheriff of the County of Devon, the Governor of our Prison at Holloway and all others whom it may concern. By her Majesty's command:
> Whereas Thomas Dudley and Edwin Stephens were at a

general gaol delivery holden at Exeter on the 1st day November 1884 before the Mr Baron Huddleston tried on an indictment for murder, and the jury having found Special Verdict, they were bound over to appear at the next assizes for Cornwall for sentence after judgement had been pronounced by the Queen's Bench Division at the High Court of Justice.

And whereas the said Thomas Dudley and Edwin Stephens did on the 4th day of December 1884 appear before the Queen's Bench Division of the High Court of Justice, and were by the said Court adjudged guilty of murder, and on the 9th day of December 1884, were sentenced to death and were by the said Court ordered to be detained in our prison at Holloway.

We, in consideration of some circumstances humbly represented unto us, are graciously pleased to extend Our Grace and Mercy unto them and to grant them Our Pardon for the crime of which they stand convicted, on condition that they may be imprisoned, without hard labour, for the term of six months, to be reckoned from the date on which judgement was pronounced upon them, namely from the 4th day of December 1884.

Our will and pleasure therefore is that you do give the necessary directions accordingly, and for so doing, this shall be your warrant. Given at our Court of St James the 11th day of December 1884, the 48th year of our reign.

Far from a relief, the term of imprisonment came as a brutal shock to both men, who had believed Collins's assurances that they would be released immediately. Philippa had visited Tom on Friday afternoon, and though he appeared in low spirits, he told her they expected to receive the Queen's Pardon and be home on the Sunday.

She had been preparing to leave home at ten on the Saturday morning, to make a final visit before his release, when a telegram was delivered giving news of the six-month sentence.

Before their sentence was confirmed, Tom and Stephens had been treated as 'first-class misdemeanants', allowed to exercise together in the grounds, receive visits and letters, wear their own clothes and have food brought in. Now they were deprived of all their previous privileges and placed under the numbing silent regime, in which even the brutality of hard labour would have been some relief from the darkness and silence of their cells. Separated from each other and all their fellow inmates and forbidden to speak, they were locked up for twenty-three hours a day, released only for divine service and silent exercise in the prison yard.

Tom's bleak state of mind was not improved by the knowledge that his carefully accumulated savings had been consumed in the cost of his defence and that, as the wife of a convicted murderer, Philippa was barred from resuming teaching at Newtown Board School or any other establishment.

Tom wrote to the home secretary from gaol, on the standard form supplied by the prison, detailing the date and place of conviction, the crime, the sentence. His rambling, impassioned plea for greater clemency was received by the Prison Commission on 8 January 1885.

To the Right Honourable Sir William Vernon Harcourt, Her Majesty's Principal Secretary of State for the Home Department.

I beg to call your attention what our terrible sufferings while in our 15 feet boat for 24 days. The only food we had for the first 11 or 12 days was one half pound of Turnips and, say, at the most three pounds of raw Turtle each, and you may say next to no water, only our owen urin to drink day after day.

For the next 8 days not any food whatever and five days of which, not one drop of water. Can any one on shore judge the state of our bodys and what must our poor brain and mind have been when that awful impulse came to put the poor lad out of his misry?

For he was dying at the time, the salt water killed him and the terrible deed was done for the sake of somthing to eat and exist upon. That gastly food, it makes my blood run cold to think about it now, and would to God I had died in the boat. I should have saved the pain from those belonging to me whatever.

I can assure you I shall never forget the sight of my two

unfortunate companions over that gastly meal. We all was like mad wolfs, who should get the most. For men, fathers of children, to commit such a deed we could not have our right reason, and it cannot be expected that we had, straining our eyes day and night over the horizon looking for help. What mortal tongue can tell our sufferings but our owen?

About the 15th day, when lots was spoken about and we all was about the same in bodly health, Brooks must admit that I offered my life did the lot fall to me. I was quite prepared to die, I have God for my witness, but no one else would hear of it.

But it was not to be done until the last possable moment and I feel quite sure had we not that awful food to exist upon not a soul would have lived until we was rescued.

But as I have said before, I wished I had died rather than to have pain cast on those who are dear to me, or had let the poor lad died we should not have had many hours to wait I am sure.

Then to be rescued just at death's door, and receive every kindness from the hands of strangers for 38 days, and to be landed in our owen native country and tell the truth as I did of our sad tale to be cast into prison but thanks to God not for long. We were allowed to return to our happy homes then, to live extra well to get up our bodly strength for three months. But then comes the pain again that recalls all the terrible past. It makes my sad affair doubly hard to bare.

I therefore beg of your further consideration: First, that I trust you may see fit to advise our Gracious Majesty the Queen to grant her humble servant a free pardon, and let me return to my happy home and get my living honistly as I have done at sea since I was not ten years old.

I can say that neither man or woman can say I ever done either an unjust action and every master living I have served since a lad was at Exeter to speak on my behalf. Three came all the way from Scotland but was not allowed.

Secondly, if you cannot advise a pardon, I pray the sentence may be dated from the day I was tried at Exeter, November 6th.

Thirdly, that you will advise an exception and allow me to hear from and write my wife or see her at stated times you may think fit to sanction on my behalf, different from the regulations of the prison. Then my mind would be at rest to know all was well home.

Fourthly, I further pray you will allow an exception to the diet and allow me one good meal daily, namely the hospital dinner that I was supplied with at first for a few days, or that you will allow me to provide one at my expense.

I trust favours asked will receive your merciful consideration, and that you will take into account the unhappy circumstances that have placed me in this position, and that I may receive a favourable reply.

I am, Sir, your obedient servant, Thomas Dudley.

He was granted the right to receive letters and occasional visits from Philippa, but Harcourt rejected the other requests. The home secretary also received numerous other petitions on behalf of the two men from all over the country, including the places most closely associated with the tragedy: Tollesbury, Falmouth and Southampton.

We the undersigned of Tollesbury in the county of Essex, unanimously resolve that a petition should be presented to you, Sir, asking your intercession with Her Most Gracious Majesty the Queen, begging for a free pardon on behalf of Thomas Dudley, now lying in Holloway Jail.

Thomas Dudley is a native of this place and is respected by all who know him. We ask this on account of his hitherto almost blameless life, the terrible ordeals through which he has passed, the fact that medical evidence was altogether excluded at his trial and that his further incarceration will preclude him from the chance of taking up business offered him by a relative in the Colonies.

The home secretary also received,

The humble petition of the Mayor, Magistrates, Corporation and Inhabitants of Falmouth on behalf of Dudley and Stephens, Captain and Mate of the ill-fated yacht *Mignonette*.

These poor men ought to have the sentence of six months imprisonment commuted and a free pardon granted with an immediate order for their release. Independent of their terrible sufferings in an open boat on the high seas for twenty-four days, the subsequent trial and imprisonment has been to them no ordinary punishment.

There was also a petition from John Burton of the Curiosity Shop in Falmouth, who had met Harcourt when he visited Falmouth two years earlier: 'May I ask the favour of your sympathy for Dudley and Stephens? Trusting yourself and Lady Harcourt are well, I might here add I am the person who stood bail for Dudley and Stephens.'

A number of other individuals also petitioned Harcourt. Miss Alice Maud Lever wrote from Cheshire asking for a free pardon for them and enclosing fifty pounds to be sent to their families 'as a New Year's gift'.

Harcourt was unimpressed. 'Write to the lady to say that the sentence on these men was carefully considered and cannot be changed, and return the money to her. It is not necessary to give her any address as I do not wish to encourage presents of this kind. Have the letter carefully registered as in its present state the cheque is payable to the bearer.'

Despite his efforts, Miss Lever made contact with Philippa and passed on her donation. She also enlisted her brother, Ellis Lever, an industrialist and philanthropist, to petition the home secretary. He wrote a letter containing, 'a suggestion which might be advantageous in preventing any such deplorable mishap in the future'.

His idea – that ship-owners should in future be compelled to stock their lifeboats with provisions and water – was eventually adopted, but a law requiring the provision of an adequate number of lifeboats had to await a more terrible tragedy, the sinking of the *Titanic*.

Ellis Lever also sent a petition to,

Her Most Gracious Majesty Victoria. The case to the prisoner's wife and children is so exceptional and heartrending and as to the man himself, it should not be forgotten, he unreservedly and voluntarily stated to his most terrible disadvantage the whole circumstances. So constant and remorseful a memorial is likely to endure, not for six months, but for all time to come during his life, that I do most earnestly and humbly beseech Your Majesty so to relax the ordinances of justice in this case, as to be pleased to give directions that the term of imprisonment to Captain Thomas Dudley may be curtailed, if it be even for one moiety of the unexpired portion of that term.

Lever enclosed with his own petition a letter written to him by Philippa.

... Every yacht owner has testified in his favour, in fact all who came in contact with him respected him, and it was his boast that no man, woman or child could look in his face and say, 'Tom Dudley, you have wronged me.'

He often urged me to give up school duties because of the anxiety attending them but while his position was uncertain, I preferred working. . . .

On June 3rd I received a telegram from him at Madeira saying 'All is well'. That was the last communication received until the receipt of the telegram of September 6th speaking of the accident and terrible sufferings undergone.

In the meantime, the yacht had foundered on July 5th, twelve hundred miles from the Cape. He with his companions had suffered indescribable agony in the open boat for twenty-four days and nights, the latter being the most terrible death staring them in the face, every billow threatening to engulf them, while the fear that the sharks would knock in the bottom of the boat constantly haunted them.

The very elements seemed to mock their sufferings. As he often described it, they would eagerly watch the clouds gather and seem ready to pour rain down in abundance and then while the poor sufferers in agony watched, the clouds dispersed and left them in despair. Was not that a time of delirium and fever? Poor victims to misery, can their situation be conceived? Their tongues were swollen and black. He said they were like wild animals.

Without wishing to speak slightingly of his fellow sufferers but in justice to my husband, his wonderful forethought, bravery and unselfishness were very prominent. He it was who stayed in the yacht procuring provisions until almost too late. He constructed the sea anchor with which to break the force of the huge waves and prevent them engulfing them. He cut off the bottoms of his trousers to stop the hole in the boat. He urged the men to give up a garment apiece to be used for sails and on their refusal erected all the wood that could be spared from the bottom of the boat. After constant entreaties they gave up their shirts which with his own he erected for a sail.

The men, hopeless and tortured, were bent on committing suicide but were buoyed up by him, and after the deed was committed both Brooks and Stephens grasped his hands many scores of times in the day saying he had saved their lives and how they would show their gratitude on reaching home if they ever did so.

When picked up they were as weak and helpless as infants, having to be carried to berths and nursed with wonderful skill. If not so treated they must have perished. They were on board the *Moctezuma* receiving all possible attention for nearly six weeks, consequently no idea could be formed of their pitiful condition at the time of rescue.

On September 6th they landed at Falmouth and Tom immediately made his deposition before the Magistrates, not palliating a single circumstance, though entreated never to divulge it. That the bravest and most honest should suffer must seem hard when one who, too cowardly to do, was not too scrupulous to share, yet could be permitted to go unpunished and then make a market out of the misery of his companions. . . .

After being summoned to Exeter to await his trial, he returned home November 6th, from then until December 4th he bore a month of suspense. At that time Winifred was attacked with congestion of the lungs and he nursed her night and day. We were doubtful of her recovery when he had to go to Holloway again to undergo another ordeal, still more trying. On the 9th December, being sentenced to death, he was taken back to Holloway, there receiving sentence of six months imprisonment.

. . . I feel doubtful if he will ever be so strong as before. Now he is eager to leave England as soon as possible. We trust soon to settle our affairs and make a fresh start in Australia.

Although managers of public places of amusement have offered him large sums of money to induce him to exhibit himself, he has refused. The publicity and misery of the tragedy have been too painful almost for human endurance.

I beg to enclose letters for private perusals. Permit me to sign myself, Sir, I am your obedient and grateful servant. Philippa Dudley.

A Home Office official noted on the file containing the letters from Ellis Lever and Philippa: 'It is said that he will go with his wife to Australia as soon as he is released. His wife's letter giving an account of her anxieties etc. is very pathetic.'

Harcourt's view remained unaltered. 'Nil. This is a melancholy case but the sentence is a light one and cannot be altered.'

Stephens, in poor physical and mental health, had written no less than twenty-three petitions to the home secretary. The last read:

In consideration of his past troubles and the recommendations accorded him at Exeter both by the Judge and jury, he hopes he may still meet with further favour and that some portion of his unexpired sentence may be remitted.

Your petitioner prays that during the remainder of his imprisonment, he may be allowed to write and receive letters and visits from his family at more frequent intervals than are prescribed in the ordinary prison regulations. Your petitioner will ever pray . . .

The unsigned petition ended abruptly at that point.

Harcourt noted, 'Granted the same privileges as regards letters and visits. Nil as to the rest of the petition.'

After the failure of their petitions, Philippa wrote to thank Ellis Lever for his efforts.

I beg to acknowledge the receipt of your favour and learn from it that all your kindly efforts on our behalf have not succeeded.

I feel confident had it been possible you would have so accomplished it.

It has of course been a disappointment. I learned Mr Bates [a reprieved murderer] had been set at liberty and thought that perhaps that of Tom and his companion might follow. At any rate, his term will expire on the anniversary of the voyage that has cost him twelve months' loss and suffering.

Under favour, I may mention that I have not been at all well but am thankful to say I am better. Again thanking you and your family for your many kindnesses which have made me more hopeful. I am, dear Sir, your obedient and grateful servant. Philippa Dudley.

CHAPTER 23

Prisoners 5331 and 5332 were eventually released from Holloway on 20 May 1885, a year and a day after the *Mignonette* had sailed from Southampton on its final voyage.

Still bitter at his treatment, Tom left England for ever, sailing for Australia with his wife, children and one of Philippa's sisters, on the steamer *Austral*. It left Gravesend on 19 August 1885 and passed the Royal Portsmouth regatta the next day, where the yacht *Marguerite*, with Daniel Parker restored as a crewman, was competing.

To Philippa's relief, the *Austral* only retraced the *Mignonette*'s course as far as the Bay of Biscay, before taking the usual steamer route through the Mediterranean. It passed through the Suez Canal, and took on coals at Aden before steaming across the Indian Ocean to reach Sydney on 5 October 1885.

Tom joined his wife's aunt in business and prospered as T. R. Dudley and Company, oilskin, sail, tent, tarpaulin and flag-makers, yacht and boat outfitters and riggers, carrying on business firstly at Clarence Street and later at 47, 49 and 51 Sussex Street, near the junction with Erskine Street. He also had a slipway to the Parramatta river in the grounds of his house in Cambridge Street, Drummoyne. By 1900 he was employing over forty people and was well known in Sydney yachting circles as a large-scale sail and tarpaulin contractor.

Philippa had given birth to three more children and though one of them, a boy, died in infancy, two more girls – Elizabeth and Charlotte – survived.

However, the family's happiness and prosperity was to be brief. A pandemic of bubonic plague erupted in Hong Kong in 1894 and, carried by shipborne rats, it spread to every country in the world, killing thirteen million people. It reached Sydney early in 1900. The first signs were hundreds of dying rats around the wharves of the Union Shipping Company and the slums and crumbling wharves of Darling Harbour.

The means by which the plague was spread were still barely understood, but Dr Ashburton Thompson, president of the Sydney Board of Health, was an authority on the disease.

> Symptoms of the plague are shivering, rise of temperature, aching in the head, back and limbs, and a sickness. Great weakness succeeds with mental disturbance leading to coma or delirium. Death often occurs, however, before any characteristic symptoms are developed.
>
> At an early stage dark spots or patches often appear on the skin produced by subcutaneous haemorrhage, and bleeding may also take place from the various mucous membranes. Bleeding from the lungs, though rare in recent epidemics, was regarded as a characteristic symptom of Black Death in its most virulent form.
>
> By the second or third day the most distinctive features develop: one or more glandular swellings usually in the neck, armpits or groin. These generally break and lead to prolonged suppuration. In a few cases, carbuncles develop at a later stage of the disease.
>
> There can be no doubt the disease can be conveyed from one person to another but it is exceedingly doubtful if contagion can be thus conveyed directly without some intermediary. The general opinion now is that rats are an essential intermediary for carrying the disease.
>
> The plague may be conveyed from rats to humans by the intermediary agents of fleas sucking the blood of the rodents and afterwards inoculating the individual. If any dead rats are found about the premises, boiling water should be first thrown

over the carcase to kill any fleas and then the rats can be destroyed without danger.

Such measures as white-washing houses and cleansing gutters and sewers are not really of the slightest effect in allaying the spread of the plague. As a precautionary measure it is advisable to use disinfectants freely in order to get rid of fleas and such like vermin. Cleansing a neighbourhood, however, may have the ultimate effect of driving rats into another district, so distributing the infected rodents over a wider area.

There must be no half-measures. If we want to get rid of the plague we must kill the rats. Material for disinfectant is a weak solution of oil of vitriol – sulphuric acid – in water, say a five per cent solution. Within houses other things are more suitable and necessary. Out of doors sulphuric acid will be all that is necessary and it is very cheap.

At Dr Thompson's urgings, the city authorities began an extermination campaign, concentrating first on the wharves and stores alongside the harbour. All the people employed were inoculated against the plague and paid well above the normal rates. Floors were pulled up to remove dead rats, streets were cleaned of refuse and 179 loads 'above the normal scavenging of the city' were taken to the tip.

The *Sydney Mail* editorialized:

The attack of plague could prove a lasting service to our metropolis, what with the killing of vermin in all directions, the overhauling of our sanitary appliances and machinery, the cleansing of wharves, sewers, drains and streets, the disinfecting of dirty areas, the compelling of the City Council to shut up the vile garbage tip at Moore Park and devise more modern methods of dealing with refuse than Proverbial in old Jerusalem, and the warning which people have got to keep themselves clean, we should expect that in years to come Sydney will never be quite such a dirty, ill-kept and ill-managed city as it has been up to the present.

Despite the authorities' efforts to eradicate infected rats, the first recorded human case of the outbreak of bubonic plague, a dock labourer, Arthur H. Payne, a labourer for the Central Wharf Company at Dawes Point, was placed in quarantine on 26 January. However, he had only a mild case of the disease and later recovered.

Tom became the second victim. His first-floor premises in Sussex Street lay just behind the harbour and the toilet drained through a broken pipe into the water. On the morning of Tuesday, 13 February, he removed five dead rats from the room. He fell ill while at work the following Saturday and remained at Sussex Street for two days before being taken home to Drummoyne. He died on the afternoon of Thursday, 23 February 1900, at the age of forty-six.

He had fallen heavily at work a few days earlier, damaging his abdomen, and at first doctors suspected peritonitis, but the speed and suddeness of his death, coupled with the earlier case of plague, led to a hasty post-mortem examination. It was carried out at three thirty that afternoon by Dr Frank Tidswell.

From specimens of blood taken from the body, Dr Thompson confirmed the cause of death as bubonic plague, contracted from the fleas the dead rats had carried. According to the doctor, such a sudden death was not unusual for the plague. 'The symptoms may be rather mild but the poison takes its special effect on the heart.'

Tom was the first Sydney fatality from the outbreak. By the end of June over a hundred further deaths from plague had been recorded in the city.

Within an hour of the completion of the post-mortem, police had sealed off Tom's business premises and home, and put his family and everyone else found there into immediate quarantine. Five policemen stood guard on the house, where thirteen people had been isolated.

Among them were Philippa and Julian Dudley, now aged seventeen, Alexander Parker, a clerk in the railway department, and his wife, Archibald McDonald, a handyman employed at the house who was ill with stomach pains and being closely watched for symptoms of bubonic plague, Mrs Hoskins, Mrs Ludgate, Peter Gorman, Thomas Carrie and three boys, George Grear, Norman Mackie, and James Cox, who had arrived at the slip in a yacht that morning with a Japanese man by the name of Erakwa Bush. Several of them had gone to the house only to express their condolences, but all were taken into quarantine.

Four more people were quarantined at the premises in Sussex Street:

Tom's daughter Philippa and Arthur Wilson, a friend of the family she was later to marry, Mr Shannon, a sailmaker, and the book-keeper, William Wetherill.

All of them, together with two more people later identified as at risk – an eighteen-year-old girl called Maggie Beattie and Frederick Glebe, a haberdasher who had visited the house during Tom's illness – were taken to the quarantine station on the North Head above the entrance to Sydney Harbour.

The house and business premises were fumigated by the authorities and Dr Thompson reported that the sewerage in Sussex Street was defective. 'One morning Captain Dudley removed from the premises no fewer than five dead rats, being assisted in the work by one of the men now at the quarantine station.'

Inadequate sewerage was not unique to Tom's premises. A reporter extracted a statement from a Board of Health spokesman that not more than one house in every twenty-two was properly connected with the sewers. The statement was hastily withdrawn, but the board later admitted that it had prosecuted 440 owners or occupiers whose sewerage arrangements were 'insanitary or incomplete' since the start of the year.

Dr Thompson and Dr Pinkburn supervised the arrangements for Tom's funeral and interment. His body was wrapped in a sailcloth soaked in a 5 per cent solution of sulphuric acid and placed in a watertight coffin, which was then filled to the brim with more sulphuric acid and the lid sealed down. The coffin was enveloped in a succession of sailcloth sheets saturated with the same ferocious disinfectant and a jacket of 'asphalt cloth' was then wrapped around it.

The coffin was removed that Saturday evening, 24 February, and taken by water, towed in a skiff by a launch, to the quarantine station on the North Head. The interment took place later in the evening, in the cemetery inside the grounds of the quarantine station, a steeply sloping site high above the water, commanding a view of South Head.

Neither Philippa nor any other members of the family were allowed to attend the burial. After the briefest of services, the coffin was committed to the earth, buried in an unusually deep grave, officially known as number 48, with all its numerous wrappings undisturbed.

EPILOGUE

In all the years since Tom Dudley and Edwin Stephens were sentenced, there have been only two further recorded cases of the custom of the sea.

On 4 January 1893, three of the four survivors who had been clinging to the waterlogged hulk of the *Thekla* for thirteen days drew lots and killed the fourth. His legless and headless body was still hanging from the rigging when they were rescued. The Norwegian authorities carried out an investigation, but no formal proceedings were instituted either against them, or the survivors of the *Drot*, which foundered in a hurricane off Mississippi in 1899.

Six of the crew constructed a raft from the wreckage and cast themselves adrift. One went mad and threw himself overboard. Another, apparently dying, was killed and his blood drunk, and the same fate befell a third man shortly afterwards. The three remaining men then cast lots for the next victim. The loser, a German seaman, accepted his fate and bared his breast to the knife, or so the two survivors said after their eventual rescue. The German consul sought their arrest and extradition for murder, but the US authorities first delayed then quietly dropped proceedings, on the grounds that 'these unfortunate sailors have suffered enough'.

No twentieth-century cases have been recorded, but despite great advances in the safety of ships, survival techniques and search-and-rescue operations, there is no doubt that such incidents have occurred, particularly during the Second World War. Tom Dudley's prophecy to

Arthur Collins, 'Never again will men return to these shores and freely confess what they have done,' has proved correct.

There was an echo of the case of the *Mignonette*, however, at the inquest into the sinking of the ferry, *Herald of Free Enterprise*, at Zeebrugge in 1987. During his summing up, the coroner referred to the evidence of an Army corporal who had been trapped with dozens of other passengers. Their only way of escape from the rising waters was by means of a rope-ladder but it was blocked by a man who had frozen in panic while climbing it. After repeatedly shouting at him to move, the corporal ordered those below him to pull the man off the ladder. They did so and he fell into the water and drowned, while the others made their escape.

No criminal proceedings were ever contemplated against the corporal or any of the other people involved and, although the coroner conceded that, 'I think we need to at least glance in the direction of murder', he went on to describe certain killings as 'a reasonable act of what is known as self-preservation . . . that also includes in my judgement, the preservation of other lives; such killing is not necessarily murder at all.' Necessity – 'the great law of Nature and self-preservation' – rejected by the most senior judges in England a century before, might be a defence, after all, against a charge of murder.

Tom Dudley's body still lies under the rocky soil of the North Head above the mouth of Sydney Harbour, but the inscription on the small gravestone marking his last resting place has weathered away. Nothing now remains to indicate the spot but a few fragments of crumbling stone.

If the *Mignonette*'s dinghy, the knife with which Tom killed Richard Parker, or the letter he wrote to Philippa on the back of the chronometer certificate have survived to the present day, their whereabouts are now unknown.

However, the sextant and its case in which Edwin Stephens scratched a farewell note on the fifteenth day in the dinghy turned up in an auction in Adelaide, South Australia, 25 years ago. The sextant 'from a deceased estate in Sydney' – presumably the estate of one of Tom Dudley's children – was in a decrepit condition and was knocked down for 60 Australian dollars (about $40 US), but the English purchaser was fascinated by the inscription and set out to discover the story behind it. After careful restoration, its new owner used it to teach himself the art of celestial navigation.

Philippa Dudley was released from quarantine on Tuesday, 6 March 1900. She survived her husband by twenty-eight years, dying at Chatswood in North Sydney in 1928 at the age of eighty-six. The two daughters born to her and Tom in Australia died before her, but their three elder children survived her, and their son Julian ran the family business until 1946. It continued trading in other hands until the 1970s.

The other leading characters in the case of Regina versus Dudley and Stephens met with mixed fortunes. Early in 1885, while the two men were still serving their sentence in Holloway, Arthur Collins was duly awarded the knighthood he had been promised. He was elevated to the bench as Chief Justice of Madras the same year. He served there for fifteen years, and was also vice-chancellor of the university from 1889 to 1899, before retiring to England. He died, aged eighty-one, on 12 September 1915.

Sir William George Granville Venables Vernon Harcourt's tenure as home secretary ended with the defeat of the Gladstone government at the general election of 1885, but he later served as chancellor of the exchequer in 1886 and again from 1892 to 1895, and was leader of the House from 1893 to 1898. He died in 1904.

Samuel Plimsoll continued his indefatigable campaigns even after resigning his seat in the Commons in 1880 to spend more time with his ailing wife, Eliza, but public attention had moved on to other issues, and he was defeated when he attempted to return to the House as member for Central Sheffield in 1885, following Eliza's death. The hero of a decade before was now a largely forgotten, peripheral figure. He died in 1898.

Mr Baron Huddleston's age and failing health – coupled perhaps with a touch of snobbery about his origins and a suspicion that he lacked the dedication and gravitas required of a Lord Chief Justice – denied him his ultimate ambition.

'The Last of the Barons' died on Friday, 5 December 1890, aged seventy-three. His obituary in *The Times* reported that 'His digestion had become much impaired and it was dyspepsia which brought about the end. He had gone through his judicial work for some time past with great discomfort from pain and sleeplessness but he adhered, perhaps too resolutely, to office.'

His memorial was the leading case of Regina versus Dudley and Stephens with which his name is associated and which remains familiar to every student of the law to this day.

Tom's two crewmates survived him, but neither lived out their days in happy circumstances. Two days after his release from prison, Edwin Stephens again wrote to the Board of Trade, attempting to renew his certificate of competence.

> I now again beg to renew my application for my certificate as I am unable to obtain employment until I am in possession of the same, and having a wife and family dependent upon me, I am naturally anxious to gain that employment as soon as possible.
>
> Trusting that in considering my application, the Board of Trade will take into consideration the trials that I have lately undergone, and grant me the renewal of my certificate as soon as practicable.

A Board of Trade official made the grudging annotation, 'I suppose we should return the certificate.'

Still in poor physical and mental health, Stephens turned down Jack Want's offer of a free passage to Sydney and did not go to sea for the rest of that year, surviving on occasional shore jobs and the money his wife was able to earn. He returned to the sea the following spring as master of the *Madeline*, a yacht sailing out of Cowes, and was back on the ocean later that year, making two voyages to deliver steam yachts to Alexandria in Egypt.

In the early 1890s he worked occasionally on the Atlantic run, but his voyages were punctuated by longer and longer periods ashore, as his mental health deteriorated and he grew more dependent on alcohol. Under those pressures, his marriage had also failed and he left Southampton, living for a while in Leytonstone, north-east London.

He made his last voyage in 1898, at the age of fifty, serving as mate on the steamship *Jourcoing* on a voyage from Portsmouth to Sardinia. He never went to sea again. Prone to continued and increasingly severe fits of depression and alcoholism, he found work of any sort hard to come by, and died a pauper in Hull, aged sixty-six, on 25 June 1914.

Ned Brooks continued to exhibit himself in museums and travelling freak shows for a few more months, but as the case of the *Mignonette* faded from the public memory and the showmen sought ever newer and more exotic attractions, he soon found himself out of work. He returned to Southampton and the money he had earned brought him no lasting benefit.

No record exists of the wife and children he was rumoured to have abandoned at the time of the *Mignonette*'s voyage, but he did marry in 1891, and found work as a rigger and yacht hand, and as a seaman on the Isle of Wight ferries. He even sailed on a yacht, the *Una*, for a while with a cousin of Richard Parker.

He continued to live in and around Southampton and at one point was living in Richard's old village of Itchen Ferry, in a house on Smith's Quay. 'Curly' Bedford, another relative of the dead boy, reported that he would often hear Brooks staggering home drunk and crying out in the night, 'I didn't do it.'

Like Edwin Stephens, Brooks died in poverty, succumbing to a heart attack in Southampton Parish Infirmary on 22 July 1919, aged seventy-three.

In memory of Richard Parker, an inscribed tombstone was placed over the previously unmarked graves of his parents in Pear Tree Churchyard, Itchen Ferry. It was maintained in pristine condition for many years. No one in the parish knew who cleaned the stone and tended the grave at dead of night, but local tradition had it that, before leaving England, Tom Dudley had arranged for someone to do so. Although Tom was in poor financial straits at the time, he retained none of the surplus money from the defence fund, donating it, as he had pledged, to pay for the education of Richard's sister Edith.

The inscription on the boy's gravestone originally read: 'Sacred to the memory of Richard Parker, aged seventeen years, who died at sea after nineteen days' dreadful suffering in an open boat in the tropics, having been shipwrecked on the yacht *Mignonette*'.

Beneath it was a quotation from the Book of Job: 'Though he slay me, yet will I trust him.'

At the insistence of Richard's elder brother, Daniel, a second inscription, from Acts VII: 60, was added: 'Lord, lay not this sin to their charge.'

AUTHOR'S NOTE

The sinking of the *Mignonette* and the death of Richard Parker were real events, and much of the dialogue has been based on the court transcripts and other papers accumulated at the time of the trial.

I have omitted the surname of the Falmouth pilot Gustavus Lowry Collins to avoid confusion with Tom's defence lawyer of the same surname, but all the events are true or, when re-created, are based on contemporary accounts and the similar experiences of other shipwrecked sailors.

ACKNOWLEDGEMENTS

This is not an academic treatise and the text has not been burdened with footnotes. The primary and secondary sources I have drawn on in researching this book are detailed in the bibliography, but no one can write about the *Mignonette* without acknowledging a considerable debt to Professor A. W. B. Simpson and his splendid book on the legal aspects of the case of Regina versus Dudley and Stephens: *Cannibalism and the Common Law*.

The disproportionate glow of achievement I felt when unearthing a document or reference that Professor Simpson had not already discovered and annotated is its own tribute to the thoroughness of his meticulous research. I am also grateful to him for permission to quote from his interview with a distant relative of Richard Parker, Ivor Bedford, from whom comes the story of Ned Brooks crying out in the night, and from his interview with Vernon Cole. Frank Robb's *Handling Small Boats in Heavy Weather* is an invaluable guide to avoiding and surviving shipwreck, and the accounts of many survivors are contained in E. C. B. and Kenneth Lee's excellent *Safety and Survival at Sea*. David Thornton's *Plough & Sail* is an affectionate remembrance of the Tollesbury area in the nineteenth century, and George Peters's *The Plimsoll Line* is a lucid account of Samual Plimsoll's lifelong campaigns on behalf of seamen.

Stan Hugill's *Sailortown* vividly re-creates the murky dockside world of Victorian seamen. Those interested in delving further into freak shows and 'museums' should consult Robert Bogdan's splendid *Freak Show: Presenting Human Oddities for Amusement and Profit*. The Victorian prison system is explored in Anthony Babington's *The English Bastille: A History of Newgate Gaol and Prison Conditions in Britain 1188–1902*, and John Camp's *Holloway Prison*.

My personal thanks go to Mark Lucas and Sally Hughes at Lucas Alexander Whitley in London, and in New York to Kim Witherspoon at Witherspoon Associates and Emily Loose and the rest of the team at John Wiley & Sons. Their professionalism and enthusiasm make it a pleasure to work with them.

My thanks also to Pete Metcalf for information on the law and court procedures in the nineteenth century, Robin Poulier for his advice on the physiological effects of drinking sea-water and urine, Ian Platts and Gavin Craig for helping this landlubber to understand something of yachts and sailing, Simon Wilkinson for finding a photographer at five minutes' notice and Jo, Julie, Belle and Bridget at Just A Sec for transcribing my inaudible tapes into a workable typescript.

My thanks also to two individuals who contacted me after reading the British edition of *The Custom of the Sea*. Barbara Boon showed me the only painting (as far as I know) of the *Mignonette,* and Trevor Ryan told me the tale of finding Tom Dudley's sextant and the moving message inscribed in its case, in an Adelaide auction room.

I am also grateful to Kathy Wallace and Alex Hooper at the Falmouth Art Gallery, the staff of the Falmouth Public Library, Captain George Hogg, Roger Stephens and the staff of the Falmouth Maritime Museum, Mr Peter Gilson, Honorary Librarian at the Royal Cornwall Polytechnic Society, the Woodrolfe Shipyard at Tollesbury, the Curator of the Brightlingsea Museum, Helen Langley of the Department of Special Collections and Western Manuscripts at the Bodleian Library, and the staffs of the British Library at St Pancras, the British Library Newspaper Section at Colindale, the Public Record Office at Kew, the National Maritime Museum at Greenwich, Ilkley Library, Bradford Reference Library, Leeds Reference Library and the innumerable other institutions and individuals who have given willingly of their time and knowledge in dealing with my endless queries.

BIBLIOGRAPHY

Newspapers

Bristol Gazette; Bristol Mercury; Colchester Chronicle; Colchester Mercury and Essex Express; Commercial Shipping & General Advertiser; Cornubian; Daily Recorder; Daily Telegraph; Devon Evening Express; Essex Standard; Exeter & Plymouth Gazette; Falmouth News Slip; Falmouth Packet; Falmouth & Penryn Weekly Times; Field; Fun; Graphic; Hunt's Yacht List; Hunt's Yachting Magazine; Illustrated London News; Illustrated Police News; Limerick Star & Evening Post; Limerick Times; Liverpool Weekly Post; Mariner's Mirror; Morning Post; National Review; New York Herald; New York Times; Pall Mall Gazette; Penny Illustrated Newspaper; Philadelphia Public Ledger; Pictorial News; Pictorial World; Plymouth Weekly Mercury; Police Guardian; Punch; Royal Cornwall Gazette; Saturday Review; Singapore Daily Times; Southampton Observer & Winchester News; Southampton Times & Hampshire Express; Southern Echo; Spectator; Standard; Straits Observer; Sutton Herald; Sydney Gazette; Sydney Mail; Sydney Morning Herald; Sydney Daily Telegraph; The Times; Weekly Mercury; West Briton; Western Weekly News.

Official Reports and Manuscripts

Federal Cases, United States v Holmes, Case No. 15,383

Regina v Dudley & Stephens, (1884) Queens Bench Division 273, (1885) 560, 1

Select Committee Appointed to Inquire into the Causes of Shipwrecks 1826

Report from the Select Committee on Shipwrecks of Timber Ships 1839

First and Second Reports from the Select Committee on Shipwrecks 1843

Preliminary Report from the Royal Commission on Unseaworthy Ships 1873

Final Report of the Royal Commission on Unseaworthy Ships 1874

Report of the Outbreak of Plague at Sydney, 1900, by the Medical Officer of Health

Archive Sources

Public Record Office, Kew: ASSI 21/71; BT 99/90; BT 108/14; BT 109/204; BT 122; CO 273/76, 80; CUST 31/244; CUST 67/11; DPP 4/17; FO 27/634; HO 34/35; HO 34/52; HO 144/141 A36934; IND 6687/2; KB 6/6 (2); MT 9/101/M257/75; MT 9/112/M13696/75; MT 9/257/M9658 85; RG 9/1091; RG 10/1675; RG 10/1196; RG 10/1778; RG 11/1217; RG 11/1206

Bodleian Library, Oxford: The Harcourt Papers, MS Harcourt Dep. and MS Harcourt Dep. Adds.

Books and Periodicals

Adams, W.H.D., *Great Shipwrecks: A Record of Perils and Disasters at Sea, 1544–1877*, London, 1877

Alexander, Michael, *Mrs Fraser on the Fatal Shore*, Michael Joseph, London, 1971

Arens, W., *The Man Eating Myth: Anthropology and Anthropophagy*, Oxford University Press, New York, 1979

Ashley, F.W., *My Sixty Years of Law*, John Lane, London, 1936

Babington, Anthony, *The English Bastille: A History of Newgate Gaol and Prison Conditions in Britain 1188–1902*, Macdonald, London, 1971

Baker, Sherston, *The Judgement in the* Mignonette *Case, National Review* 4, 1884–5

Barker, James P., *The Log of a Limejuicer*, Pitman, London, 1934

Bennet, George, *Journal of the Voyages & Travels by the Rev. Daniel Tyerman and George Bennet, Esq*, compiled by James Montgomery, vol. 2, London, 1831

Bisset, J., *Sail Ho!*, Hart-Davis, London, 1961

Bogdan, Robert, *Freak Show: Presenting Human Oddities for Amusement and Profit*, University of Chicago Press, 1988

Bombard, Alain, *The Bombard Story*, translated by Brian Connell, André Deutsch, London, 1953

Bombard, Alain, *The Voyage of the Hérétique*, Simon & Schuster, New York, 1954

Bond, Richard, *The Ship Steward's Handbook*, J. Munro, Glasgow 1918

Camp, John, *Holloway Prison: The Place and the People*, David & Charles, Newton Abbot, 1974

Chase, Owen, *The Wreck of the Whaleship 'Essex': A Narrative Account by Owen Chase, First Mate*, ed. Iola Haverstick and Betty Shephard, Harcourt, Brace, Jovanovich, New York, 1965

Coppleson, Victor, *Shark Attack*, Angus & Robertson, London, 1959

Dana, Richard Henry, *Two Years Before the Mast*, J.M. Dent Everyman Library, London, 1972

Davis Ralph, *The Rise of the English Shipping Industry*, Macmillan, London, 1962

Dean, John, *A Narrative of the Shipwreck of the* Nottingham Galley *in Her Voyage from England to Boston*, Provincial Press, Portland, Maine, 1968

Dean, John, *A Narrative of the Suffering, Preservation and Deliverance of Capt. John Dean and Company in the* Nottingham Galley *of London, cast away on Boon Island, near New England, December 11, 1710*, London, 1711

Dickens, Charles, *The Old Curiosity Shop*, Oxford University Press, Oxford, 1951

The Dictionary of National Biography, Bulletin of the Institute of Historical Research, London, 1966

Elms, Charles, *Shipwrecks & Disasters at Sea, or, Historical Narratives of the Most Noted Calamities, and Providential Deliverances from Fire and Famine on the Ocean*, Philadelphia, 1849

Elms, Charles, *The Tragedy of the Seas: or Sorrow on the Ocean, Lake and River from Shipwreck, Plague, Fire and Famine*, New York, 1841

Engels, Friedrich, *The Condition of the Working Class in England*, London, 1892

Fiedler, Leslie, *Freaks: Myths and Images of the Secret Self*, Penguin Books, Harmondsworth, 1981

Gilbert, William S., *The Bab Ballads*, George Routledge & Sons, London, 1898

Gilbert, P.W., *Sharks & Survival*, D.C. Heath & Co., Lexington, 1963

Gray, Thomas, *Fifty Years of Legislation in Relation to the Shipping Trade and the Safety of Ships and Seamen 1836–1886*, London, 1887

Harrison, Brian, *Drink and the Victorians: The Temperance Question in England, 1815–72*, Faber & Faber, London, 1971

Harrison, David, *The Melancholy Narrative of the Distressful Voyage and Miraculous Deliverance of Captain David Harrison of the Sloop Peggy*, London, 1766

Hassan, David, *Sailing to Australia: Shipboard Diaries by Nineteenth Century Emigrants*, Manchester University Press, Manchester, 1994

Hefferman, Thomas, F., *Stove by a Whale: Owen Chase and the Essex*, Wesleyan University Press, Connecticut, 1981

Hocking, Charles, *Dictionary of Disasters at Sea During the Age of Steam, 1824–1962*, (2 vols) Lloyds Register of Shipping, London, 1969

Hugill, Stan, *Sailortown*, Routledge & Kegan Paul, London, 1967

Huntress, Keith, *Narratives of Shipwrecks & Disasters 1586–1860*, Iowa State University Press, Iowa, 1974

Jennings, Cyril, *An Ocean Without Shores*, Hodder & Stoughton, London, 1950

Johnson, Peter, *The Encyclopaedia of Yachting*, Dorling Kindersley, London, 1989

Kemp, P., *The British Sailor: A Social History of the Lower Deck 1588–1905*, London, 1971

Langman, Christopher, *A True Account of the Voyage of the* Nottingham Galley *of London, John Dean Commander, from the River Thames to New England*, London, 1711

Layson, J.F., *Memorable Shipwrecks and Seafaring Adventures of the Nineteenth Century*, London, 1884

Lee, E.C.B., and Kenneth, Lee, *Safety & Survival at Sea*, Greenhill Books, London, 1989

Leslie, Edward, *Desperate Journeys, Abandoned Souls*, Macmillan, London, 1989

Lewis, Michael, *The Navy in Transition: A Social History 1814–1864*, Hodder & Stoughton, London, 1965

Lloyd, Christopher, *The Nation & the Navy: A History of Naval Life and Policy*, Cresset Press, London, 1954

The Lifeboat: The Journal of the Royal National Lifeboat Institution, 1 July 1867 and 1 November 1870

MacCormick, Donald, *Blood on the Sea*, Frederick Muller, London, 1962

Marcombe, David, *The Victorian Sailor*, Shire Publications, Princes Risborough, Bucks, 1985

Marriner, Brian, *Cannibalism, The Last Taboo*, Arrow, London, 1992

Melville, Herman, *Moby Dick or the White Whale*, Dent Everyman's Library, London, 1907

Neider, Charles (ed.), *Great Shipwrecks & Castaways*, Harper & Bros, New York, 1952

Newby, E., *The Last Grain Race*, Secker & Warburg, London, 1956

Ortzen, Len, *Stories of Famous Shipwrecks*, Arthur Barker, London, 1974

Paine, Ralph D., *Lost Ships & Lonely Seas*, Century Co., New York, 1921

Peters, George, *The Plimsoll Line: A Biography of Samuel Plimsoll*, Barry Rose Publishers, Chichester, 1975

Plimsoll, Samuel, *Our Seamen: An Appeal by Samuel Plimsoll, MP*, Virtue & Co., London, 1872

Poe, Edgar Allen, *The Narrative of Arthur Gordon Pym of Nantucket*, ed. Harold Beaver, Penguin Classics, London, 1986

Pool, David, *What Jane Austen Ate and Charles Dickens Knew*, Robson, London, 1998

Rediker, Marcus, *Between the Devil and the Deep Blue Sea*, Cambridge University Press, Cambridge, 1987

Robb, Frank, *Handling Small Boats in Heavy Weather*, Quadrangle Books, Chicago, 1965

Rogers, Stanley, *Crusoes & Castaways*, Harrap, London, 1932

Saunders, Ann, *Narrative of the Shipwreck and Sufferings of Miss Ann Saunders*, Z.S. Crossman, Providence, 1827

Schofield, Brian and Louis, Martyn, *The Rescue Ships*, Blackwood, Edinburgh, 1968

Marine Research Society, *The Sea, the Ship and the Sailor: Tales of Adventure from Log Books and Original Narratives*, Salem, Massachusetts, 1925

Shea, Michael, *Maritime England: The Nation's Heritage*, Country Life Books, London, 1981

Shurtleff, William, *Distressing Dangers and Signal Deliverances, Religiously Improved*, Boston, 1727

Simpson, A.W.B., *Cannibalism & the Common Law*, University of Chicago Press, Chicago, 1984

Slocum, J., *Sailing Alone Around the World*, Hart-Davis, London, 1948

Smith, C. Fox (ed.), *Adventures and Perils of the Sea: Being Extracts from the 100-years-old Mariner's Chronicle and Other Sources Descriptive of Shipwrecks and Adventures at Sea*, Dodge Publishing Co., New York, 1937

Smith, J.C., and Hogan, Brian, *Criminal Law*, Butterworth, London, 1996

Snow, Edward Rowe, *True Tales of Terrible Shipwrecks*, Alvin Redman, London, 1964

Stevens, R.W., *On the Stowage of Ships and their Cargoes*, Plymouth, 1891

Tannahill, Reay, *Flesh and Blood: A History of the Cannibalism Complex*, Hamish Hamilton, London, 1975

Thomas, R. (ed.), *Interesting and Authentic Narratives of the Most Remarkable Shipwrecks, Fires, Famines, Calamities, Providential Deliverances, and the Lamentable Disasters on the Seas, in Most Parts of the World*, Hartford, Connecticut, 1850

Thompson, E.P., *The Making of the English Working Class*, Gollancz, London, 1963

Thompson, F.M.L., *The Rise of Respectable Society: A Social History of Victorian Britain*, *1830–1900*, Fontana, London, 1988

Thornton, David, *Plough & Sail*, Owl Printing Company, Tollesbury, Essex, 1987

Tiira, Ensio, *Raft of Despair*, Hutchinson, London, 1954

Who Was Who, vols. I and III, London, 1920

Williams, G., *A Commentary on R. v Dudley and Stephens*, Cambrian Law Review 8, 1977

Williams, Walter, *The Loss of the* Mignonette*, A Terrible Tale of the Sea*, London, 1884

Wood, Walter, *Survivors' Tales of Famous Shipwrecks*, Geoffrey Bles, London, 1932

313

PICTURE CREDITS